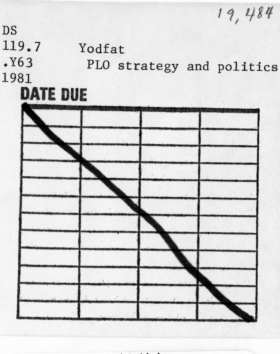

PLO
Strategy and Tactics

Aryeh Y. Yodfat
and
Yuval Arnon-Ohanna

ST. MARTIN'S PRESS NEW YORK

©1981 Aryeh Y. Yodfat and Yuval Arnon-Ohanna

St. Martin's Press, Inc., 175 Fifth Avenue, New York, NY 10010
Printed in Great Britain
First published in the United States of America in 1981

Library of Congress Cataloging in Publication Data

Yodfat, Aryeh, 1923-
    P.L.O. strategy and tactics.

    Bibliography: p.207
    Includes index.
    1. Munaẓẓamat al-Taḥrīr al-Filasṭīnīyah.
2. Jewish-Arab relations- -1973-   I. Arnon-Ohanna,
Yuval, joint author.   II. Title.
DS119.7.Y63 1981   322.4'2'095694   80-22200
ISBN 0-312-61761-5

CONTENTS

Appendix Two: Documents

Preface

The role of the Palestinian organizations — and in particular of their roof organization, the Palestine Liberation Organization (PLO) — extends beyond the context of the Palestine question and the Arab-Israeli conflict into broader aspects of Middle Eastern power politics and strategy.

The PLO has developed in the course of fifteen years from a small and marginal organization totally dependent on the Arab States into an independent organization granted international status and recognized by Arab States as 'the sole representative of the Palestinian people!'

Nevertheless, because it is heterogeneous, it is also fissiparous, with a consistent record of splits and internal struggles. Furthermore, its status as the sole legitimate representative of the Palestinian people is not acceptable to all the Palestinians themselves — for example, those who live in Jordan.

Although the PLO is one of the most spoken-about and controversial organizations in the international arena, there is a remarkable dearth of published material on an academic level on the ideology, political views and sources of power of the PLO, about its social and administrative structure and analyzing the internal struggles within it.

This book attempts to present a comprehensive study of the PLO, in terms of a systematic research discipline. It attempts to present and analyze the different Palestinian organizations, their strategy and politics, their positions and activities, their history and ideology, organizational structures, leading personalities and their roles, internal struggles and disputes, relations with the Arab world, involvement in inter-Arab affairs and relations with great powers — the United States, the Soviet Union and the Peoples' Republic of China.

The book begins with a comparatively brief but comprehensive survey of the PLO and the Israeli-Egyptian peace process, as a prologue to the description of the emergence and growth of the PLO and an examination of its ideology, strategy and relationships with the major world powers and within the Arab bloc. The epilogue reviews developments up to early 1980, including PLO ties with Khomeyni's regime in Iran, the Arab summit meeting in November 1979, on the PLO's status in Lebanon, the deterioration in PLO-Libyan relations and oscillating currents in PLO relations with the US, USSR and Western Europe.

Based mainly on primary, especially Arab sources, the book has been carefully edited and annotated in order to provide the reader and the scholar with correct reference material. A balanced selection of PLO documents and resolutions is included in the Appendix, and an outline of the principal Palestinian organizations within the framework of the PLO. Wherever possible, PLO material and statements by its representatives have been traced to the original source and where this has not been possible, an indication to this effect is given to the reader.

The authors wish to thank the Reuven Shiloah Research Center for Middle East and African Studies of the Tel-Aviv University, the Middle East Department of Haifa University, Mr. Harold Blumberg, our editor and publisher, and Ms. Maureen Shalit who typed the manuscript.

A. Y. Yodfat
Y. Arnon-Ohanna

Abbreviations

AAPSO – Afro-Asian People's Solidarity Organization
AFP – Agence France Presse
ALF – Arab Liberation Front
ANM – Arab Nationalists Movement
AP – Associated Press
ARR – Arab Report and Record (London)
ASU – Arab Socialist Union (Egypt)

BBC – British Broadcast Corporation

CC – Central Committee
CENTO – Central Treaty Organization
CIA – Central Intelligence Agency (USA)
CP – Communist Party
CPSU – Communist Party of the Soviet Union
CSM – Christian Science Monitor (Boston)

DFLP – Democratic Front for the Liberation of Palestine
DPA – Deutsche Presse Agentur (West German News Agency)
DR – Daily Report

EC – Executive Committee

FBIS – Foreign Broadcast Information Service (USA)
FLN – Front de Liberation Nationale (Algeria)

GA – General Assembly (UN)
GC – General Command
GDR – German Democratic Republic
GRU – Glavnoe Razvedovatel'noe Upravlenie, Main (Military) Intelligence Directorate (USSR)

IHT – International Herald Tribune (Paris)
IRA – Irish Republican Army

KGB – Komitet Gosudarstvennoy Bezopasnosti, Committee for State Security (USSR)
KUNA – Kuwaiti News Agency
ME – Middle East
MENA – Middle East News Agency (Egypt)
MER – Middle East Record (Shiloah Center, Tel Aviv University)

NATO – North Atlantic Treaty Organization
NCC – National Consultative Council (Jordan)
NCNA – New China News Agency
NY – New York

OLS – Organisation of Lebanese Socialists
OPEC – Organisation of Oil Exporting Countries

PASC – Palestinian Armed Struggle Command
PCC – Palestine Central Council
PDFLP – Popular Democratic Front for the Liberation of Palestine
PDRY – People's Democratic Republic of the Yemen
PFLOAG – Popular Front for the Liberation of Oman and the Arabian Gulf
PFLP – Popular Front for the Liberation of Palestine
PFLP-GC – PFLP-General Command
PLA – Palestine Liberation Army
PLF – Palestine Liberation Front
PLO – Palestine Liberation Organisation
PNA – Palestinian National Assembly
PNC – Palestinian National Council
PNF – Palestine National Front
POLP – Popular Organisation for the Liberation of Palestine
PRC – People's Republic of China

QNA – Qatar News Agency

SANA – Syrian Arab News Agency
SU – Soviet Union

TASS – Telegraph Agency of the Soviet Union

UAR – United Arab Republic (Egypt)
UC – United Command (PLO)
UN – United Nations
UNIFIL – UN Interim Force in Lebanon
UNRWA – UN Relief and Works Agency
UPI – United Press International
USA – United States of America
USSR – Union of Soviet Socialist Republics

WAFA – Wikalat Al-Anba Al-Filastiniyya (Palestinian News Agency)
WFTO – World Federation of Trade Unions

PLO AND THE PEACE PROCESS

CHAPTER ONE

IMPACT ON PLO OF CAMP DAVID AGREEMENT

The Palestine problem was the main cause for the deadlock in the Middle East political process that existed on the eve of the visit to Jerusalem on November 1977 by President Anwar Al-Sadat of Egypt. The Palestinian issue has also been the most difficult problem in the implementation of the Israeli-Egyptian peace treaty.

The Palestine Liberation Organization (PLO) greatly strengthened its position between the October 1973 war and the 1977 Sadat initiative in both the inter-Arab and international arenas. This flowed from the recognition of the PLO as the "sole legitimate representative of the Palestinian people" by the Arab states, leading to an international recognition of the PLO by the UN, and other international bodies.

Increasing recognition for the PLO aggravated the deadlock in the political process. The PLO's adherence to its ideology that denied the existence of Israel and called for the establishment in place of it of an Arab Palestinian state led to Israel's opposition to any contacts with the PLO, at the same time as Arab states insisted that the PLO join the negotiating process. The US and the USSR were divided on this question and while the former supported Israel, the latter upheld the Arab view, leading the political process into a cul-de-sac.

The paradox is that, whereas from 1948 to 1967 the Arab states ignored the question of Palestinian identity, they moved in a different direction in 1967 and moved still further after the October 1973 war. Arab states granted to the PLO the right to decide *for them* when to end *their* struggle against Israel. In the secret resolutions of the Arab Summit Conference in Algiers (November 26–28, 1973), with the exception of Jordan, all the Arab states committed themselves "to restore the legitimate rights of the Arab people of Palestine *as will be decided by the Palestine Liberation Organization*".   The secret resolutions of the Rabat Arab Summit (October 26–29, 1974), this time with Jordan's support, confirmed the commitment to restore the national rights of the Palestinian people *"in accordance with resolutions that will be accepted by the PLO"*.[1] At both those summits Arab states not only gave to the PLO the right of exclusive representation of the Palestinian people but also bound their own hands by delegating to the PLO the exclusive decision as to when the Palestinians' rights have been met. This meant, in effect, that as long as the PLO would not be fully satisfied with the Middle Eastern arrangements, Arab countries must continue the struggle against Israel, even if their own interests would require them to act otherwise. It was tantamount to giving to the PLO a right to *veto* any solution of the conflict, even if it were to be acceptable, by any, or most, or all Arab states.

At that time the Geneva Conference was regarded as the main arena for a future peace settlement. The conference, convened immediately after the war of October 1973, was never resumed. Arab states refused to go to the conference without the PLO, while Israel refused to accept the PLO as a negotiating partner, and both co-chairmen of the Conference, the US and the USSR, had different positions on this matter. Another obvious paradox was that, even if invited, the PLO could hardly join the Conference, as negotiations with Israel would mean recognition, expressly ruled out in PLO ideology.

The Sadat initiative to conduct direct Egyptian–Israeli talks was initially confronted with the same problems and was an attempt at finding a way out of that vicious circle.

It is instructive to examine what happened in the PLO camp since President Sadat's 1977 initiative, on the following levels: changes in PLO position; PLO reactions; PLO inter-Arab relations; PLO internal developments.

● Changes in the PLO position since the Sadat initiative

Two phases of the PLO's operation can be distinguished since the Sadat initiative: a decline that began in November 1977 and continued till about the summer of 1979; an upward swing, from the summer of 1979 onwards, with the prolongation of the Israeli–Egyptian peace talks and the emergence of difficulties in the autonomy negotiations.

Israeli–Egyptian negotiations had a far reaching influence on the PLO, both in the international and inter-Arab arena. The process of quick advances in the international position of the organization since 1973 came to a halt. The international forum that had to be the framework for negotiations, the Geneva Conference, in which Arab states and the two super-powers were to participate, was replaced by Israeli–Egyptian–American contacts in which PLO participation seemed remote. The USSR, the patron of the PLO, was pushed aside, while the USA, playing a leading role in engineering the contacts, had no official ties with the PLO. President Carter declared that the PLO had been excluded from the political process because of its extreme position.[2]

The greatest impact of President Sadat's initiative on the PLO status and position was in the inter-Arab arena. Sadat proved that in order to achieve progress in the Arab-Israeli conflict, there was a need to circumvent the Algiers and Rabat resolutions. He insisted that the Israeli-Egyptian settlement would not be a separate one but that it must also deal with the Palestinian problem, without conditioning it upon PLO cooperation, knowing that this would freeze the political process.

Thus, President Sadat openly repeated what Jordan's King Hussein had done furtively a few years earlier, in his secret contacts with Israel and his "United Arab Kingdom" proposal of 1972.[3] Israel introduced unofficially the "Allon plan," which guided the policy of her former government, and the autonomy proposal of the present one. The three proposals are entirely different, but they share one common characteristic: a separation between the great mass of the Palestinian population that lives in Palestine itself and the radical organizations of Palestinians living outside of Palestine.

President Sadat's position, however, was ambiguous. On the one hand, he pushed aside the PLO, but on the other, kept the option open for its future integration in the negotiations. During the peace negotiations, President Sadat appealed to Palestinians – as had King Hussein before him – to dissociate themselves from the PLO, to take their future into their own hands and to accept the autonomy proposals, which he considered to be a stage towards a future independent Palestinian state. Time and again, echoes were heard of the proposals of 1937 and 1947 to divide Palestine into Jewish and Arab states, – which Palestine Arabs, who followed the radical Grand Mufti Haj Muhammad Amin Al-Husseini, refused to accept.[4] When writing these lines, in the last weeks of 1979, the position of the Palestinian population in the West Bank and that of the PLO is quite clear in its firm opposition.

President Sadat circumvented the Algiers and Rabat resolutions. He did not mention the PLO in his address to the Knesset in Jerusalem on November 1977[5] and did not insist on its cooperation in the negotiations that developed later. He moved further, proposing a return of the West Bank to Jordan and of Gaza to Egypt for a period of five years after the signing of the agreement. The Camp David agreements (September 17, 1978) provide that the parties to the negotiations to solve the Palestinian problem will be Egypt, Israel, Jordan and "the representatives of the Palestinian people". The same definition appeared in a letter of Begin and Sadat to Carter on March 26, 1979, that was a part of the Israeli–Egyptian peace treaty. It said that Israel and Egypt will proceed with the implementation of Camp David agreements relating to the West Bank and Gaza strip. They invited Jordan to join the negotiations and reiterated that "the delegations of Egypt and Jordan may include Palestinians from the West Bank and Gaza Strip or other Palestinians as mutually agreed." The PLO was not mentioned by name. The reference to "other Palestinians" might be construed as a reference to the PLO, but the further statement "as mutually agreed" excluded such a possibility.

On the other hand, Sadat in his address to the Knesset on November 20, 1977, called on Israel to implement "the legitimate rights of the Palestine people" and specifically proposed the establishment of a Palestinian state. He did not mention the PLO and did not ask for it to join the negotiations – but he left the option open. In the Aswan formula that was accepted by him and by President Carter on January 8, 1978, references were made to a solution of the Palestinian problem in "all its aspects", a recognition of the "legitimate rights" of the Palestinian people and their participation in deciding their future.

Furthermore, Egypt continued to refer to the PLO as the "sole legitimate representative of the Palestinian people". Those Egyptian statements have one more dimension. After the rejectionist conference in Tripoli (December 2–5, 1977) Egypt froze her diplomatic relations with all participants in the conference, but not with the PLO. Said Kamal, the PLO representative, was the only "rejectionist" envoy who continued to sit in Cairo after the break in relations between Egypt and the PLO that came after the signature of the peace treaty. The PLO office in Cairo was closed but reportedly reopened again. In a discussion in the Egyptian cabinet on April 8, 1979, after the signature of the peace treaty, acting Foreign Minister Butrus Ghali said that Egypt can help the PLO because she recognizes the organization and it leads a liberation struggle.[6]

In conclusion, the status of the PLO was undoubtedly affected as a result of the Sadat initiative. During the earlier phase of the Israeli–Egyptian negotiations, the PLO was down-graded to a waiting position, but by the summer of 1979 its "international rating" had gone up again. The Rabat resolutions were flouted by proofs that it was possible to sign an Israeli-Arab treaty, one that embraces the Palestinian problem, without the cooperation of the PLO and in spite of its opposition to it. On the other hand, Egypt did not renounce her recognition of the PLO and may yet ask its participation in the negotiations on autonomy.

In the autonomy talks conducted between Israel and Egypt, the two sides took up quite different positions. Israel was for an administrative autonomy for the people of the West Bank and Gaza, that would enable them to conduct their internal affairs. Egyptian proposals gave the autonomy a character resembling an independent state. The US, fearing a breakdown of the agreement, looked for additional supporters in the Arab world. The potential candidates, Jordan and Saudi Arabia, preferred to remain in the framework of the all-Arab consensus that was against the agreement. West Bank and Gaza Arabs, too, adhered to that consensus in their opposition to the autonomy proposals.

The talks conducted by Austrian Chancellor Bruno Kreisky and Socialist International Chairman Willy Brandt with PLO leader Arafat in Vienna on July 6–8, 1979 were not coincidental. It certainly seemed as if the Vienna meeting came about with the encouragement, or at least the approval of the US administration.

The UN Security Council had to deal on July 31, 1979 with the Palestine problem, when the US showed increasing concern that the autonomy negotiations were about to reach a deadlock. Americans concluded that there was a need in some way to appease the PLO in order to make the process move forward. A pre-condition for that was seen in introducing a new draft proposal in the Security Council that would replace (or supplement) the 242 resolution, to which the PLO had consistently objected.

In a late July 1979 meeting of UN representatives of the US, Kuwait and the PLO it was decided to defer the Security Council's debate to August 23, 1979. In a parallel move, a Kuwait initiated draft proposal that was accepted by the PLO was sent to the Security Council. USA representative, Andrew Young, initially denied that such a meeting — contrary to his instructions and the US position not to conduct negotiations with the PLO as long as it does not recognize Israel and the 242 resolution — had taken place. After it became publicly known that the meeting had been held, he resigned in mid-August. The mere fact of his coordinating moves with the PLO reflected a change very much for the better in the PLO position. (See CHAPTER SEVEN: US–PLO)

● PLO Reactions to Israeli-Egyptian Negotiations

The PLO found itself waiting in the wings for the most part during the Israeli-Egyptian negotiations unable to influence meaningfully the course of events.

The basic position of the PLO and of the "Rejectionists" on the negotiations had been entrenched at the Tripoli (Libya) Summit Conference, December 2–5, 1977. The PLO additionally adopted two courses: a military course involving violent activities aimed at undermining the peace process and at frightening those who would like to join it; and a political course mainly directed towards a public image of moderation and readiness to participate in future negotiations.

Simultaneous with its signature on a joint document with the "rejectionist" countries at Tripoli, the PLO formulated its own position in the framework of the Tripoli Conference, endorsed by all its component organizations. This position was summed up in a "six clause agreement", of which the fifth clause had a particular importance. These clauses were:

- establishment of "a united front" with Libya, Syria, Iraq, Algeria and the PDRY (South Yemen) to oppose "capitulation to imperialists, Zionists and those Arabs serving them",
- condemnation of any Arab party participating in the Tripoli Conference but opposed to the establishment of this front (a reference to Iraq),
- rejection of UN Security Council resolutions 242 and 338,
- rejection of all international committees based on those resolutions, including the Geneva Conference,
- "action to implement the right of the Palestinian people to return [to Palestine] and to self-determination in the framework of a national independent state in each part of Palestinian land that will be liberated — without granting peace or recognition or involvement in negotiation,"
- imposition of a political boycott on the Sadat regime.[7]

The PLO was able to adopt resolutions of this kind but was incapable of performing any meaningful political activity against the political process. It was, in fact, politically paralyzed and was compelled to be a passive spectator, unable to influence events.

The PLO fears were compounded by Sadat's Jerusalem visit, when it saw a possibility of a quick signing of an Egyptian-Israeli peace treaty. The only option open to it was to try to undermine the process by violent activities. At a later period when it became clear that negotiations would take a long time, the PLO returned to the political arena.

It could be assumed that the PLO would strengthen its military struggle mainly against Israel and as a second priority, against Egypt. But its activities were in fact directed primarily against the Palestinians, with the aim of preventing their cooperation and support of the peace initiative and autonomy proposals. Later they were directed against Egypt and only after that against Israel.

With the publication of the Tripoli "Six Clauses", Salah Khalef (Abu Iyad), Arafat's deputy, warned West Bank and Gaza notables not to violate these resolutions, "as it is possible to liquidate them easily". A short time afterwards, when listing the future tasks of the PLO, Abu Iyad listed also the following task:

"Revolutionary masses have to implement all kinds of revolutionary violence to frighten the hesitant".[8]

Reports soon appeared that the PLO had compiled a list of 24 Palestinian personalities, residents of the West Bank and Gaza Strip who expressed support for the Sadat initiative and that the intentions were to liquidate them. It also became known that notables of the West Bank wrote a petition to Yasir Arafat in which they asked him to cancel that decision, but he refused to reply to their request.[9]

Within a short time, internal terror activities were staged. After December 1977, Palestinian personalities were assassinated in the West Bank and the Gaza Strip, most notably the Deputy Head of the Education Office in the West Bank, Hamdi Al-Qadi, a declared pro-Jordanian, who was assasinated on December 26, 1977; Nur Al-Din Jankhu who was assassinated in Ramallah on February 7, 1978, was one of the best known Palestinian notables who had advocated cooperation with Israel[10]; Hashim Al-Khuzendar, the Imam of Gaza, who supported the Sadat initiative and who in December 1977 organized a delegation of Gaza notables to Egypt, where they were received by Sadat and expressed support for his policy, was assassinated on June 2, 1979. A PLO spokesman praised the assassination saying it was a fulfillment of a mission. Three sons of Khuzendar were PLO members.[11]

The fear that a number of Palestinians would share in the general enthusiasm for the peace initiative led to an activating of internal terror, not only in the Israeli administered territories, but also against PLO members who had expressed moderate positions in the past or a readiness to establish contacts with Israel.

The PLO is a conglomeration of a number of organizations that are to a large extent a reflection of inter-Arab divisions (see Appendix). Such divisions were still more visible when supported by Iraqi organizations in the PLO, as the Arab Liberation Front and members of the organization of Abu Nidhal which had embarked on the liquidation of people who were suspected of being moderate.

The first victim was Sa'id Hamami, PLO representative in London, who was assassinated on January 4, 1978. A day after the assassination, an anonymous caller to the United Press International identified himself as speaking in the name of the Palestinian revolution and said that Hamami had been executed because he was involved in negotiations with Israel, adding that this was "only a beginning".[12]   George Habash, leader of the Popular Front for the Liberation of Palestine (PFLP), said a day later that the liquidation of traitors and of supporters of Sadat will continue energetically.[13]   After Hamami's assassination, further assassinations of more Palestinian personalities led to an outbreak of a terror war, of killings and reprisals between the PLO mainstream, and pro-Iraqi organizations in the summer of 1978.

Relations between the PLO and Egypt became strained immediately after Sadat's visit to Jerusalem, but deteriorated still further after PLO adherents assassinated the Chairman of the Cairo Daily, Al Ahram, former Egyptian Education and Information Minister Yusuf Al-Siba'i on February 18, 1978. They also took as hostages participants in the Afro-Asian People's Solidarity Organization (AAPSO) Conference, of which Al-Siba'i was Secretary General, which took place in Nicosia. During the negotiations concerning the hostages, an Egyptian commando force arrived in Cyprus and attempted to release the hostages by force. In the shooting between them and Fath forces, some Egyptian commandos were killed.

Egypt reacted sharply and her information media appealed to the world "to sweep out the terrorists from human society". An Egyptian paper accused the "Black September" organization of seizing hostages and committing murder.[14] It was clear that it was an indirect accusation of Fath, as it was already well known that "Black September" was a cover for Fath activities, with which Fath had no interest in identifying itself publicly and openly. Arafat denied that he had anything to do with the assassination of Siba'i and promised to hit with an "iron fist" those who were guilty of it, thus accusing the organization of Abu Nidhal. Egyptian media then asked "if Arafat is not able to control the various PLO groups, how does he dare to claim an exclusive representation of all Palestinians?"[15]

The hitting of Egyptian targets continued also after Egypt had signed the peace treaty with Israel, not only by al-Fath. On July 13–15, 1979, a group which identified itself as Eagles of the Palestinian Revolution (a cover for Syrian-controlled Al-Sa'iqa) attacked the Egyptian Embassy at Ankara, seizing there many hostages, including the Ambassador. They asked, as a condition for their release, an annulment of the Israeli-Egyptian peace treaty, a recognition by Turkey of "the legitimate rights of the Palestinian people" and the opening of a PLO office in Ankara. Egyptian media sharply reacted.[16] Negotiations ended with the release of hostages, and a PLO office was opened in Ankara on August 15, 1979.

On March 11, 1978, PLO members in a seaborne incursion into Israel, murdered a number of Israeli civilians. They entered Israel from the Mediterranean, took over a tourist bus which they seized on the highway not far from the coast and forced it to go in the direction of Tel-Aviv. On the way they fired in all directions, hitting people indiscriminately. The bus was blown up, causing many casualties. Arafat, visiting the USSR and East Germany at the time, told his hosts that he did not know anything about plans of this kind and that he had been informed about the attack only through the media. According to a well-informed Western commentator he had been placed in a delicate situation. Had he known about it and not mentioned it to his hosts it would have implied that he did not trust them. Had he not known about, it would have meant that he did not control his own organization.[17]

Israel reacted, beginning on March 14, 1978, with the "Litani Operation" that gave her military forces the control of most of South Lebanon. Israeli forces withdrew about two months later back to the international border, ending the withdrawal on June 14. UN forces arrived in South Lebanon, *inter alia*, with the aim of preventing the PLO from re-entering the area and conducting activities against Israel from there. UN forces attempted to prevent their return, but there were also instances of cooperation between UN personnel and Palestinians, such as selling them arms and of smuggling sabotage equipment to Israel.

On April 22, 1979, members of the "Palestine Liberation Front" (PLF) organization of Abu Al-Abbas (that split from the PFLP – General Command, headed by Ahmad Jibril) entered Nahariya on the northern Israel coast, and killed two civilians.

A few weeks later Israel proclaimed a new activist policy against the PLO, announced in an address by Prime Minister Begin in the Knesset on May 7, 1979. The policy was not only to react and retaliate but to initiate a continuous offensive. In that address Begin also proposed peace talks with Lebanon.

In the period since the Sadat initiative the PLO lost three of its military leaders, including the former head of PFLP "foreign operations" Wadi' Haddad who died a natural death in April 1978.[18] During the years when he was active, he was responsible for hijackings of planes and other terrorist acts, some of them in cooperation with European terrorist organizations. Another victim was a Fath leader considered to be the head of "Black September" organization, Ali Hasan Salama – who had been responsible for the murder of Israeli sportsmen in the 1972 Munich Olympic Games – killed when a car blew up in Beirut on January 22, 1979. The third was Zuhair Muhsin, head of Al-Sa'iqa organization and of the PLO Military Department. Muhsin was shot on July 25, 1979 near the entrance to his apartment in Cannes on the French Riviera by two unidentified persons.

To sum up – PLO military activities were directed firstly against Palestinians on the West Bank and in the Gaza Strip, and later against Egypt and Israel. Undeterred, Egypt and Israel continued their negotiations and signed a peace treaty. The Palestinians, under the PLO threats, were indeed prevented from cooperating with Israel, supporting Sadat's initiative, and participating in the proposed autonomy negotiations. It is however difficult to say how far the

PLO threats alone contributed to the Palestinians' attitudes. There were probably additional factors such as Jordan's opposition to the autonomy proposals, the united stand of most Arab countries against Sadat's initiative and the general tendency to avoid cooperation with Israel under any circumstances.

As time passed after Sadat's Jerusalem visit, and it became clear that Israeli-Egyptian negotiations would be lengthy, the PLO extended primarily its political activities. The PLO understood that no matter what the results of the negotiations – a failure or a success – the Palestinian problem will be the next subject on the agenda. Therefore, whenever it seemed that Israeli-Egyptian negotiations had reached a turning point, the PLO switched to political activities with a view to improving its position for the next stage.

The way that the PLO chose to go was the same which it had pursued with much success in the years 1975–1977, i.e. before Sadat's peace initiative: to dabble in moderate declarations to show its tendency to flexibility, but simultaneously to preserve the official ideology, which called for a destruction of Israel without any modification. When it seemed in Spring 1978 that Israeli-Egyptian negotiations were unsuccessful and it looked as if they were coming to an end, Labib Tarazi, the PLO UN representative, declared on May 5, 1978, that the aim of the organization was not the establishment of a Palestinian state in all of Palestine. He argued that after the establishment of a Palestinian state in the West Bank and Gaza Strip, a new situation would appear in the Middle East and the Palestinian state would then recognize Israel's borders.

With the publication of the Camp David agreements in September 1978 the PLO's immediate reaction was to join Arab states in condemning them. But in November 1978, at the time of the Blair House Conference in Washington, when an Israeli-Egyptian peace treaty was seen to be a matter of days – PLO proclamations were made similar to those of Tarazi, this time by more senior personalities. Arafat said in a conversation in Damascus on November 25, 1978, with US House of Representatives member, Paul Findley, according to the latter, that the PLO was ready to end its armed struggle and to recognize Israel *de facto* if an independent Palestinian state in the West Bank and Gaza linked by a corridor would be established. The PLO, he said, will however continue to use non-violent methods (political and diplomatic) to establish a secular state in all of Palestine.[19] It was said in a similar vein by PLO representative in France, Ibrahim Sus and by Arafat's deputy Salah Khalaf (Abu Iyad).[20] It expressed itself in particular in the meeting of Arafat with Kreisky and Brandt referred to earlier.

It should be noted that in not one of those statements was it said that the PLO would be ready to recognize Israel's right to exist. Moreover, Arafat declared at a mass meeting in Syria, on November 19, 1978, less than a week before his talks with Mr. Findley, that the PLO stood by "the continuation of the revolution to liquidate Israel with the force of arms" and added that the organization will not agree to any surrender, partial solution or plans for an autonomy.

● **PLO in Inter-Arab Relations**

The PLO participated in all inter-Arab rejectionist conferences held after President Sadat's visit to Jerusalem: in Tripoli (December 2–5, 1977), Algiers (February 2–5, 1978), in Damascus following the Camp David agreements (September 20, 1978), and in the Baghdad Summit Conferences (November 2–5, 1978; March 27–31, 1979) and again in Tripoli (November 20–22, 1979). At all those conferences, the PLO status as the sole legitimate representatives of the Arab people of Palestine was re-affirmed as well as their legitimate rights to return to Palestine and to their former homes, to self-determination and to establish an independent state. At all those conferences, it was decided to continue the struggle against Israel.[21]

Thus the PLO integrated into the Arab camp which rejected the peace initiatives. However, it could not escape involvement in internal rifts within that camp and was embroiled in a series of wars of assassination with Iraq.

The assassination of the PLO representative in London, Sa'id Hamami on January 4, 1978, was followed by declarations by a number of rejectionist spokesmen that this was only the beginning. After Hamami's assassination by Iraqis, more PLO personalities, all of whom had adopted a more moderate political line, like Izz Al-Din Qalak, PLO representative in Paris, were assassinated. Most disturbing for the PLO was the attempt on June 15, 1978, on the life of Ali Yasin, one of Arafat's closest friends, and PLO representative in Kuwait. The PLO reacted with attempts on the lives of Iraqi representatives. The cycle of assassinations soon increased, as did attacks on missions and embassies in Europe and the Far East. On August 2, 1978, an attempt by PLO members was made on the life of the Iraqi Vice-Consul in Karachi. Iraqis reacted by raiding the PLO mission in Islamabad on August 5. The series of assassinations virtually ended after the September 1978 Camp David Agreements. Both Syrian and Iraqi opposition to those agreements and their fear that they might soon lead to a peace treaty led to a Syrian-Iraqi reconciliation, and an end to the tension between the PLO and Iraq.

The principal PLO achievements included its role in the revolution in Iran and in an improvement in relations with Jordan.

Iran is not an Arab country and is outside the framework of inter-Arab relations, but the influence of the Iranian revolution on Arab positions was considerable, The PLO had at the outset of the campaign been against the Shah, siding openly with Khomeyni. In spite of the PLO's declared policy many times over many years that it would not interfere in the internal affairs of Arab countries, after its role in Jordan (1970), in Lebanon (1976), this was the third major PLO involvement in attempts (this time successful) to change Middle East regimes.

PLO aid to the opposition to the Shah regime was military, financial and political. Members of Iran's opposition groups received training in PLO units, the organization transferred arms and ammunition to Iran and gave open support to the revolutionaries before the Shah's downfall.[22]   This was not a one way street. Khomeyni had early on declared that "Arafat enjoys the support of the Iranian people in his efforts to regain Palestinians' rights and to return Muslim lands to Muslim hands".[23] Arafat was the first foreign leader who went personally to Khomeyni to congratulate the latter on his success. Arafat asked and received from Khomeyni approval to convert the building where the Israeli legation had been housed in Teheran into the PLO office. The PLO regarded Khomeyni's takeover as heralding a major strategic change in the whole area. When Arafat in Teheran praised the great Muslim victory and the new common Muslim front, he clearly caused embarrassment to George Habash, Na'if Hawatimah and other PLO Christian leaders. Conscious of this, Arafat quickly dispatched to Teheran, Archbishop Capucci — who had been tried and found guilty by Israel of direct sabotage activities while representing the Catholic Church in Jerusalem and had been released by the Israel Government at the personal request of the Pope, on condition that he would not be active in the Middle East — in order to calm any potential inter-sectarian tension within the PLO.

Aware of the long record of Jordanian-Israeli contacts, both open and secret, since the 1940's, the PLO was concerned after Sadat's visit to Jerusalem that Jordan might follow Egypt and join in the negotiations. The PLO's concern on this score was strengthened when Jordan did not initially react to Sadat's visit and failed at the very outset to join in the attacks on him. There was even talk emanating from Amman that Sadat had broken the psychological barrier between Israel and the Arab countries and that the position taken by Sadat in his address to the Knesset in November 1977 corresponded to Jordan's position, and to the position of all the Arabs and that he should not be condemned for what he had said but only for the fact that he had visited Jerusalem at all.

An authoritative Jordanian position was given by King Hussein when time passed after the Sadat visit and it was becoming clearer that an agreement would not be reached between Egypt and Israel quickly. Hussein declared that he would join Egyptian-Israeli negotiations on condition that he would know in advance their final outcome. He insisted on a full Israeli withdrawal to the 1967 lines and self-determination for the Palestinians.[24]   On another occasion, he said that he would be ready to take responsibility for the people of the West Bank and Gaza (in violation of the Rabat decisions) if the interests of the Palestinian people would require it, but only if his pre-conditions on complete withdrawal were met.[25] Jordan's Prime Minister Mudar Badran also said that Jordan might join negotiations if Israel would declare her readiness to withdraw from all territories and to implement the rights of the Palestinian people. To this he added that Jordan was conducting unofficial negotiations with the PLO.[26]

This was indeed the first admission by Amman of Jordanian-PLO contacts. PLO personalities including Zuhayr Muhsin, Head of the pro-Syrian Al-Sa'iqa organization, denied their existence, but it emerged clearly that they had taken place and that Muhsin himself had played a role in them.

Jordan took a big step towards rapprochement with the PLO when she established on April 16, 1978, a National Consultative Council (NCC). It was to be a substitute for the Jordanian parliament, dissolved after the Rabat Conference had granted to the PLO the right to be the sole legitimate representative of the Palestinian people. The NCC, like the previous parliament, consisted of 60 representatives — 30 from the West Bank and 30 from the East Bank. The most conspicuous novelty was the inclusion in the NCC of members of the Palestine National Council (the PLO supreme body — see Appendix) living in Jordan. From that time on, they were members of both a Jordanian official consultative body and of the PLO's official supreme body. Later press reports confirmed that even before the establishment of the NCC, there had been secret contacts between Jordan and the PLO. Evidence of this could be seen in the fact that the PLO had not condemned the establishment of that Council. Participation in the Jordanian NCC by members of the Palestine National Council (PNC) was seen to facilitate an indirect PLO participation in future negotiations with Israel, in which Jordan might take a part.

The first change in the PLO's attitude towards Jordan emerged following the "Litani Operation" in which Israeli forces for a brief period took over control of South Lebanon up to the Litani River. That led to a situation in which the PLO actually lost the last territorial base it had in south Lebanon and found itself pushed back to the north, to areas that were under Syrian control. This highly inconvenient situation for the PLO might have contributed to the change in its thinking and to its response to Jordanian signs to enter negotiations with her.[27]

The thaw in the enmity between the PLO and Jordan was accelerated by their common opposition to the Camp David agreements, to the subsequent Israeli-Egyptian peace treaty and to the autonomy plans. For the first time since September 1970, the PLO and Jordan had common aims and mutual interests. This commonality did not bridge the gap between them nor did it allay deep suspicions which each had of the other, as they had always had. It did, however, encourage common actions towards achieving a common aim — to strengthen the "steadfastness" (in Arabic — sumud) of the Palestinians in the West Bank against the peace process.

High level contacts between the PLO and Jordan began in summer 1978. Hussein and Arafat met several times: at the Baghdad Summit (November 1978) and during three short visits, each of a few hours that Arafat made to Jordan during which he met Hussein at the Mafraq airport (November 1978; March, September and November 1979). On the first two visits Arafat was not allowed to continue to Amman and he left Jordan for Syria immediately after the airport talks. Only in September 1979 was he invited to stay in Amman — and then for a very brief time. In the interim between those meetings, PLO leaders' led delegations to Jordan: Khalid Al-Fahum, Zuhayr Muhsin and Mahmud Abbas

(November 1978), Hamad Abu-Sitta (December 1978), Khalid Al-Fahum and Abd Al-Jawad Salah (January 1979) and Faruq Qaddumi (February 1979), and Khalid Al-Fahum again (August 1979). Joint PLO-Jordanian statements were issued during these missions, both sides declaring their adherence to the resolutions of the Rabat and Baghdad summits, called to implement Palestinians' rights and to assist the people of the Israeli-administered territories. A "working charter" was signed on December 24, 1978 to coordinate activities against Israeli-Egyptian agreements and autonomy plans. On the eve of Arafat's second visit, Jordan released a few hundred PLO prisoners. Jordan refused, however, to respond to PLO requests to permit the PLO to return to the positions in Jordan which the PLO had occupied prior to 1970, for military training and to enable the PLO to conduct her activities against Israel from Jordanian territory. Cooperation was restricted at this stage to rallying the resistance of the inhabitants of the West Bank to the peace treaty and the autonomy plan.[28]

● **Internal PLO Developments**

Since the Sadat initiative and until the spring of 1979, Arafat's personal status and influence in the PLO seemed to have eroded somewhat, culminating in the convening of the 14th Palestine National Council session in January 1979. Subsequently, with the improvement in the position of the PLO, during the summer of 1979, Arafat's status improved also.

The erosion in Arafat's status became visible when different personalities and groups staged independent activities without any coordination with him. Arafat was accused by rejectionists of following too moderate a line towards the Sadat initiatives. When groups in the PLO began to conduct terror activities they did not bother to inform him about it. Examples were the assassinations of Siba'i and Hamami and the bus massacre in Israel.

Arafat's situation deteriorated after the Litani operation, when PLO adherents infiltrated in south Lebanon and conducted activities without coordination with Arafat. This followed after Arafat had declared on June 2, 1978, that he would not permit his people to open fire from Lebanon on Israeli territory. Arafat adopted this line because he was interested in an Israeli withdrawal from south Lebanon and did not want to give Israelis a pretext to delay it. He also agreed to the stationing of UN forces at the PLO controlled Beaufort fortress.[29] On June 5, 1978 the Rejection Front, reacting to Arafat's agreement, published a statement to the effect that Arafat does not represent them and that they would not agree to cease activities against Israel.

Internal differences also appeared in the dialogue between the PLO and Jordan. The Rejection Front opposed these negotiations, finding support from the PDFLP.[30] The difference over the negotiations with Jordan developed several times from verbal disputes to violent clashes between Palestinian organizations.[31]

Criticism against Arafat reached a point where on May 24, 1978 the Rejection Front organizations published an open letter jointly with the PDFLP in which they asked to elect a new PLO leadership that would not be autocratic as the present one was.

The rivalry reached its major expression at the 14th Palestine National Council session that was convened between January 15—23, 1979, for the first time, not in Cairo, but in Damascus. Arafat asked for an extension of his authority and the Fath organization asked to increase its representation in the PLO institutions and to increase its share in the distribution of funds received by the PLO. Neither of these demands were granted.

The short-lived improvement in relations between Syria and Iraq had its impact during the Palestine National Council session as the organizations supported by Syria and Iraq, the pro-Syrian Al-Sa'iqa and the pro-Iraqi Arab Liberation Front, coordinated their positions and established a united front against Fath. They opposed Fath demands and stressed their reservations on the "autocratic rule" which, they said, "Arafat had introduced in the PLO".

Internal struggles during the session sharpened and pressure on Fath strengthened as a result of demands by two more organizations — the Palestine Liberation Front of Abu Al-Abbas and the Front of Palestinian Popular Struggle of Samir Ghoshe, both of them rejectionist organizations tending towards Iraq — to join the PLO and its institutions. In the past, Fath had managed to keep them out although at that time those two organizations were supported by the pro-Iraqi and pro-Syrian organizations in the PLO.

The result of such internal struggles and differences was that the Palestine National Council ended its meetings without reaching significant political decisions. [32]

NOTES TO CHAPTER ONE

1. The secret resolutions of the Algiers Arab Summit Conference were leaked by Al Nahar (Beirut), December 4, 1973. The secret resolutions of the Rabat summit were leaked by Al Safir (Beirut), November 30, 1977.

2. President Carter said on December 15, 1977:

"The PLO have been completely negative. They have not been cooperative at all. In spite of my own indirect invitation to them and the direct invitations by Sadat and by Asad, by King Khalid of Saudi Arabia, the PLO have refused to make any move towards a peaceful attitude. They have completely rejected UN resolutions 242 and 338. They have refused to make a public acknowledgement that Israel has a right to exist, to exist in peace. So I think they have, themselves, removed the PLO from any immediate prospect of participation in a peace discussion".

This, however, did not exclude Palestinians from the negotiations, and in spite of Carter's strictures, he added that "we want to be sure that at least moderate Palestinians are included in the discussions". (*Department of State Bulletin*, January 1978, p. 14).

3. King Hussein introduced the "United Arab Kingdom" plan on March 15, 1972. It provided for a division of Jordan into two regions, one on the Western Bank and the other on the Eastern Bank. Each of them had to be autonomous but both of them would be united under the Hashemite Crown. (see Appendices)

4. The Peel Commission's partition plan for Palestine was presented on July 7, 1937. It called for the establishment of an Arab state in the central hill country and in the whole of the south. A Jewish state was to include the Galilee, the surrounding valleys and coastal plain to the south of Jaffa (but not including that town). Jerusalem and Bethlehem together with a wide corridor to Jaffa were to remain under British Mandate Administration.

The partition plan accepted by the UN General Assembly on November 20, 1947, called for the establishment in Palestine of two states, one Arab, one Jewish, with Jerusalem as an international area. In the north, the Arab state would have the west of the Galilee and the Jewish state the east of it. In the center, the Jewish state would have the coastal plain and the Arab state the hills and mountains. The Negev would be in the Jewish state, but Beersheba and the Gaza strip would be in the Arab state.

5. *Ha'aretz* (Tel-Aviv), November 21, 1977.

6. UPI, Reuter, April 8, 1979.

7. Radio Voice of Palestine from Damascus, December 5, 1977.

8. *Al Safir* (Beirut), December 11–15, 1977.

9. *Al Yaqza* (Kuwait), January 9, 1978.

10. *Ha'aretz* February 8, 1978.

11. UPI, AP, June 2, 1979.

12. UPI, January 5, 1978.

13. *Ha'aretz*, January 8, 1978.

14. *Al Jumhuriyya* (Cairo), February 20, 1978.

15. See Egyptian press of February 19–21, 1978.

16. Anis Mansour – close to Sadat – proposed that Egypt should learn from Israel how to react in such cases (October, Cairo, July 14, 1979).

17. *Yediot Aharonoth* (Tel-Aviv), March 26, 1978. See also: Paul Wohl, "Brezhnev and Tel-Aviv", *Christian Science Monitor* (weekly international ed.), April 10, 1978, p. 30.

18. Reports appeared that Wadi' Haddad had been poisoned by a "slow-acting poison" (Al Hawadith, Beirut, April 6, 1978). According to the Voice of Palestine (August 24, 1978) Wadi Haddad had been poisoned by Iraqi Intelligence. Iraq had been trying to control Haddad's organization and to limit its movements.

19. *Middle East Reporter* (Beirut), November 27, 1978 (AFP and UPI)

PLO spokesman in Beirut, Mahmoud Labadi said on December 2, 1978 that the Findley report was "not completely accurate," but declined to elaborate.

20. *Le Monde* (Paris), January 6, 1979.

21. Concluding statement of the Tripoli Conference.
Radio Damascus, December 5, 1978; statement at the conclusion of the Baghdad Conference, Radio Amman, November 5, 1978; Radio Baghdad, March 31, 1979.
22. Hani Al-Hassan, one of the prominent PLO personalities declared openly that the organization supplied arms and munition and provided military training to the opposition to the Shah. *Al Safir* (Beirut), December 5, 1978.
23. Khomeyni interview to the Lebanese *Monday Morning*, January 6, 1979, as quoted by UP and Reuters, January 6, 1979.
24. King Hussein interview by CBS, January 1, 1978.
25. King Hussein interview by *Al Mustaqbal* (Paris) February 11, 1978.
26. Mudar Badran interview by *Al-Ray Al-Amm (Kuwait)*, February 26, 1978.
27. Al Qabas (Kuwait), April 9, 1978.
28. Radio Amman, November 18 and 29, 1978, March 17, 1979; Radio Damascus, November 18, 1978, March 17, 1979; Arafat interview by *Al-Nahar*, February 3, 1979.
29. Radio Voice of Israel, June 2, 1978; *Al-Nahar*, June 3, 1978.
30. See sharp PFLP criticism of PLO-Jordanian negotiations in Al-Nahar, December 12, 1978.
31. For example, the clashes in the refugee camps Nahr Al-Bard and Al-Badawi, between Fath and PDFLP members on January 4–6, 1979.
32. *Al-Safir, Al-Nahar*, January 18, 19, 22, 23, 1979; Radio Beirut, January 23, 1979.

EMERGENCE
IDEOLOGY
SOCIAL BACKGROUND

CHAPTER TWO

EMERGENCE, GROWTH AND REPRESENTATION

When the British Mandate over Palestine terminated in May 1948, the Palestinian national movement was in a deep crisis. In contrast to what had happened in other Arab countries which succeeded in creating for themselves a secular-political leadership, the Palestinians supported a religious-political leader, the Grand Mufti of Jerusalem, Haj Muhammad Amin Al-Husseini.[1] This course led to failures, disappointments and continuing difficulties. Non-Muslim Arabs (Christians and others) had generally refused to accept him. An opposition developed against him, also from within the Muslim population, by the Nashashibis (whose role is fully defined in CHAPTER FOUR: Social Background). The internal relations between the two factions went from bad to worse and during the Arab Revolt of 1936–1939 about two thirds of the Arabs who lost their lives, died in internal Arab clashes, not in operations against the British authorities.

On October 1, 1937, the British deposed Haj Amin, outlawed all the Palestinian political bodies and organizations, arrested most of their leaders and exiled many of them.[2] The exiled leaders (mainly to Syria and Lebanon) were threatened by the possibility that another, alternative leadership might arise among the masses of the Palestinian population who had remained in the country. They tried hard to prevent it, mainly by sending in groups which engaged in a merciless internal terror. They thus succeeded in preventing the rise of any other leadership, but the result was, in fact, an absence of any leadership at all.[3] This leadership vacuum was exploited by other Arab states. At the St. James Conference, convened by the United Kingdom in London in 1939 to deal with the Palestine problem, several Arab states enjoyed the status of equal partners with Palestinians. Within a year, these Arab states had achieved a position of patronage vis-a-vis the Palestinians. These Arab "patron states" relegated the Palestinians and their problems to lower priorities in the years of the Second World War.

When "the Palestinian problem" came up before the United Nations Organization, the UN General Assembly adopted a resolution on November 29,

1947 for the establishment in Palestine of Jewish and Arab states. The Jews accepted the resolution but the Palestinians and Arab states rejected it. A Jewish state named Israel was proclaimed on May 15, 1948, the day of the termination of the British mandate. The Palestinians joined the armies of Egypt, Trans-Jordan, Syria, Iraq, Saudi Arabia, Lebanon, and Sudan in an invasion of the country to end Israel's existence. From the outset, the invasion was turned back by the Israelis and in agreements that were concluded between Israel and the Arab states, control of central Palestine was given to Trans-Jordan and of the Gaza Strip to Egypt.

King Abdullah of Trans-Jordan convened a conference in Jericho on December 1, 1948, at which Palestinian notables repudiated recognition of the Supreme Arab Committee and asked Abdullah to annex the Arab part of Palestine, that was known later as the West Bank, with Jordan. This was done, *de facto,* in 1949 and *de jure* on April 1950. The name of the state changed from Trans-Jordan (only one bank of the river) to the Hashemite Kingdom of Jordan (the two banks). Only the United Kingdom and Pakistan recognized that annexation.

A similar situation prevailed in the Gaza Strip. The Palestinian Supreme Arab Committee announced on September 22, 1948 in Gaza, the establishment of "a Government of All Palestine". It adopted, on October 1, 1948, the flag of Sherif Hussein of Mecca of 1916 as the flag of Palestine and declared Palestine's independence in the area "between Syria and Lebanon in the north, Syria and Trans-Jordan in the east, the Mediterranean in the west and Egypt in the south". The government was dissolved with the arrival of Egyptian forces — and all its decisions were declared invalid. Egypt did not annex Gaza but left it under Egyptian military rule.

The Arabs of Palestine, then about 1.2 million, comprised those on the West Bank and in Jerusalem (since 1950 a part of Jordan) numbering about 600–700,000, including 250,000–300,000 refugees — a great number of them in the course of time, settling on the East Bank.

— those in the Gaza Strip, under Egyptian rule, numbering about 250,000, of whom about 150,000 held refugee status.

— Arabs in the state of Israel, numbering about 160,000.

— those in other countries — about 100,000 in Lebanon, about 50,000 in Syria and small numbers elsewhere in the region.[4]

A state of Palestine was not created though more than 70% of its area — according to the UN plan of partition — remained in Arab hands from the crucial period of 1947/1948 till 1967. Thirty years later, in 1976, a resolution was accepted by the Arab states to grant Palestine the status of a member-state in the Arab League. ("Palestine" had enjoyed only observer status in this organization.)

At the time of the 1948 Arab-Israeli war, about 500,000 Arabs of Palestine sought refuge in neighbouring countries, believing it to be only temporary and that they would soon return with the victorious Arab armies (see CHAPTER FOUR: Social Background). Israel, absorbing at that time about 1.2 million Jewish refugees from the Arab countries, allowed some of them to return but most of them who stayed in the Arab countries remained in refugee camps. Jordan and

Israel were the only countries that gave Palestinians citizenship, election rights and representation in their parliaments. Jordan also encouraged a great number of them to move from the West to the East Bank. They thus constitute half the population of Jordan. Other Arab countries treated them as foreigners and second rate citizens, tried to prevent their absorption by the local population, and refused them even provisional rights of settlement. Everything was done to defer a solution to the Palestinian refugee problem, a handy stick to beat Israel with, at any and every opportunity.

Consequently, the problem of Palestinian Arabs ceased to be only a local problem. Their status became a pan-Arab problem and Palestinian politics a part of pan-Arab politics. Finidng ways to solve the problem was seen as a pan-Arab prerogative. Palestinian Arabs were precluded from using their own initiative and instead, became pawns on the chessboard of Arab politics.

The stand that was taken by Egypt's President Jamal Abd al-Nasir and under his influence by the Arab summit conferences was that a war against Israel must wait until the Arab states had established a military superiority. As a facet of the Egyptian-Syrian "cold war" after the break-up of the Egyptian-Syrian union (1958–1961), it led to Syrian accusations that Egypt was neglecting the Palestinian problem and to Egyptian denials.

These accusations were levelled again in 1963, at the time when Israel laid a water pipeline to carry water from the Kinneret to the Negev. Arab states threatened to go to war if Israel began to pump water, but war did not break out when pumping by Israel began. Instead, Nasir called for the first Arab Summit Conference in Cairo in January 1964. A resolution to divert the Jordan River was adopted there, to thwart Israel's plans.

In order to preserve the "Palestinian entity" from extinction and to keep it under Egypt's effective control, a decision was adopted at the conference to convene a founding conference of the "Palestinian entity". A Palestinian congress was convened in Jerusalem on May 25–June 2, 1964, with delegates appointed by Ahmad Shuqayri participating. It announced the establishment of a Palestine Liberation Organization (PLO), adopted a Palestine National Covenant (or Charter), and decided to establish a Palestine Liberation Army (PLA). Shuqayri was elected Chairman of the PLO Executive Committee.

The PLO, which was largely under Egyptian control, stressed political activity that fitted Egypt's policy of that time. Shuqayri supported Egyptian positions, and the PLO obligated the Egyptians with a Palestinian cause to further their own aims. A Lebanese comment aptly termed the PLO "the Palestinian branch of Nasirism", continuing that Shuqayri was the nominal head of the PLO, but President Nasir was its real leader.[5] However, neither the PLO nor the PLA enjoyed any real power to conduct independent activities. The PLO appointments, organization, training and activities were decided by the Arab League and in fact by Egypt. This situation changed later, after the Fath took over control of the PLO in 1968.

The PLA comprised separate regiments stationed in Arab states. They were manned by Palestinians who lived in those countries and were subordinated to local military commands. They were supported financially by the host countries. The Palestinian recruits suspected that these Arab countries allowed lower budgets for the PLA than for their own units, provided them with second-rate training, and at the same time, gave them duties to perform which they did not want to do themselves.[6]

Syria's attitude to the PLO was reserved and her support was given to another Palestinian organization — Al-Fath, "the conquest", the word being made up from the initials in reverse order of Harakat Al-Tahrir Al-Filastini — the Movement for the Liberation of Palestine.

Al-Fath was established towards the end of the 1950's by Yasir Arafat, then a student at Cairo University, Khalil Al-Wazir (Abu Jihad), Salah Khalaf (Abu Iyad) and Faruq Al-Qaddumi (Abu Lutf). By calling Al-Fath a movement and not an organization, its founders emphasized that it would include as many Palestinians as possible.[7] The ideological basis of Al-Fath was deliberately weak in order to prevent factions and splits.[8] Unlike the PLO which was involved in inter-Arab affairs, Al-Fath tried not to adopt positions on internal Arab social and political affairs, which it deemed to be a diversion of attention from the main aim — the struggle against Israel in order to liberate Palestine.

Al-Fath, from the start, emphasized the military thrust of its movement carried out by its military arm, Al-Asifa (the Storm). The first military operation was made on January 1, 1965, and this day was proclaimed as its founding day.

When, in February 1966, the left wing of the Ba'th party came to power in Syria in a coup, Al-Fath was an immediate beneficiary. The new leadership adopted the doctrine of "People's Liberation War" as its declared policy. Al-Fath was given the backing of the Syrian army, including supplies of arms and training facilities. This brought it increasingly under Syrian control (more specifically — under the control of Syrian Army Intelligence). The Syrians had an interest in provoking clashes between Jordan and Israel and used Fath to that end. They were infiltrated to Jordan and from there to Israel. Israel retaliated against Jordan, in accordance with its policy to hold the country from which the infiltrators came as responsible for their operations. The Israeli raid into the West Bank village of Samu' on November 1966 was the major operation of its kind at that time.

Another Palestinian group in the service of Syria's intelligence, most of whose work was to gather information for them, was the Palestine Liberation Front (PLF). It was a small group, established in 1959 by Ahmad Jibril, a former officer of the Syrian army, and Ahmad Za'rour, a former Jordanian officer, with the aim of waging a guerrilla war against Israel. When Al-Fath launched its first operations in the beginning of 1965, contact was established between the two groups, but this coordination was short-lived.[9]

Al-Fath, and still more the PLF, achieved little in operations in Israel, but the chain of attack and counterattack that followed contributed much to the sharpening of tension in the area and indirectly to the outbreak of the June 1967 Six Day War. Knowing that with their small and limited power they would never have any chance of beating Israel by themselves, the Palestinian organizations tried to push the Arab states to an open war against her. That war broke out on June 1967, but its results were opposite to the Palestinian organizations' hopes.

● June 1967–September 1970 – High Tide

In Arab thinking the military defeat of Egypt, Syria, Jordan and Iraq in June 1967 called for a total reconstruction of their regular forces in order to continue the struggle and just as important, in order to raise morale and to demonstrate that the Arabs were not acknowledging defeat. Arab "confrontation states" and Egypt in particular concentrated their efforts on the restoration of the status quo ante June 1967. However, the heavy defeat of the four Arab armies made it clear that the regular armies alone could not meet Israeli military superiority. Thus the Arab states resolved to support guerrilla warfare against Israel. As a rebuttal to accusations that they were therefore abandoning the Palestinians, increasing commitments were made to those who represented "the Palestinians' struggle" – the fida'i organizations.[10]

Al Fath, representing the "activist" fida'i trend, was thus considerably strengthened as an alternative to the PLO. Under pressure, Ahmad Shuqayri resigned on December 24, 1967, as PLO Chairman and Yahia Hamuda was elected acting Chairman. On July 1968 Al Fath representatives joined the PLO's principal bodies. Less than a year later, thanks to good relations with Arab states and the aid received from them, Al-Fath was in a dominant position in the PLO and on February 1969 took over the PLO leadership. Al Fath leader, Yasir Arafat became chairman of the PLO executive committee.

Al Fath opted for "small war tactics" as the most rewarding strategy in the struggle against Israel. Its military doctrine was to a large extent based on Chinese and north Vietnamese principles of guerrilla warfare. Terms such as "people's war", "base area" and "self-reliance" were frequently found in Al Fath propaganda. It demanded that Arab states bordering Palestine play the role of Hanoi in the Vietnamese revolution.[11]

Attempts were made by Al Fath to build an image of a military organization unaligned to any ideological or political tendency. It called for the mobilisation of all forces in the struggle against Israel and the deferment of a resolution of internal differences to a later stage. For Palestinians, it said, this is the stage of national liberation, of liberating their country. When this stage will be over, it will be followed by the next stage of social and economic liberation. In the present stage, Palestinians must cooperate with all Arab regimes and not interfere in their internal affairs and must put pressure to receive aid but not allow themselves to become completely dependent on Arab regimes. Palestinians must try to use Arab supporters and not be used by them.

In the discussion whether the struggle should be all-Arab or Palestinian, Al Fath stressed the Palestinian motivations. Palestinians were to take the leading role in the struggle by taking the initiatives. The rhetorical stress on self-reliance was a reaction to their bitter experience of being abandoned by one or another Arab country or leader when convenient to them.

Al Fath attracted mainly the nationalist and Muslim activists who were not motivated by some specific left creed or ideology. It enjoyed the support of the more conservative Arab states like Saudi Arabia, Kuwait and the Persian Gulf principalities.[12] It was, however, not a right-wing movement but can be compared to the Algerian FLN in its early stages. Islamic motivations were present, but the leaders tried to present a revolutionary image to the outside world (at least outside Saudi Arabia and other conservative Arab states), as the international friends of Al-Fath were nearly all left-wing circles in Europe and the governments of communist countries.[13]

The image that Al Fath assiduously built for itself was not endorsed by the "Popular Front for the Liberation of Palestine" Al-Jabha Al Sha'abiya Li-Tahrir Filastin (PFLP) which looked upon Al Fath as a conglomeration of Palestinian bourgeois and Muslim Brotherhood members identified with reactionary Arab regimes.

The PFLP, headed by George Habash, was established on December 7, 1967, by a merger of three organizations: the Vengeance Youth — the Palestinian branch and military arm of the Arab Nationalists Movement (ANM)[14] — headed by George Habash; the Heroes of Return, a pro-Egyptian military faction set up in late 1966 by anti-Shuqayri members of the PLO, based in Lebanon; the Syrian sponsored and based Palestine Liberation Front (PLF) headed by Ahmad Jibril and Ahmad Za'rour.

The PFLP adopted a Marxist-Leninist ideology, terminology and slogans.[15] It aimed to fight not only against "Zionism" (Israel) but also against "imperialism", (the US in particular) and "Arab reactionaries" (Saudi Arabia, Jordan, etc.). The latter were not to be trusted, as the basic contradictions were between it and the Arab masses and not between it and Israel, allied with its ally, the "imperialists". The PFLP saw itself a part of "world revolutionary forces" with its allies, the Cubans, the Vietnamese, North Koreans and Chinese, but less so, the Soviets because they were advocating a political settlement. The struggle "to liberate Palestine" was considered by the PFLP to be a part of a general world revolution that will be both political and social. Palestinian struggle against "Zionism" is seen by it to have a class and not only a national character because "only the toilers are its faithful carriers".

While Al Fath stressed Palestinian interests first and only after it Arabism — the PFLP reversed the priorities, stating the long term aim to be not the establishment of a Palestinian State but the consummation of Arab unity. It considers cooperation with most existing Arab regimes impossible, as basic differences emerge constantly and lead to divisions among them. However, it retained connections with Iraq and the Popular Republic of South Yemen (PRSY). It has an interest to implicate Arab states and involve them in the Arab-Israeli conflict.[16] The more they will be involved in the struggle, the more chances will be there for their radicalization and eventual overthrow. The short-term PFLP aim was — and still is — the establishment close to Israel, of an "Arab Hanoi" in Jordan or in South Lebanon, which would help to defeat Israel in concert with an armed mass struggle inside the "Israeli Saigon".[17]

Believing in world revolution, the PFLP engaged in foreign operations which involved parties not directly concerned with the Arab-Israeli conflict, leading to ties with terror organizations such as the Irish IRA, the German Bader-Meinhoff group, the Japanese Red Army and the Italian Red Brigades.

PFLP was engaged in a series of hijackings of planes that began with the hijacking of an El Al plane to Algeria in July 1968. The most notorious hijackings took place in September 1970 when four airliners were hijacked, one was blown up at Cairo airport and three were flown with about 500 hostages, near Zarqa in Jordan. The PFLP justified such operations by saying that they keep the Palestinian problem alive and make the world conscious of its existence. But sometimes such operations harmed the Palestinian organizations more than they helped them. For example, the hijackings in September 1970 gave King Hussein a pretext to attack them and to rally world support for his actions. In the midseventies, the PFLP stopped the hijackings.

Since its establishment there had been a dispute between a Left and Right wing in the PFLP. The Left, headed by Na'if Hawatimah failed to take over the leadership from the "Center" led by Habash, who provided some kind of balance between the Left and the Right in the former PLF headed by Ahmad Jibril. Habash pursued an anti-Syrian line and was arrested by Syrians at the beginning of 1968. A former Engineers officer in the Syrian Army, Jibril, who had many connections with the Syrians, rejected the Habash line. He broke with the PFLP in October 1968, establishing the "Popular Front for the Liberation of Palestine — General Command" (PFLP — GC — Al-Qiyada Al Amma Lil-Jabba Al-Sha'abiyya Li-Tahrir Filastin). It was a small pro-Syrian organization with a restricted membership, but rated to have a high military preparedness level. It used leftist slogans similar to those of the PFLP, but, with scanty attention to their relevance. Political issues were considered to be a waste of time, a deflection from military activities and the active struggle against Israel.

This was the opposite of the position taken by the PFLP Left wing led by Na'if Hawatimah (a non-Palestinian Christian from Trans-Jordan), which broke away from the PFLP in February 1969 establishing the "Popular Democratic Front for the Liberation of Palestine" (PDFLP — Al-Jabha Al Sha'biyya Al Dimoqratiyya Li-Tahrir Filastin). The split occurred when Habash, released from a Syrian gaol, returned to the PFLP to find that Hawatimah had usurped his command; after a fierce struggle between the two leaders, Hawatimah left the PFLP with his followers and set up the new organization.

The PDFLP adopted an extreme Marxist-Leninist ideology[18] and established ties with Arab Left and Communist parties.[19] Its political doctrine was based more on Vietnamese and Cuban innovations, rather than on Marxism-Leninism on the Moscow model. It called on the overthrow of not only the so-called "reactionary" Arab regimes, but also the Moscow-oriented "progressive" Arab regimes (as in Egypt, Iraq, Algeria). The latter were considered by the PDFLP not much different from the "reactionary" regimes as all of them had failed in achieving necessary national and social goals.[20] The PDFLP was more doctrinal than the PFLP which it scorned for shallowness and impetuosity in place of ideological thinking. The PDFLP paid more attention to Leftist political education, and its members were required to study the works of Lenin and theoreticians of the popular struggle. It stressed the ideas of the Left, rather than Arab nationalism and advocated a "democratic state" in Palestine, as a strategic aim and not only as a tactical move to receive international support. The PDFLP, unlike other Palestinian organizations was ready to grant the Jews of Israel a certain cultural autonomy in a future Arab Palestinian state.

When Arab states were faced with the growth of a strong Palestinian movement enjoying considerable prestige, they took steps to have a foothold and an influence in this movement. Several states, including Egypt, Saudi Arabia, Syria and Iraq established "their own" Palestinian organizations but only the last two met with success. Syria established the Al Sa'iqa and Iraq, the Arab Liberation Front.

The organization called the "Vanguards of the Popular Liberation War", Tala'i Harb Al-Tahrir Al-Sha'bi better known as Al Sa'iqa, was established by the Syrian Ba'th regime by merging three small existing organizations in December 1968. It was based on Ba'th members of Palestinian origin and its theory and ideology were identical to those of the Syrian Ba'th. Syria provided it with finances, weapons, manpower, training courses, facilities and instructions. Al Sa'iqa saw the "Palestinian revolution" as part of a pan-Arab revolution and saw no justification for the establishment of a separate Palestinian state, opting for union with other Arab countries under Syria's leadership. Hence the word "Palestine" is missing from the organization's name. Second in size in terms of manpower and equipment, it presented itself as an alternative to Al-Fath and has been trying ever since to take over the political and military lead from it.

At the outset, the organization was headed by Colonel Tahir Dablan, a Syrian officer of Palestinian origin. But by the end of 1968 he was deposed.[21] At the end of 1970, General Hafiz Al-Asad who took over power in Syria, nominated Zuhayr Muhsin, a Palestinian by origin and a member of the Syrian Ba'th party "national leadership" as the head of the organization.

The establishment of Al-Sa'iqa fulfilled several needs of the Syrian Ba'th party: to free the party from internal pressures of extremists who were demanding more activities against Israel, to enable Syria to intervene indirectly through Al-Sa'iqa in the Palestinian arena, in Lebanon and in Jordan, and most important — as an instrument of internal Syrian politics. It was established at the time of a power struggle in Syria between the civilian wing of the Ba'th party headed by the party's Deputy Secretary General, Salah Jadid (then Syria's "strong man") and the military wing headed by Defence Minister Hafiz Al-Asad[22], and became to a great extent an instrument in the struggle between the two wings.[23] Al-Sa'iqa was attached directly to the Ba'th party (after being linked to the army whose Palestinian officers had been transferred to it earlier) serving its civilian wing as a counter-weight to the army. The Jadid wing tried to strengthen Al Sa'iqa by asking party organizations and affiliated mass groups, especially student organizations (even if not of Palestinian origin) to join Al-Sa'iqa training courses.

With the increase in the rivalry between the Syrian and Iraqi Ba'th regimes — the latter came to power in Iraq in July 1968 — Iraq decided to follow the Syrian example and to establish "their own" Palestinian organization. Iraq's reply to Al-Sa'iqa was the establishment in April 1969 of the "Arab Liberation Front" (ALF) — Jabbat Al-Tahrir Al-Arabiyya — from the pro-Iraqi Ba'th party cadres. The Front, as the absence of "Palestine" in its name also indicated, stressed the Arab rather than the Palestinian character of its movement and opposed the creation of Palestine as a new and separate state. According to its ideology, Palestine should be liberated, but must be simultaneously merged into existing Arab territories, in the interest of grand Arab unity, under the leadership of the Iraqi Ba'th party. The majority of its members came from Arab countries and only a minority were of Palestinian origin. It was always dependent on Iraq and served as an instrument of her inter-Arab policy. Its leader was 'Abd Al-Wahhab Al-Kayyali, later to be replaced by Abd Al-Rahim Ahmad.

• Jordan — A Lost Citadel 1970–1971

During the first six months after the Six Day War Palestinian organizations aimed at concentrating their activity in the newly occupied West Bank and the Gaza Strip. Believing in the slogan of Chairman Mao that "the revolutionary must act among his fellow people as a fish in the water", the organizations proclaimed a "popular armed revolution" whose purpose was to stir up civil rebellion among the Palestinians in those territories. However, the local population clearly rejected this call.

Most of the Al-Fath cells in the West Bank were discovered and in January 1968, Israeli forces reached the base in Ramallah in which Yasir Arafat was hiding, but he escaped in the nick of time, crossed the Jordan River and found refuge in Amman. Thus ended the "popular armed revolution".[25]

The Palestinian organizations then concentrated their activities in Jordan, in which they enjoyed a certain political independence and a territorial base which enabled them to continue an active military struggle against Israel.

At the beginning of 1968, they were concentrated mainly in the Jordan Valley, close to the Israeli-Jordan border. Ousting the local villagers, they converted the principal villages in the valley into armed bases. But in March, 1968, after an Israeli schoolbus hit a mine laid by Al-Fath, causing many casualties, Israeli forces attacked the principal Palestinian base at Karama. Again Yasir Arafat, who was at the base, fled in time, leaving his men behind. From then on, the Palestinian organizations opted for dispersion in various areas in Jordan, rather than concentration in a single place.

Palestinians were granted Jordanian citizenship and absorbed among the population. But while Jordan hoped to take over "liberated Palestine" radical Palestinians were counting on a later take-over. Even more significantly, radical organizations such as the PFLP or PDFLP raised the slogan that "the road to Tel-Aviv leads through Amman". Rating Jordan to be weaker than Israel, they saw in a revolution in Jordan the first step towards "the liberation of Palestine".

Organization	Social Ideology	Palestinism vs Arabism	Ties to Arab States	Class that Bears Struggle	Party	Struggle against Israel	Democratic Palestinian State	Historical Explanation of Weakness
AL FATH	Lacking, but gradually turning to the Left	Stressing of Palestinism, Arabs only help and support		All Palestinian People	No need for a party; the state will be established by those who struggle	is the Palestine revolution	As an Arab State	Leaning on Arab states and not on Palestinians
PFLP	Marxism-Leninism	Arabism and after that Palestinism	Iraq	Workers in particular, but petty bourgeoisie should not be rejected	Unity of Party and Strugglers	is the way to an Arab revolution	A tactical slogan only; a part of Arab unity	Lack of a scientific class approach
PDFLP	Marxism-Leninism	Palestinism and after that Arabism; sees itself internationalistic		To rely only on the proletariat	The struggle is a tool of policy	has a class meaning	A central principle	Lack of a scientific class approach
AL-SA'IQA	"Scientific Socialism"	Arabism under the Syrian Ba'ath hegemony	Syria	Each Arab of the working class that believes in Ba'th principles	The party leads	a part of all-Arab struggle and of liberating Palestine & the Arab world from reaction and imperialism	A strategic principle: required by progressiveness	
ALF	Socialism coming from Arab nationalism	Arabism under the Iraqi Ba'ath hegemony; the stressing of Palestinism considered anti-nationalist	Iraq	Workers in particular, but need a revolutionary vanguard; not to reject national bourgeoisie	The party leads	will succeed if it will adopt the idea of all-Arab unity	Sharply rejected; no separate state has to be established	A separation of Palestinian problem from Arabism; divisions in the Arab world

Other organizations in the service of Arab states, like Syria and Egypt worked hard to influence Jordan to subordinate her policy to that of the countries which supported their respective organizations.

Jordan's policy became a function of the interplay of two fundamentally opposed factors: inter-Arab pressures for freedom of action of Palestinian organizations versus Jordan's attempts to safeguard her sovereignty. In the period up to September 1970, the Palestinian organizations gradually increased the scope of their activities, becoming a sort of "state within a state". Numerous tasks, ordinarily the domain of the state, were performed by them alongside the regular Jordanian offices. Palestinians operated welfare and health services, established courts of justice and formed their own police forces.[26] They, however, went beyond the freedom of action granted to them and over-estimated their forces and chances to come to power.[27]

Al-Fath seemed initially willing to avoid an open confrontation with the Jordanian army, but the PFLP and PDFLP were not prepared to accept any control whatsoever, and staged clashes with the army in the hope of forcing Fath to join in and believing that Palestinians would emerge victorious from any showdown with the Jordanian government. In the summer of 1970 the PDFLP raised the slogan of "All Power to the Resistance" (on the pattern of the Russian Bolshevik 1917 slogan of "All Power to the Soviets" before their coming to power in October 1917) and on September 1, 1970, made an attempt on King Hussein's life. On September 6, the PFLP gained control of an airfield near Zarqa, where three planes hijacked by them were forced to land.

The northern part of Jordan, the Irbid area in particular, became increasingly controlled by the Feda'yun. In and around Amman the situation was on the verge of chaos, with Palestinian organizations on the point of becoming the dominant element in the capital. On September 16, a Palestinian "liberated area" was proclaimed in the northern part of Jordan.[28]

The Jordanian army, particularly the officers from a Bedouin background, were not ready to accept that situation and pressed the King hard to bring an end to it. After considerable hesitation, a military government was formed on September 16. The next day heavy fighting broke out between the Jordanian army and Palestinian organizations. The latter were assisted by an armed invasion of Syrian forces on the night of September 18–19. The Syrians sent a regular armoured brigade as well as their own PLA brigade, Hittin, crossing the border and engaging in battle with the Jordanian Army. In the clash, the Jordanians had the upper hand and the Syrians retreated, suffering casualties. When Syria began to organize other units for dispatch to Jordan, Israel concentrated her force near the border, warning Syria not to intervene again. The Syrians left Jordan on September 23. The next day the Feda'yun accepted a cease-fire. They were saved from complete annihilation only by the intervention of Arab states. Jordanian sovereignty was gradually restored at the espense of the Feda'yun who in July 1971 were eventually forced to leave the country. Their territorial base in Jordan was completely lost.

The grave results of the war between Jordan and the Palestinian organizations brought the latter to a re-appraisal of the situation. Some Palestinian personalities, including Arafat, took consolation in "the ill wind that blows no good" spirit by contending that "the unity of the rifles" of the more important organizations had been forged while the smaller factions had been eliminated.[29] But the more important message was clear: it was proved that in an open confrontation between an established State and an underground organization — the latter does not have much chance to win. The lesson that was learned was the need to establish as far as possible regular military forces in order to prevent a similar defeat in the future. This was undertaken after 1971. When the Fath found a new territorial base in Lebanon, it established there semi-military forces — the battalions "Karameh", "Kastel" and "Yarmouq".

Another much more important result of the war was on the political plane. The fighting against Jordanian military forces came at a time of a cease-fire in the "War of Attrition" between Israel and Egypt, tendencies in Egypt towards a political solution and the death of Jamal Abd al-Nasir. There were many in the PLO who argued that King Hussein had dared to make an open stand against them because of the "political climate" in the Middle East. There is no doubt that had the cease-fire and the political process come a year or two earlier, when the PLO was more popular, its reaction would have been stronger, perhaps also more violent. But this time, its military power smashed, it could no longer ignore these contrary opinions. In fact, some modifications towards a political process were introduced in the ideology.

The National Covenant, valid since 1968, spoke about armed struggle as "the only way" to liberate Palestine. Resolutions at the Eighth Palestinian National Congress of March 1971 defined armed struggle as the "principal way" to liberation, which inferred that there were other ways too.[30]

● Lebanon – The Last Territorial Base

Palestinian infiltration in Lebanon was carried out during the second half of the 1960's, even before the events of the "Black September" in Jordan. However, it is clear that these events accelerated that process. The situation in Lebanon, while in some respects similar to that in Jordan, was also different in other important aspects.

Unlike Jordan, Lebanon was never regarded by the PLO as a part of Palestine. Moreover, there had been no sizeable and rooted Palestinian minority among the local population. About 160,000 Palestinian refugees had lived in Lebanon since 1948, but unlike in Jordan, they had no citizen rights, and had never reached any key positions in the Lebanese government, economy or society.

On the other hand, the pluralist, internally divided Lebanese society facilitated infiltration by the PLO. The PLO found Beirut more convenient than Amman as a political center. The local Muslim and Left factions were decidedly more sympathetic, mass communications were better developed and the Lebanese authorities, who were afraid of any change in the delicate balance between Christians and Muslims, could be more easily manipulated.

Now, after 1970, Lebanon became the last territorial base of the PLO and the last confrontation border through which the organization could carry on its military activities against Israel.

In effect, however, the course of events was similar to that in Jordan. Within a short period, the PLO created also in Lebanon "a state within a state", smuggled weapons and ammunition to the refugee camps, turned them into *de facto* ex-territorial areas, and brought the country into the vicious circle of Palestinian attacks against Israel and Israeli retaliation.

Towards the end of 1968, some Palestinian organizations such as the Fath, Sa'iqa and the PFLP entered into the wild, thinly populated region of ravines and caves on the western slopes of Mount Hermon. The area was on the Lebanese side of the converging borders of Israel, Syria and Lebanon.[31] The Arabic name of the area is 'Arqub', but "Fathland", a sobriquet given to it by a Western journalist — was readily adopted by the mass media in the West. Syrian aid and supplies were given to the organizations, through a path which was called "the Arafat path". Lebanese authorities, especially Prime Minister Abdullah Al-Yafi, tried at first to ignore this process.[32] However, Palestinian armed penetration continued and also spread to the refugee camps on the coastal plain of Lebanon and into Beirut, the heart and capital of the country.

The stronger Palestinian organizations became in Lebanon, the greater were their claims. They asked to have training centres in the refugee camps, to maintain there arms and to act freely against Israel from Lebanese territory. Arab states pressed Lebanon into permitting strikes against Israel from her territory. Lebanon, whose border with Israel had been the quietest since 1948, showed no interest in the PLO proposals. The result was the outburst of clashes during 1969 between Lebanese military forces and Palestinian groups, the most violent of them occurring in October 1969 in Beirut, south Lebanon and in the refugee camps. At that stage, President Charles Helou appealed to Jamal Abd al-Nasir, asking him to mediate. The Lebanese Chief of Staff, General Emil Al-Bustani, hastened to Cairo and in the negotiations between him, Arafat and Egypt's Foreign Minister Mahmud Riyad, an agreement was reached on November 3, 1969, that is known since then as the Cairo agreement. Its text was never officially published, but it was soon leaked in a Lebanese newspaper.

The Cairo agreement, which continues to be in force at the time of this writing, expressly stipulated PLO recognition of Lebanon's sovereignty and the authority of its government. But it also officially recognized the organizations' right to act from Lebanon against Israel (in spite of the existence of an armistice agreement between both countries). The agreement called for a census of the members of Palestinian organizations in Lebanon at that time. Joint PLO-Lebanese units were to be established to supervise its implementation.[33]

The Christian Rightists (the Phalangists and the National bloc) opposed the Cairo agreement and resolved to annul it. This led to further clashes during 1970. Such incidents developed in May 1973 into a violent struggle. The Lebanese army intervened, using heavy arms, tanks and the air force. Syria closed her border as a means of pressure on the Lebanese authorities. The waves of violence ended with the Melkart agreement of May 1973, which supplemented the earlier Cairo agreement. It limited the number of armed PLO members in different areas of Lebanon, with the exception of 'Arqub (Fathland), restricted the quantity of arms which organizations were permitted to hold in refugee camps to only light weapons; prohibited medium and heavy arms, prohibited the PLO to wear uniforms and carry arms while visiting towns and to block roads inside Lebanon.[34]

Within a short time, new clashes broke out, this time as a result of disagreements in interpreting the Melkart agreement. The question was whether the limiting of the number of armed PLO men and arms referred to the situation that existed in Lebanon in 1973 — at the time of the Melkart agreement, or because it was a supplement to the Cairo agreement — according to the situation in 1969. The clashes ended only with the outbreak of the Arab-Israeli war of October 1973.

It is instructive to examine internal aspects of the PLO and the Palestinian presence in Lebanon during that period.

The PLO was dominated by Al-Fath in a coalition with Al-Sa'iqa and the PDFLP. Pressure was exerted on Palestinian organizations by Arab states to unite or at least increase cooperation among them. It led to attempts to act together in areas of military, financial and information activities and appropriate departments were established in the PLO apparatus to deal with this coordination. A certain measure of cooperation in the military field was achieved in Lebanon in which all organizations had an interest to continue to keep their semi-independent status.

Al-Fath continued to be the largest and the dominant organization in the Palestinian arena. It maintained close relations with almost all Arab regimes, radical and conservative alike, trying to keep away from controversial social and political affairs. The only exception was with regard to Jordan, Al-Fath endorsing the PFLP position that the downfall of the regime in Jordan is a necessary precondition to the "liberation of Palestine" — a reaction to the events of July 1971, when Palestinian organizations were forced to stop their activities in that country.

The "Black September" organization (named after the harsh measures by Jordanian authorities against Palestinian organizations in September 1970) was a cover for Al-Fath activities, as Black September was headed by members of Al-Fath's inner circle. It appeared publicly for the first time while assuming the responsibility for the assassination in Cairo of Jordan's Prime Minister, Wasfi Al Tal (November 28, 1971). Later, in December 1971 the organization shot and slightly wounded Jordan's Ambassador in London, Zeid Al Rifa'i (who later became Jordanian Prime Minister), blew up a gas plant in the Netherlands, oil tanks in Hamburg and an oil pipeline in Trieste. In May 1972 it hijacked a "Sabena" airliner and forced it to land at the Lydda Airport. On September 5, 1972, the organization murdered Israeli sportsmen at the Olympic Games in Munich; on December 28, 1972, it seized the Israeli Embassy in Bangkok, taking six hostages. In 1973 it attacked and occupied Saudi Arabian embassies in

Khartoum and Paris.   Although Al-Fath subsequently also undertook such activities, it proclaimed responsibility neither for its own acts nor for those of "Black September".

Al-Sa'iqa gained in importance when the center of activity of the Palestinian organizations moved from Jordan to Lebanon.   Syria could, through Sa'iqa, influence developments in the Palestinian and Lebanese arenas.   She did so, by creating tension and bringing about a deterioration in relations between Palestinians and Lebanese authorities.   It enabled Syria to intervene on behalf of Palestinians and in that way gain an influence both in Lebanon and among Palestinian organizations.   Al-Sa'iqa also served as an instrument of internal Syrian politics.   Before staging the "bloodless coup" in November 1970 which gave him supreme power in Syria, General Hafiz Al Asad sent military units to surround Al-Sa'iqa bases under the control of the rival party's civilian wing and made them powerless.   After Asad came to power, he removed pro-Jadid elements from the Sa'iqa command and replaced them with "his people."   Since then, it was led by Zuhayr Muhsin.

The PDFLP, opposed to existing Arab regimes and to any compromise, strongly influenced other Palestinian organizations to the extent that relations between them and Jordan and Egypt rapidly deteriorated.   By 1972 the PDFLP admitted the error of its ways, and moved closer to Al-Fath advocating a unity of Palestinian organizations, and an improvement of relations with Syria, Iraq, Arab communist parties and with the USSR.   Consequently, the USSR began to provide some aid to the Front.

The PDFLP nevertheless continued to maintain good relations with China and in July 1973 sent a large delegation to Peking.

Simultaneously, the PFLP widened the scope of its foreign operations which included inter alia the hijacking of a "Lufthansa" plane in Bombay in February 1972 and the murder of passengers at the Lydda Airport — the latter perpetrated on its behalf by the Japanese "Red Army".   The PFLP also cooperated with other international terrorist organizations including the German Bader-Meinhoff group, and the IRA.

Arab Communist Parties (CP's) made efforts to establish their own Palestinian organization and in November 1969 the CP's of Jordan, Syria, Iraq and Lebanon established the "Al-Ansar" (partisan) Forces (Quwwat Al-Ansar).[35] The organization was small and its role was minimal, if it indeed amounted to anything at all.   It was not recognized by major Palestinian organizations and the PLO leadership refused to grant it membership, although Fa'iq Warrad, an Al-Ansar member, was accepted *ad personam* as a member of the Palestine National Council.   In due course, the group ceased its activities completely and nothing further was heard of it.

The Palestine National Front (PNF) was established by the Jordanian CP in the West Bank on August 15, 1973, as its "front organization".   It was joined by non-communists and posed itself as representing people of the West Bank. Initially, the PLO did not take a favourable view of increasing communist influence among Palestinians fearing competition from it, but in time accepted the

PNF and its members were invited to join the PLO Executive Committee, principally due to the small number of PLO members coming from the West Bank, since the PLO had been established in the main by refugees from the coastal plain who had left Palestine in 1948 (see CHAPTER FOUR: Social Background). The acceptance of the PNF by the PLO made it easier for the PLO to claim that it represented all Palestinians.

The Front's activities were in staging demonstrations against the Israeli authorities, spreading leaflets, writing slogans on walls and terror acts. Most of its leaders were arrested by Israel and some of them were deported to Lebanon and Jordan. Some PNF members when undergoing Marxist studies in the USSR were also given military training. On their return they established a CP military arm, with the aim of preparing political and military cadres for the time of Israel's withdrawal and the establishment of a Palestinian state.[36]

Following the first two splits in the PFLP in 1968-1969, when the PFLP-GC and PDFLP left the organization, a third split occurred in March 1972. The Popular Revolutionary Front for the Liberation of Palestine (PRFLP) headed by Abu Shihab, came into existence. Each organization blamed the other for ideological deviations, but it was quite clear that a personal struggle was the main reason for the split. In the mid-seventies, the organization ceased its activities, and some of its members returned to the PFLP.

• Civil War in Lebanon

An incident in early March 1975 in the port of Sidon when fishermen supported by a Leftist Muslim Group came into conflict with the town's security forces sparked the civil war which converted democratic and Westernized Lebanon into a battlefield, involving local and foreign forces, to the present day.

The Sidon incident was followed by clashes between Palestinian organizations among themselves. The most serious of them occurred in Ayn Rumana when a PDFLP bus, returning from a funeral procession was ambushed by another organization. Al-Fath tried at the beginning of the civil war to keep out of direct involvement, but already by April some organizations mainly from the Rejection Front supported Muslims and Leftists in their fight against the Christian Right.

From April 1975 until the end of the year, the clashes were sporadic, characterized by many cease-fires in which unsuccessful attempts were made to bring a permanent end to the fighting. There were no fewer than 51 proclamations of a cease-fire and all of them were broken.[37]

Stronger fighting broke out in 1976. Lebanon's central government soon ceased to function and the country in fact divided into parts.

In January 1976 Lieutenant Ahmad Al-Khatib proclaimed his desertion from the Lebanese army and the establishment of a Lebanese Arab Army which fought on behalf of the Left and the Muslims. Christian soldiers also deserted Lebanon's military forces and joined Christian militia. On May 5, 1976, Christian leader Elias Sarkis succeeded Suleiman Franjiyah as president of the Lebanese Republic after the latter had refused repeated appeals to him to resign.

By 1976, the PLO was directly involved in the fighting. Radical "rejectionist" organizations and also Al Fath and those in the PLO center fought on the side of Lieutenant Khatib. The Lebanese Leftists comprising the Socialist Progressive Party of Druze leader, Kamal Jumblat, communists and "Nasirites" fought the predominantly Christian regime. Palestinian organizations which had been accepted in Lebanon as "guests" became active in an internal civil war and contributed to the disintegration of the State. It was clearly spelt out not only by radicals, but by Abu Iyad, second-in-command in Fath, adopting the slogan used five years previously when Jordan was to be the victim, that "the way to Palestine" leads through Lebanon.

— "We accept in this country only the Lebanese Arab Army . . . The way to Palestine passes through Lebanon . . . it passes through Ain Tura and Ayun Al-Siman [Christian strongholds] and it must reach Junya [the Christian capital] ."[38]

Syria had traditionally considered Lebanon to be part of Greater Syria torn away from her in 1920 by the French Mandate. This was her chance to reverse the situation. In January 1976, Syria intervened in the Lebanese civil war with the Palestine Liberation Army (PLA) units, Hittin and Qadissiyya and the Sa'iqa organization, having control over both. Within a short time, both these units had disintegrated, because of their unwillingness to fight their fellow Palestinians. In June 1976 Syrian regular forces intervened directly, supporting Christians and fighting Syria's "natural allies" — the PLO, Muslims and Leftists. By the end of 1977, there were 22,000 Syrian soldiers in Lebanon[39] — and they are still there.

The Arab summit conferences in Riyadh (October 18, 1976) and Cairo (October 26, 1976) resolved to end the fighting in Lebanon and gave an inter-Arab legitimacy to a permanent Syrian presence in Lebanon, in the framework of an inter-Arab military force, predominantly Syrian. The summits reaffirmed the 1969 Cairo agreement and the right of Palestinian organizations to have a presence in Lebanon in accordance with that agreement.[40]

With an inter-Arab legitimacy for her forces in Lebanon in hand, Syria turned again towards her former allies and resumed aid for the PLO, the Muslims and the Leftists in their fight against the Christians.

Nevertheless, the Syrian invasion of Lebanon was a grave threat to the PLO, which stood to lose its last territorial base. As the PLO reflected inter-Arab divisions and conflicts, it split in 1976 in conformity with these divisions.

The pro-Syrians, the Sa'iqa, PFLP-GC and parts of the PLA preferred to fight alongside Syria against their Palestinian brothers. On the other hand, a strange coalition appeared comprising all the other organizations: Egypt sent the 'Ain Jalud PLA brigade over which she had control, to fight in Lebanon against Syria, alongside Al Fath, the PDFLP and other rejectionist organizations which leaned towards Iraq, such as the PFLP and the ALF. The PFLP-GC of Ahmad Jibril split and his deputy Abu Al-Abbas established a new group, the Palestine Liberation Front. Pro-Syrian brigades of the PLA Qadi'siyya and the

Hittin, disintegrated completely, as did Al-Sa'iqa, but in 1978, the Syrians painstakingly started a process of reorganizing them once more.

Southern Lebanon was mostly quiet during the civil war. After the Syrian invasion of Lebanon, Palestinian organizations entered this area. Regular Syrian forces which had an interest in the control of this area held back from entering because of Israel's objection to Syrian forces close to her border. On the other hand, there was virtually no Lebanese authority in the area. The Palestinian organizations entered this vacuum, and southern Lebanon thus emerged as their last territorial base. In March 1978, after the PLO had struck at an Israeli bus, Israel occupied this area for about three months (see CHAPTER ONE: PLO and the Peace Process), withdrawing its forces by June 14, 1978. UN (UNIFIL) forces were stationed in the area committed to prevent Palestinian armed groups from returning. But such groups gradually infiltrated again and their number was estimated in summer 1979 to be about 3000.

● The Question of Representation

In the October 1973 war as in the June 1967 war, the PLO was hardly a factor. But the PLO scored in the aftermath of both wars. Whereas, the PLO made material gains out of the 1967 war its gains were primarily political from the October 1973 war, as its political position improved considerably after 1973.

The organization received extensive international recognition, opening offices in many countries, in the Third World bloc in particular. By fall 1979, 106 States had given it some form of recognition. The PLO had achieved *ad hoc* status in the United Nations Organization and the Palestinian problem was frequently dealt with in the UN General Assembly, Security Council, Committees, specialized agencies and organizations. A specific committee of 20 UN members was established to deal with this problem.

This extensive international recognition did not, however, enable the PLO to achieve one of its principal aims in its struggle against Israel. While Western powers recognized Israel's right to exist and saw a recognition of Israel and of UN resolution 242 as a precondition for establishing ties with the PLO, the PLO's assessment was that it was too heavy a price to pay.

The situation was totally different in the inter-Arab arena. Here the PLO succeeded where Palestinians had failed again and again since the end of the 1940's. For the first time since Arab states had deprived the Palestinians of their right to represent themselves, they granted that right to a Palestinian organisation, namely the PLO. This was a radical reversal — from expressly denying Palestinians the right to act on their own behalf, from denying them any rights to determine their own destiny — there was not only a *de facto* transfer of control over Palestinian affairs to a Palestinian body, but more than that an entrenched veto given to the Palestinians on matters concerning Arab states and their vital interests. However, the PLO's right to represent Palestinians depended on a number of prior and binding conditions with limitations. In other words, it amounted mostly to rhetoric and was to prove very difficult to implement.

"Who speaks for the Palestinians?" had been an unanswered question since the end of the British Mandate over Palestine in 1948. A number of Arab states claimed to have such a right. The Hashemite regime which had annexed the West Bank to Jordan claimed that "Palestine is Jordan". Palestinians were given Jordanian citizenship, including representation in government bodies. Jordan, however, avoided any recognition of the existence of a Palestinian people, as such recognition would have dangerous consequences for her. Syria stressed often that she saw Palestine as her own southern territory. It was clearly defined as such by President Hafiz Al-Asad.[41] A close advisor of his, Sami Al-Atari declared:

"The citizen of Syria regards Palestine as southern Syria and the Palestinian citizen regards Syria as northern Palestine . . . One cannot consent to continue with the frontiers traced by the Sykes-Picot agreement. The Palestine problem is a Syrian problem and an Arab problem".[42]

The Iraqi Ba'th regime held the same view — there should be no separate Palestinian identity since Palestine is part of the united Arab world. Inevitably Iraq wanted Palestine to be included in its sphere of influence and not in the Syrian sphere.

President Sadat's Egypt feared an independent Palestinian state which might become a destabilizing factor in the area and a Soviet base and thus undermine any political settlement, or chance for a settlement in the Middle East. Egypt and also Saudi Arabia and Kuwait — preferred to see in the occupied territories, instead of a separate state a Palestinian "entity", linked to Jordan. Algeria and Libya, distant from the Arab-Israeli confrontation arena are not really influential factors, and while they are prepared to fight Israel for the establishment of a Palestinian state it would be a fight "till the last Egyptian or Syrian soldier" and not by Algerians or Libyans.

It thus seems clear that while nearly all Arab states pay lip-service to the idea of an independent Palestinian state, none of them with any effective means to help bring it about, want it. A piquant illustration of this came in a statement by President Carter in the late summer of 1979 (see CHAPTER SEVEN: US and PLO).

Different Arab outlooks and inter-Arab rivalries, on the question of a Palestinian state reflected among Palestinians led to differences among Palestinian organizations and within the PLO itself.

Al-Fath consistently claimed the existence of a Palestinian people, clamoured for efforts to be made to establish a Palestinian state and asserted that the organization represents the Palestinian people on its way to their future state.

A quite different position was taken by Zuhayr Muhsin, the leader of Al-Sa'iqa, the second largest organization in the PLO, and head of the PLO military department. He said:

"As Golda Meir denies the existence of a Palestinian people, I argue that such a people does exist and is different from the Jordanian. But actually there are no differences between Jordanians, Palestinians, Syrians and

Lebanese. We all constitute a part of one people. We speak about a Palestinian identity only for political reasons because Arabs' national interest is to encourage the existence of a separate existence of Palestinians ... Jordan, having fixed frontiers, cannot for tactical reasons, claim to have rights to Haifa or Jaffa, but I, as a Palestinian, can claim Haifa, Jaffa, Beersheba and Jerusalem ... "[43]

Similar thinking appeared among the Iraqi Ba'th party's client faction, the Arab Liberation Front. The absence of the word "Palestine" in the name of what purports to be a Palestinian organization and the substitution of the term "Arab" is more than a semantic exercise. This organization considers that even if a Palestinian state would be established, it would soon disintegrate and merge in a untied Arab state (under Iraqi hegemony). The establishment of an independent and separate Palestinian state would, in its view, only increase divisions in the Arab world. Close to this way of thinking, even if not expressing it so baldly are the PFLP, the Front of Popular Struggle of Samir Ghoshe and the pro-Iraqi group of Abu Nidhal.

Some, mainly tactical needs led Arab leaders who did not genuinely want the establishment of a Palestinian state to call for its establishment. Egyptian spokesmen frequently referred to the possibility of a future Palestinian state (and not only an entity). In Syria the Ba'th party's ideological organ presented such a possibility saying that it will force Israel to withdraw from the West Bank and Gaza and would constitute a stage to her complete elimination. It avowed that:

"Insistence on the independence of the Palestinian state, today's possible form of Palestinian self-determination, is not a Palestinian rejection of Arab unity nor a Palestinian rejection of Jordan. It is, quite clearly, a meticulous guarding of the full national and historic rights of the Palestinian Arab people. It, in its Palestinian personality, will be able, from the UN rostrum and in the field of battle, to claim the areas of Galilee, the Little Triangle and the Negev, in other words, over half of the territory of 'Israel' before 1967. It will also be able to demand the return of a million Palestinian refugees to Israel, namely more than the number of Zionists that are to be found on the soil of Palestine. This will create the material basis for the secular and democratic Palestinian state ... But this Palestinian people will not be able to achieve this if this entity 'melts' into another Arab state. In this situation, the problem will be transformed into a harder dispute between a number of Arab states and Israel ... Hence the right of self-determination in the sense of the creation of an independent and sovereign Palestinian state on the West Bank and in Gaza does not mean a re-partition of the Arab homeland ... and it should not be regarded as a step that is in opposition to the current of Arab unity... The annexation of the Palestinian state to another Arab state is a step opposed to Arab unity because it is conditional upon the granting of legitimacy to Israel".[44]

Thus, support for Palestinian claims was based on tactical considerations and seen as a step towards a further aim. Similar positions prevailed in other Arab states. In spite of that, a paradoxical situation developed in which all Arab states without exception, granted the PLO the right of exclusive representation of the Palestinian people and committed themselves to continue with their struggle against Israel until "the legitimate rights of the Palestinian people" will be granted to them. Defining those rights was left by them to the PLO.

How did this siutation come about? What is its meaning? Could this right of exclusive legitimate representation be implemented?

The first step in this process came at the Algiers Arab summit conference, a short time after the October 1973 war. Terms such as "Palestinian people" and their "inalienable national rights" were used in the published statement of November 28, 1973, at the winding-up of the conference. The PLO was not mentioned at all. Nor were there any explanations defining those rights.[45] There were, however, secret resolutions also at the Algiers conference defining for the first time the Arab strategy of an offensive against Israel to camouflage the final aim — an end to her existence (see CHAPTER THREE: Ideology). The Arab States transferred to the PLO the exclusive right to represent the Palestinian people, gave it the right to interpret the meaning of "national rights" of Palestinians and committed themselves to action to restore those rights. Only Jordan expressed reservations on those resolutions.[46]

The acceptance of the Algiers secret decisions was in fact a declaration of intent to perpetuate the Middle East conflict. The transfer to the PLO of the exclusive rights to represent the Palestinian people contributed to a hardening of Israel's position. The PLO had proclaimed as its central ideological aim the destruction of Israel. In the light of the Algiers resolutions, Israel reached the conclusion that she had no partner for a dialogue and that it made no sense to hand over territories to those committed to her destruction. The PLO's right of veto on the positions taken by and actions of Arab states in fact implied political stagnation. The very declaration that the PLO is the sole legitimate representative of the Palestinians implied inter-Arab legitimacy to the disintegration of Jordan, since the PLO and not the Hashemite administration was now the legitimate representative of about fifty per cent of the citizens of the East Bank of Jordan.

What led Arab states to adopt such extreme decisions? Arab leaders seemed to have been aware of the severity of those decisions judging by the fact that they were not published. Did the outcome of the October 1973 War engender arrogance at Algiers?

The first Arab leader who refused to accept those resolutions was King Hussein of Jordan, but he was soon joined by President Sadat, who had consistently interpreted the 1973 War as a means of achieving political aims. At their meeting in Alexandria on July 16—18, 1974, the two leaders tried, for the first time, to bypass the Algiers resolutions. The joint statement that was published at the end of their talks said, inter alia:

"The two sides declare that the PLO is the legitimate representative of the Palestinians, except for those Palestinians residing in the Hashemite Kingdom of Jordan".[47]

The statement did not speak about "Palestinian people". It did not clearly define whether Jordan was both on the Eastern and Western Banks, although it stated clearly that the PLO does not represent Palestinians of Jordan.

In that way Sadat and Hussein indicated their readiness to open a door for a political settlement, particularly since they went further, calling in the statement for steps "to reach a disengagement agreement on the Jordanian front as a first step towards a just peaceful solution".[48]

The two leaders wanted here to neutralize the dangers to Jordan's regime and to a possible political process in the Middle East conflict inherent in the Algiers resolutions.

But the Alexandria decisions held for only about two months, until on September 20–21, 1974, a tripartite conference was held in Cairo of the foreign ministers of Egypt (Ismail Fahmi), Syria (Abd Al-Halim Haddam) and the Head of the PLO's Political Department (Faruq Al-Qaddumi). Under Syrian and PLO pressure a decision was adopted on the Palestinian problem that straightened the line again in accordance with the Algiers summit resolutions:

"Starting from the resolutions of the sixth Arab summit at Algiers, the conference agreed on the following . . . Persistance in backing the PLO in its capacity as the sole legitimate representative of the Palestinian people [49] . . ."

Ratification was given a few days later at the seventh Arab summit conference convened at Rabat on October 26–29, 1974. Its secret resolutions gave to the PLO a right to interpret the meaning of "legitimate rights" of the Palestinians and to determine how far Arab states were to be committed to achieve those rights. This time in the published decisions, the PLO was proclaimed to be the "sole legitimate representative of the Palestinian people". Jordan accepted the decisions, however reluctantly.[50]

The Rabat decisions are still in force, having been reaffirmed at the Tripoli and Baghdad Arab summit conferences in 1977 and 1978 respectively. With the exception of Egypt, no Arab state has retreated from them, and Egypt has never officially stated that she does not consider them to be valid any longer. President Sadat has expressed a number of times, since the beginning of his peace initiative, his support of the PLO and has even stated that he did not go beyond the bounds of the Rabat decisions. In fact, Egypt by-passed the Rabat decisions by her readiness to conclude a peace treaty with Israel and to involve Israel in bilateral negotiations about the future of Palestinians. Sadat said a number of times that the PLO had excluded itself from the peace process and appealed to Palestinians to see King Hussein as their leader.[51] All this may not exclude the possibility that Egypt will turn once more to the PLO as she did at the tripartite conference after the Alexandria declaration, but Egypt sees the PLO as impeding the peace process.

Do other Arab states express an adherence to the Rabat decisions to grant the PLO the right of exclusive representation of Palestinians? Do they enable the PLO to implement this right?

Arab representatives reiterate in international forums, conferences and meetings, in the framework of the UN and outside it, in joint statements with non-Arab countries, addresses and interviews, that the PLO is the sole representative of the Palestinian people. It was accepted by the UN in resolution 3236 in 1974 and was since then reaffirmed on various occasions.

However, many problems have arisen in the practical implementation of those rights. Even five years after Rabat, the Arab world has not yet fully and sincerely implemented the decision granting the PLO the exclusive right to represent all Palestinians.

Jordanian reservations are obvious. In Jordan and in other Arab countries in which there are large numbers of Palestinians, such as Lebanon, Syria, Saudi Arabia and Kuwait, such monopoly for the PLO might endanger internal security, if not the regimes in those countries, leading to the establishment of ex-territorial areas in which Palestinians living there would recognize only the authority of the PLO.

Claims of this kind, to grant the PLO full authority over Palestinians living in Lebanon, appeared thus, in a PFLP organ, in early 1977:

"As the PLO is the sole legitimate representative of all Palestinians, it is also responsible for the Palestinians in refugee camps [in Lebanon] and has the right to implement its rule over its citizens."[52]

This in effect claims the areas of Palestinian refugee camps in Lebanon are ex-territorial, to be under the jurisdiction of the PLO and not of the Lebanese authorities — a state within a state.

The PLO did not even attempt to conceal its aims to bring an end to Jordan's regime. An article in the PLO organ *Shu'un Filastiniyya*, written about a year after the Rabat conference indicated clearly and openly what Jordan may expect if she allows the PLO to re-enter her territory and as "the sole representative of her Palestinian citizens".

The article said that the PLO has to overthrow the regime in Jordan and turn her territory into a main base and springboard for activities in the rest of Palestine, similar to the role that was played by North Vietnam as a base against the South's regime. No Arab state will agree, the article said, to such a base because "the strategy of the [Palestinian] revolution will clash with the strategy of the state". There is therefore a need to overthrow Jordan's regime.

". . . to change the entity of Jordan . . . to cancel the Jordanian entity and to establish, as a substitute, an entity of the revolution . . . the basis of Palestinian East Jordan is the building of a base toward the Great Palestine, a step that will enable Palestinians that are on the fringe of the land that has to be liberated to spread from there to the West of the river (Jordan) . . ."[53]

That citation explains resistance to the re-entry of the PLO with a possible return to the situation as it was before 1970.

But reluctance to implement Rabat decisions was due not only to internal Arab considerations but also to considerations directly related to the Arab-Israeli conflict.

Implementation of this right leads inevitably to a frozen political process, as happened with the Geneva conference that convened to serve as a forum for dealing with the Middle East conflict. The Conference could not reconvene because of the question of PLO participation. Israel refused to negotiate with an organization that aims at its annihilation, while Arab states refused to join the conference without the PLO. The result was no conference at all!

Ironically, King Hussein who had returned defeated from Rabat seemingly quickly realised that his main card is a Jordanian threat to implement the Rabat resolutions. It is one of the paradoxes that are characteristic of the Middle East. If the PLO is the sole legitimate representative of the Palestinians it means that Jordan should stop taking care of the West Bank, that Jordanian currency should no more serve as legal currency on the West Bank, that Jordanian laws should no longer be applied there, that Jordan will no longer pay salaries to officials on the West Bank, no longer needs to subsidize West Bank education, etc. Renouncing all her rights to the West Bank by Jordan would mean that the West Bank would legally no longer be an occupied territory. As Israel would probably not invite the PLO to take Jordan's place, Arab states would in fact face the loss of their portions there.

The complexities of this situation could well be presented by a brief review of the question of Palestinian representation in the National Assembly (Parliament) of Jordan.

Since the annexation of the West Bank by Jordan, the latter's Chamber of Deputies comprised 60 members elected every four years in regional elections. Half of them were from the East Bank and the other half from the West Bank. This situation persisted after Israel took over control of the West Bank in 1967. Residents of the West Bank were represented as before, in the Jordanian parliament.

At Rabat, Arab states decided that the PLO, and not Jordan, represents Palestinians. Had Hussein acted in accordance with the Rabat resolutions he would have had to immediately dissolve the existing parliament and proclaim elections to a new parliament, that would be composed of only East Bank representatives. He did not do so. The existing Parliament did not convene after Rabat, but was also not dissolved. Neither any Arab state, including the radical ones nor the PLO, protested that Hussein — through the Jordanian parliament — continued to represent the people of the West Bank, in violation of Rabat decisions.

The reasons for this silence were obvious. The thirty West Bank representatives in the Jordanian parliament preserved the statute of the West Bank as an occupied Jordanian territory.

Arab states and the PLO therefore prefer the continuation of the existing situation, in which Jordanian currency, law and influence are valid in the West Bank, even if it contradicts the Rabat resolutions that the PLO is the sole legitimate representative of Palestinians.

When Parliament's term ended in 1976, Hussein convened all its members in Amman, including Palestinians living on the West Bank. A decision was adopted that prolonged its term. Again there were no Arab protests against it.

On April 16, 1978, King Hussein proclaimed the establishment of a National Consultative Council, which too was composed of 60 appointed members, half from the East Bank and the other half from the West. This time Hussein went one step further and included in the Council, Palestinians who are PLO members and even members of the PLO supreme body, the Palestinian National Council living in Jordan. Among the appointed were Kamal Al Dajjani from Ramallah, Mahmud Al-Sharif and Widad Bulus from the Gaza Strip. Neither did any Arab state nor the PLO protest this flagrant violation of the Rabat decisions.

In conclusion, while Arab states declared a full adherence to the Rabat resolutions granting the PLO the exclusive right to represent the Palestinian people, on the level of practical daily activities, the resolutions are in fact not fully implemented.

NOTES TO CHAPTER TWO

1. Y. Porath, *The emergence of the Palestinian Arab National Movement, 1918–1929,* and Vol. 2 of the above.
The Palestinian Arab National Movement 1929–1939, (London, Frank Cass, 1974 and 1977).
2. The Supreme Arab Committee was dissolved and declared illegal by the British Mandate Administration in 1937 and re-established in 1945. It continued to exist on paper till the present. It was in fact a degenerated, weak and anachronistic body, without any ability to act.
3. Y. Arnon-Ohanna, *Fellahin in the Arab Revolt in Palestine 1936–1939* (Tel Aviv, Shiloah Centre for Middle Eastern and African Studies, 1978)
4. This was the situation at the end of the 1940's. Nabil Ali Shaath, Professor at the American University in Beirut and Director of PLO Centre for Palestinian Planning gave the following numbers of Palestinians in the early 1970's.
(*Journal of Palestine Studies,* Beirut, No. 2, Winter 1972, pp. 80–81)

Jordan	900,000
West Bank of Jordan	670,000
Gaza	364,000
Israel	340,000
Lebanon	240,000
Syria	155,000
Kuwait	140,000
Egypt	33,000
Iraq	14,000
Persian Gulf	15,000
Libya	5,000
Saudi Arabia	20,000
United States	7,000
Latin America	5,000
West Germany	15,000
TOTAL	2,923,000

The definition of Palestinians was not based here on existing citizenship or status, but on the fact that he was either an Arab born to a Palestinian father or had been a citizen of Palestine.
A large number of Palestinians obtained Jordanian citizenship. Similarly many Palestinians became citizens of various Arab or other states.

5. *Al-Nahar* (Beirut), October 31, 1967.

6. When Syria invaded Jordan in the September 1970 civil war she was going to send there, apart from her tanks, the PLA regiment Hittin. When Syria invaded Lebanon in 1976 she sent Hittin as an advance force. Egypt which wanted to contain Syria during the civil war in Lebanon sent her PLA regiment Ein Jaloud. PLA forces were then in Lebanon on both sides of the fighting — on the side of Fath and the Leftists and of Syria. Of the latter, a substantial number deserted to Fath.

7. Al-Mussawar (Cairo), January 5, 1968.

8. In July 1968 an Egyptian weekly summed up Al-Fath political thinking as follows:
    "All the views and theories come out of the rifle's barrel. As the rifle is the outer image of Al-Fath, the bullet is the ideology. Violence is the sure way, and the aim — liberation — is indisputable. That is a simple political view, which stems from a long chain of experiments: theories, views, talks, and speeches have gained [us] nothing during the [last] twenty years".

Ruz Al Yusuf, Cairo, July 1, 1968

9. Later on the PLF was merged in the PFLP. See below.

10. Fida'i, fidài'yyun — those who sacrifice themselves, are ready to die for their cause. Term used for Arab Palestinian irregulars acting against Israel.

11. Al Fath attempts to apply its military doctrines in Israel-administered territories, did not succeed much, as described by Y. Harkabi:
    "It seemed that the classical pattern of a Revolutionary War from within could now [after the June 1967 War] be applied, and that Fath's great hour had come. People and weapons were hastily smuggled to the West Bank. Yasser Arafat himself came to lead the organization of his network. Some groups began to be active. However, almost all their cells were detected by the Israeli authorities and their members were put in prison. In a matter of a few weeks the whole network collapsed. New attempts to set up an organizational network followed towards the end of the year, and these too were thwarted."
    "As Fath cells were liquidated from the beginning, they had no time to take root. Prophecies by visitors from abroad that Israel would have a 'second Vietnam', a 'second Algeria' or a 'second Aden', only reflected the predictors' national traumas, and did not come true . . . the stirring up of troubles clashed with the interests of the population. Being on the spot, they realized that resistance would harm the Arabs much more than Israel . . . Sympathy towards fidai'yuun action remained mostly on the abstract level and has not been translated into action . . . The local leaders were reluctant to forgo their position. Fatah's commanders sent from outside were in many cases considered foreigners and treated with suspicion."

(Y. Harkabi, *Fedayeen Action and Arab Strategy,* London. The Institute for Strategic Studies, Adelphi Papers No. 53, December 1968, pp. 26–27).

12. Al Fath was apparently the only fidai'yyun organization which maintained relations with the Saudi regime. Answering criticism on the part of the PFLP of his accepting financial aid from a "right wing regime", Arafat said: "I am using Saudi money to buy weapons from China". (*Al-Sayyad,* Beirut, January 23, 1969).

13. The bulk of Al-Fath arms and finances was provided by Arab countries which supplied to it USSR-made arms. Chinese arms, though on a smaller scale, were supplied directly to Al-Fath.

14. The Arab Nationalists Movement (ANM, Haraka Al Qaumiyyin al-Arab) seemed to have Egyptioan support in Egypt's expansionist "Arab Unity" period. George Habash saw Arab unity as a first stage that had to be reached in order to concentrate sufficient Arab

forces against Israel to attack and liquidate her. The movement gradually turned towards extreme left Marxist positions and slogans. The PDRY ruling party developed as the PFLP, from the ANM.

15. The then PFLP weekly *Al-Hurriya,* (Beirut), used left Marxist-Leninist terminology and slogans. It said that "the true revolutionary ideology is Marxism-Leninism because of the laws of class struggle and the material interpretation of history (*ibid.*, September 9, 1968). The Palestine resistance movement required a revolutionary ideology, hostile to imperialism, Zionism, reaction and backwardness; a scientific revolutionary ideology; a proletarian ideology". (*ibid.*, November 11, 1968). The movement's leadership should be in the hands of the proletariat. The Palestine petite-bourgeoisie could be an ally of the revolution, but must not be allowed to assume leadership (*ibid.*, November 4, 1968). "Our national revolution is an inseparable part of the World liberation movement" (*ibid.*, August 12, 1968). In January 1969 the PDFLP split from the PFLP and *Al-Hurriya* came to be its organ. The PFLP established *Al-Hadaf* as its own new organ.

16. According to *Al-Kifah,* (Beirut, June 2, 1969), PFLP policy was to implicate and cause confusion among the Arab regimes. E.g. the hijacking of the "El Al" plane to Algeria on July 23, 1968 aimed at implicating the Algerian government internationally. Also the PFLP announcement that the men who attacked the "El Al" plane in Athens (December 26, 1968) came from Beirut, provoked Israel to attack the Beirut International Airport (December 28, 1968). Similarly, the blowing up in the Golan Heights of the Tapline which carried Saudi Arabian oil to Lebanon (May 30, 1969) was aimed at implicating Saudi Arabia, Syria and Lebanon.

Referring to Israeli retaliatory actions, Habash said: "That is exactly what we want. These actions might narrow down the prospects for a peaceful solution which we do not want". (*Time*, New York, June 9, 1969)

17. *Al-Hurriyya,* September 9, 1968

18. In an interview with the Amman *Al-Masa* (June 9, 1969), Hawatimah said that the PDFLP "adheres to the Marxist-Leninist doctrine" and that its "policy towards all Palestinian, Arab and international questions stems from this doctrine".

19. In line with its Marxist-Leninist doctrine, the PDFLP formed in October 1969 its own party named the Organization of Lebanese Socialists (OLS).

20. According to *Al-Hurriya* (May 19, 1969) the (advocated by Al-Fath) principle of non-interference in the Arab regimes' affairs was becoming invalid. It proved that the clash with Arab regimes "is inevitable and that the only ally of the Palestine resistance movement was the progressive national forces which reject in principle the regimes of their countries".

21. Ehud Ya'ari, *Fath* (Tel-Aviv, 1970) p. 151.

22. Aryeh Yodfat, "The End of Syria's Isolation?" *The World Today* (London), August 1971, pp. 329–339.

23. *Al-Hawadith* (Beirut, October 3, 1969), discerned three tendencies in Al-Sa'iqa:

a) represented by Salah Jadid, sought to turn Al-Sa'iqa into a military force at his and the party's disposal.

b) represented by Hafiz al Asad, sought to neutralize Al-Sa'iqa as a force involved in the inter-party power struggle to turn it wholly into a fida'i fighting force against Israel.

c) represented by Palestinian officers who also sought to turn Al-Sa'iqa into an independent military force uninvolved in the power struggle in Syria.

24. Dr. Y. Harkabi, *Ma'ariv* (Tel-Aviv), October 21, 1970 (with certain omissions).

25. Ehud Ya'ari, *Fath,* Chapter 6.

26. According to Western press reports a precarious balance was being created between the monarchy's traditional authority and a sort of nascent Arab guerilla republic in the Jordan Valley. King Hussein was reported to be holding his throne only by the tacit consent of the organizations (*CSM,* March 8, 1968; *Observer,* March 31, 1968). The fidai'yyun became "almost a parallel government – in some parts of the country – *the* government". (*Times,* London, November 20, 1969).

According to East Jerusalem sources, King Hussein was not permitted to enter Al-Fath bases.

Following an Israeli air raid on Salt on August 4, 1968, Hussein visited the town and expressed his willingness to look in on nearby fida'iyyun bases which had been severely hit. The sources reported that the fida'iyyun refused to let the King enter their camps and that he did not press the issue (*Lamerhav*, Tel-Aviv, August 12, 1968; *Ha'aretz*, August 13, 1968).

27. Al-Fath forces were said to number in early 1969 about 5000 active members (*Times*, London, February 20, 1969). *New York Times* (February 12, 1970) reported that Israeli intelligence sources had estimated that there were 5000–6000 active fighters in all the fida'-iyyun organizations. It reported on the eve of September 1970 fighting (*N.Y. Times*, August 15, 1970) that Al-Fath had 10,000 men under arms – of whom 20 per cent were non-Palestinians.

28. Radio Damascus, Voice of the (PLO) Central Committee, September 17 and 18, 1970.

29. Arafat Press Conference in Cairo, Middle East News Agency, November 9, 1970; Arafat interviews in *Al-Mussawar* (Cairo), November 13, 1970, and *Ruz Al-Yusuf* (Cairo), November 16, 1970. See also *Al-Hawadith*, (Beirut), November 6, 1970.

30. *Al-Anwar*, (Beirut), March 5, 1971.

31. John Laffin, *Fedayeen, The Arab-Israeli Dilemma*. (London, Cassell, 1973) pp. 71–72.

32. *ibid.*, p. 71.

33. The Cairo agreement was leaked out by *Al-Nahar* (Beirut), April 20, 1970.

34. The Melkart agreement was published by *Kul Shai*, (Beirut), June 6, 1973, and by *Al Usbu Al-Arabi* (Beirut), December 15, 1976.

35. *Al-Shams*, (Beirut), May 17, 1970

36. *Ma'ariv*, (Tel-Aviv), October 2, 1974, January 13, 1975; *Yediot Aharonoth*, (Tel-Aviv), October 22, 1974; Moscow radio in Arabic, September 3, 1975. Quoted from FBIS, USSR, September 4, 1975, pp. F4–F5.

37. Y. Shimoni, *The Arab states, their contemporary history and politics*, (Tel-Aviv, 1977) p. 494 (Hebrew).

38. Speech of Abu Iyad in the Arab University of Beirut on May 23, 1976. *Al-Nahar*, (Beirut), May 24, 1976; *Al-Nida*, (Beirut), May 25, 1976.

39. Shimoni, *loc. cit.*, p. 339.

40. The resolutions of the Cairo Conference, *Sawt Al-Arab*, and *MENA*, October 26, 1976.

41. President Asad interview to *Al-Ba'th*, (Damascus), October 27, 1974.

42. Address at a meeting of solidarity with the Palestinian people in Damascus, May 24, 1978. The Sykes-Picot agreement of 1916 partitioned Arab inhabited territories of the Ottoman Empire between Britain and France. The borders between what came to be the British and French Mandated territories became the borders between Palestine and Syria.

43. Zuhayr Muhsin interview to *Trouw*, (Amsterdam), April 3, 1977.

44. *Sawt Al-Talia*, Organ of the Ba'th party in Syria, (Damascus) February 1978.

45. Resolutions of the Algiers Arab Summit Conference, MENA, November 28, 1973.

46. The secret resolutions of the Algiers Arab Summit Conference were leaked out by *Al-Nahar*, (Beirut), December 4, 1973.

47. Egyptian-Jordanian Joint Communique, *Voice of the Arabs*, (Cairo), July 18, 1974.

48. *ibid.*

49. The Joint Statement issued at the conclusion of the Tripartite conference in Cairo. *Al-Nahar Arab Report*, September 30, 1974

50. The open resolutions were published in all Arab newspapers of October 29, 1974.

51. In an interview with American TV–ABC, according to UPI, January 4, 1978. For Sadat's proposal to transfer the West Bank to Jordan and Gaza to Egypt for a five year period, see his interview with *New York Times*, May 11, 1978.

52. *Al-Thawra Mustamirra*, (Organ of PFLP, Beirut), February 19, 1977.

53. *Shu'un Filastiniyya*, September 1975.

CHAPTER THREE

IDEOLOGY AND ITS APPLICATIONS

onsiderable attention is given in the international information media to military activities and violent clashes between
Israel and the PLO, but the struggle between the two is
basically more ideological and political.

- How does the PLO define its aims?
- In which ways would the PLO choose to achieve those aims and to apply
them?

- **Ideology**

Official PLO ideology is defined primarily in the Palestinian National
Covenant, and to a lesser extent in Palestine National Council (PNC) decisions.

The Covenant defines both aims and methods to achieve them, the strategy
and tactics. Its first draft was written by Ahmad Shuqayri some three months
before the establishment of the PLO and the organization was in fact established
on the basis of this draft. It was presented at the founding conference of the
PLO on June 2, 1964. Some changes were introduced in it and it became the
official PLO programme. Since then all Palestinian organizations and groups
which joined the PLO signed the Covenant. Some articles were amended in 1968
in accordance with the altered circumstances of the Palestinians and the growing
influence of armed organizations of Al-Fath in particular. The greater radical
influence led to a greater stress of a Palestinian rather than Arab nationality
(*wataniyya* rather than *qawmiyya*), a more forceful rejection of the Jewish case
(including a narrower definition of those Jews who would qualify for the status
of Palestinians after the "liberation of Palestine"). It defined as an enemy not
only Zionism but also "imperialism", spoke about the "Palestinian revolution"

and "armed struggle" as "the only way to liberate Palestine", definitions which did not appear in the original 1964 text.

A text of the Covenant, both of 1964 and 1968, is provided in the appendices. In examining the main articles of the amended 1968 text which is valid still today, concentration must be focused on:

- Attitude to Israel and Zionism

- Palestine and its territorial bounds

- Tactics for struggle against Israel

- Future character of "Palestine" after its "liberation"

- Criteria for determining eligibility as a citizen of that state.

• Palestinian National Covenant

Much of the Palestinian National Covenant is devoted to attacking Israel and Zionism, to tactics for ending Israel's existence, to describing "the demonic character of Israel" rather than the Palestinian revival.

Article 22 says:

"Zionism is a political movement organically related to world imperialism and hostile to all movements of liberation and progress in the world. It is a racist and fanatical movement in its formation; aggressive, expansionist and colonialist in its aims; and fascist and Nazi in its means. Israel is the tool of the Zionist movement and a human and geographical base for world imperialism. It is a concentration and jumping-off point for imperialism in the heart of the Arab homeland, to strike at the hopes of the Arab nation for liberation, unity and progress."

The PLO fights this "demonic movement" and its "tool" with an aim to liberate Palestine. According to Article 15 "the liberation of Palestine, from an Arab viewpoint, is a national [qawmi] duty to repulse the Zionist, imperialist invasion . . . and to purge the Zionist presence from Palestine". There was to be no doubt what "liberation" means.[1]

"Liberation" has to be "complete" as stated in Article 21, which "rejects every solution that is a substitute for a complete liberation of Palestine".

Rejection of any territorial compromise, of a division of Palestine between Jews and Arabs, appears again and again. Article 19 says:

"The partitioning of Palestine in 1947 and the establishment of Israel is fundamentally null and void, whatever time has elapsed . . . "

The Covenant considers Judaism to be only a religion and sees Jews not as a people — "Jews belong to different nationalities and states" according to Article 20, which continues:

"The claim of a historical and spiritual tie between Jews [as individuals] and Palestine does not tally with historical realities nor with the constituents of statehood in their true sense. Judaism . . . is not a nationality . . . the Jews are not one people with an independent personality. They are rather citizens of the states to which they belong."

To sum up, there is no justification for the existence of a Jewish state and for Jews to come to Palestine . . . Those who did come have to go back to the places "to which they belong".

As Israel must, according to PLO lights, be replaced by a Palestinian state, the question arises as to where will that state be and what are its territorial boundaries.

The PLO attempted for years to avoid this question and not to give it a clear answer. If we take into consideration that the Covenant was adopted by the first PLO Conference, that convened on the territory of the Hashemite Kingdom of Jordan, it is hardly surprising that it did not speak clearly about it. No amendments were made on this subject in 1968.

Article 2 of the Covenant stated that "the boundaries of Palestine are those which existed at the time of the British Mandate", and sees them as comprising an "integral regional unit". The mandate given by the League of Nations to Britain in 1921 included both banks of the Jordan but the British White Paper of 1922 excluded Trans-Jordan from the territory to which the Balfour Declaration applied. Hashemite Emir Abdullah was the first monarch of Trans-Jordan which remained under the British Mandate. The British High Commissioner in Jerusalem retained control over and responsibility for Trans-Jordan and appointed a British subordinate in Amman to be responsible in turn to him. Only in 1946, when Abdullah was proclaimed king was Trans-Jordan officially separated from Palestine.

Article 2 of the PLO Covenant therefore includes a claim not only to all of the West Bank of Palestine, but also a not clearly defined claim to the entire Kingdom of Jordan.[2] The resolutions of the 8th Palestine National Council in Cairo in February—March 1971 staked its claim directly:

"National ties and territorial unity connect Jordan with Palestine . . . An establishment of one political entity in Trans-Jordan and another in Palestine is not based on any legality . . . The Palestinian revolution . . . did not intend to separate between the East and West banks. It did not believe that it is possible that the struggle of the Palestinian people [jamahir] will be separated from the struggle of the Jordanian masses [sha'b] . . . "[3]

Four years later, Shu'un Filastiniyya, the PLO official organ, returned to the subject, thus:

"The establishment of a Palestinian Trans-Jordan . . . is a practical step towards the establishment of the Great Palestine that will enable Palestinians . . . to spread to the west of the River in a similar way to the recent experience of North Vietnam towards her South."[4]

The question has political significance, though the PLO, for various reasons, usually tries to circumvent it. If, according to the PLO ideology, Jordan is part of Palestine, then the Palestinian claims on behalf of a people without any territory is invalid. Israel argues that the historic area of Palestine mandated to

Britain was divided in 1922 into two legal entities — Jewish and Arab — one of which became Israel and the other Jordan. Thus, the argument continues, the PLO demand for a Palestinian state in the West Bank and Gaza implies the creation of a second Arab Palestinian state in the disputed area.

Recognising its inability to achieve the elimination of Israel and the substitution of Jordan by its "Palestinian state", the PLO acknowledged the need to mobilise other Arab states to its cause.

Article 15 of the PLO Covenant states: "The Arab nation, peoples and governments . . . must mobilize all military, human material and spiritual capacities . . . [and] grant and offer the people of Palestine all possible help and every material and human support". The Palestinians will continue to assume "the vanguard role". The "armed revolution" will go on until the liberation of the "Palestinian homeland". The Covenant did not take political methods into account. Convinced that neither Israel nor Jordan would voluntarily agree to their own elimination (!), the PLO considered only a military struggle, stating specifically that "armed struggle is the only way to liberate Palestine". (Article 9)

Nevertheless, in the course of time, PLO leadership came to the conclusion that the use of political methods may bring about better results and moderated Article 9. The 12th Palestinian National Council of June 1974 decided that "the PLO will struggle by every means, the foremost [i.e. not the only one] of which is armed struggle to liberate Palestinian land".[5]

The Covenant makes scanty reference to the character of the proposed Palestinian state and tries to avoid dealing with the subject. The authors of the Covenant, having an interest in the widest possible Palestinian consensus, and the need for endorsement by all Palestinian organizations avoided references to controversial issues. An attempt was therefore made to confine such references to generalizations, and slogans which would be acceptable to all factions. Article 17 states that "the liberation of Palestine will restore to the Palestinian man his dignity, glory and freedom". Article 16 writes about establishing "an atmosphere of tranquility and peace for the Holy Land", with "no distinction or discrimination on a basis of race, color, language or religion". It provides no clue as to whether this State will be communist or capitalist, totalitarian or democratic, pro-Soviet, pro-American or non-aligned, have close ties with radical or conservative Arab states.

However, the specific question as to who will be allowed to remain in Palestine after its "liberation" is dealt with in three articles, two of them referring to Arab inhabitants (Articles 4 and 5) and one to Jews (Article 6).

Article 4 stated: "The Palestinian personality is an innate, persistent characteristic that does not disappear, and is transferred from fathers to sons". Article 5 defines who are Palestinians:

"The Palestinians are the Arab citizens who were living permanently in Palestine until 1947, whether they were expelled from there or remained. Whoever is born to a Palestinian Arab father after this date, within Palestine or outside it, is a Palestinian".

Among Arabs Palestinian identity passes from generation to generation and all Arabs who left Palestine, even many years ago, are considered Palestinian citizens and will remain such. It is not so concerning Jews. Article 6 stipulates:

"The Jews who were living permanently in Palestine until the beginning of the Zionist invasion will be considered Palestinians."

It is noteworthy that whereas here no reference is made to the progeny of those Jews, in the decisions of the 4th Palestine National Council in Cairo on July 6–12, 1968, a specific clue was given as to the date of "the Zionist invasion".

"The Council also reaffirms that the aggression on the Palestinian people and its land began with the Zionist invasion of Palestine in the year 1917 [the year of the Balfour Declaration]. Therefore the meaning of the removal of the consequences of the aggression should be the removal of all the consequences of the aggression since the beginning of the Zionist invasion and not [only those] since the war of June 1967".[6]

Article 6 would thus imply that only those Israeli Jews who arrived in Palestine before 1917 (a few old people), will after the destruction of Israel and the establishment of a Palestinian state be eligible to become Palestinian citizens. (There were only 85,000 Jews in Palestine at that time, compared with some 3 million Jews in 1979.)

Sabri Jiryis of the PLO Center for Palestine Studies in Beirut, proposed in 1975 to abolish Article 6 of the Covenant, as "the only meaning of this article is a displacement from their places of 99% of the Jews who live at present in Palestine".[7] The proposal was attacked in a PLO publication.[8] His proposal was not dealt with in any PLO forum and Article 6, with all its implications, remains valid.

The last Article (Article 33) in the Covenant states:

"This Covenant cannot be amended except by a two-thirds majority of all the members of the National Assembly of the Palestine Liberation Organization in a special session called for this purpose".

In fact, the Covenant has been amended only once – in 1968. Among the amended articles was Article 6. The earlier (1964) version had not given any limiting date for granting Jews the right of citizenship. It said that "Jews who are of Palestinian origin will be considered Palestinians if they will undertake to live loyally and peacefully in Palestine". By introducing a limiting date the amendment represented a hardening of the former version.

The Palestinian National Covenant represents clear and crystallized positions. Views are expressed from time to time that the PLO should or might amend one or more Articles in it. Basic positions, however, repeat themselves in many Articles, one similar to the other. A change in one or another Article will therefore not mean a change in the PLO outlook. Only a new National Covenant would indicate real change.

● The Covenant As An Impediment

The National Covenant in due course became an impediment to the PLO itself. It served well as an ideology as long as the PLO and the Arab states considered the exclusive use of military struggle against Israel. But that proved to be ineffective in four wars. Even the 1973 war, in which Syrian and Egyptian forces succeeded in gaining the initial advantages, ended, in military terms, with Israel holding the upper hand.

The 1973 war, was, however, a turning point. The military achievements of Arab states were indeed marginal but the political and psychological gains were enormous. The war and its outcome changed the outlook, strategy and activities of Arab states. It contributed to their adopting a more effective phased strategy of struggle against Israel. Political and military efforts jointly were to isolate Israel in the international arena and simultaneously to induce an increasing recognition of the PLO as the sole legitimate representative of Palestinians.

● The switch to a combined military-political strategy with an increasing stress on political activities, made the Covenant more a liability than an asset.

● The Covenant's sharp expressions against Israel and its declared aim to eliminate her damaged the PLO image.

● The Covenant's extremism has prevented the integration of the PLO in the political process.

● It obstructed possibilities that the PLO would be granted sovereign status without entering into any political negotiations.

● The Covenant ruled out the PLO, as far as Israel is concerned, as a negotiating partner in any circumstances.

The PLO's difficulties in entering the political process came about, however, not only because of Israeli opposition, but no less because of internal factors within the PLO itself.

The Covenant explicitly stated that" armed struggle is the only way to liberate Palestine" — Article 9 — and with that, rejected all other means of struggle. The PLO's principal difficulties in entering negotiations with Israel were however not only because of definitions, which could be by-passed, but because of fundamental political problems. Participation at the Geneva conference, or any other forum, would involve negotiations with Israel and recognition of Israel's existence. Recognition means accepting the principle that Israel has a right to exist in a part of Palestine, and this is opposed to the Covenant's ideology and the central principle that Palestine is "an indivisible territorial unit" and that "it is to be purged from the Zionist existence". Thus, even if Israel were to agree to accept the PLO as a partner to negotiations, the PLO would be prevented from negotiations by the very letter and spirit of its official ideology.

Strange and paradoxical, as it seems, the Covenant would be an obstacle for the PLO to achieve territorial gains, even if that were to be possible outside the framework of negotiations. Even in the event that Israel would be ready to withdraw from the West Bank and Gaza and to transfer the territories to the PLO, the latter in accordance with the Covenant would be prevented from accepting the transfer from Israel.

Within the PLO, there has been some awareness of this situation and sharp discussions were conducted on this subject. Some argued that the PLO in exchange for territories would have to recognize Israel in one way or another. Others argued that even if a solution could be found to by-pass that problem and the PLO would find itself in a position to accept territories and establish a state, without recognizing Israel, it should not agree to this. Their reasoning is that the Palestinian state which would be established in the West Bank and Gaza will have recognized borders and include only a part of the one and indivisible Palestine and that this contradicts the Covenant.

Such a state will have no choice but to define controversial matters. It will have to adopt a Constitution that will define who its citizens are. How then, to include in the Palestinian state also the Arabs of Israel and the people of Jordan? On the other hand, would it be possible for the PLO to see itself as a division of the Palestinian people?[9] Such a state would probably join the UN. But how would it be able to sign its Charter while it continues to adhere to an ideology that advocates the liquidation of a neighbouring state that is also a UN member?

The PLO also fears a situation in which it would cease to be a revolutionary organization and would instead, have to deal with prosaic daily problems of administration of a small country with few economic resources. Elements in the PLO have called the state that would be established in the West Bank and Gaza not *a state* (Dawla) but a *mini-state* (Duwayla).

Summing up, the Palestinian National Covenant is not only a threat to Israel, but also an obstacle to the PLO itself. It damages its international image, restricts its ability to conduct political activities and impedes the achievements of its aims. But on the other hand included in it are the general principles so central and substantial for the PLO that it is not ready to abandon or to amend it. The resultant dichotomy characterizes the behaviour of the PLO from 1973. Its dilemma is how to conceal that dichotomy, how to demonstrate on the one hand moderation, and on the other, to continue to keep the Covenant and its principles.

The National Covenant of the PLO is still considered obligatory official ideology. Parallel to that a whole series of activities are conducted with an aim to obfuscate this ideology even to the degree where it seemingly does not exist at all, and to present to the West in particular, an image of flexibility and moderation.

The PLO acts systematically in recent years to belittle the significance of the Covenant, with an attempt to make it obliterate aims as far as possible. Its spokesmen endeavour not to mention the Covenant at all. Certainly not on their own initiative. When pressed to express their positions on it, they generally present it as "ritual, as an old document from the days of Shuqayri, describing a vision of the far future, but without any current political meaning". For instance in an interview Arafat referred to the Covenant as "a dream" and blandly asked the interviewer if he has no right to dream.[10]

Such representation of the Covenant is designed only for publicity and as an exercise in public relations. For internal use, by the PLO itself, a different approach is used. Resolutions of the PNC, the PLO supreme body, often begin with a preamble that they are "on the basis of the National Covenant".[11]

Another example of Arafat's attempts to belittle the significance of the Covenant was in his UN address in 1974. He said that "the Palestine of tomorrow would include all Jews living there without discrimination, who choose to remain to live in peace". Thus he no longer demands that all Jews who came to Palestine after 1917 leave the country, but he suggests a readiness to absorb them in "the Palestine of tomorrow". Nevertheless, the Covenant and its Article 6 remains in force with no changes. (Arafat's definition of those Jews who would qualify for the status of Palestinians was even narrower, as he said that "the Jewish invasion of Palestine began in 1881'.) Arafat did not here recognize Jews as a people, he did not refer to "Israelis", but treated Jews as individuals. The meaning of Arafat's reference to the Jews "who choose to remain to live in peace" was clarified by the 13th PNC convened in March 1977. Its final statement said that Palestine will absorb the Jews, "who cast aside Zionist-racialist affiliation",[12] implying that those who will see themselves as Arabs of Jewish faith would be accepted as Palestinians.

The proposal of Sabri Jiryis to amend Article 6 that as he said, implies removal of 99 per cent of the Jews who live in Palestine, was already referred to earlier.[13] Prof. Walid Al-Khalidi proposed an establishment of a sovereign Palestinian state including East Jerusalem, having its own military forces, with a PLO participation in the government, and with Fath as "the backbone of any Palestinian government". One of the first tasks of the government will be to draw up a constitution to replace the National Covenant.[14] He sees this happening after the establishment of a Palestinian state.

A Syrian proposal to amend the Covenant came on the eve of the 13th PNC in March 1977. It was at a time of attempts to make the PLO join the political process that were supported, with some reservations, by Syria. A Syrian Ba'th party publication stated:

> "The character of the development [of the situation] ... requires the Palestine National Council to re-examine the National Covenant ... such a renewed examination does not necessarily force a moderation of national aims and does not force a break up of the ideological infra-structure of the PLO. The aim is more exactly a deepening of theoretical positions ... to enable to introduce plans for staged activities in accordance with it".[15]

It was strongly opposed by "rejectionists" and the PLO pledged not to amend the Covenant.[16] It was decided to change only the image, to stress more the strategy of stages, without abandoning the long term aims.

● A "Secular Democratic State"

The slogan of "a secular democratic state" was introduced for the first time in January 1969. At the 6th PNC (September 1969) a PDFLP proposal was made to include it as an appendix to the Covenant.[17] The proposal was rejected with the argument that it might damage Arab sovereignty over Palestine and because it ignores the numerical ratio between Jews and Arabs. Arguments were raised that if Jews would stay and be considered Palestinians the Arabness of "liberated Palestine" would be impaired because of demographic reasons. Palestinian organizations however agreed to continue to propagate the slogan, for foreign consumption in particular, because it was internationally well received and brought gains in the world's public opinion. Most organizations saw the slogan as a tactical one and only the PDFLP was ready to see in it a strategic aim.

Resolutions at the 6th PNC (Cairo, September 1–6, 1969) had stated:

"The council confirms that the aim of the Palestinian revolution is complete liberation of all Palestinian soil from Zionist occupation, from its base – Israel – and from imperialist forces backing it.

"The council declares the Palestinian people's determination to proceed with their revolution until victory and until a democratic Palestinian state, free from all forms of religious and sectarian discrimination is established".[18]

It was reaffirmed by resolutions at the 8th PNC (Cairo, February–March 1971) which stated:

". . . the future state in a Palestine liberated from Zionist colonialism will be a democratic state, where all will enjoy the same rights and have the same duties, within the framework of the aspirations of the Arab nations for national liberation and comprehensive unity . . . "[19]

The resolutions employ the slogan of a "democratic state". The term "democratic" has to be understood not as in the Western world, but rather more as in communist countries, or more accurately as in Algeria or in the PDRY. If established, it would have a single ruling party formed by the organization that would come to power, most probably Fath.

Shafiq Al-Hut, the head of the PLO Beirut office, said on this matter:

"When we speak of democracy, it must be clear that we do not mean the liberal democracy according to the one man–one vote system. Our intention is a popular democracy".[20]

The term "secular" did not appear at all in those or other PLO resolutions. Western journalists often combined the term "secular" and "democratic". Christians, like PFLP leader, George Habash, and PDFLP leader, Naif Hawatimah, have become advocates of a secular social revolution that would make them as individuals more acceptable in the predominantly Muslim Sunni Arab World, while Muslims like Arafat have relied on a strongly nationalist appeal.

The PLO often tries to emphasize its Muslim character – e.g. PLA brigades are named after the great victories won by the Muslims in the battles of Qadisiyya, Hittin and Ayn-Jalut, all of them in holy wars for Islam against non-Muslims. Professor Bernard Lewis comments:

"The imagery and the symbolism of the Fath is strikingly Islamic. Yasser Arafat's *nom de guerre,* Abu Ammar, the father of Ammar, is an allusion to the historic figure of Ammar ibn-Yasir, the son of Yasir, a companion of the Prophet and a valiant fighter in all his battles".[21]

"Al Fath", Arafat said, "had never used the term 'secular, non-religious homeland' ":[22]

> "We did not issue the slogan for the establishment of a secular state. What happened is that the French writer, Anna Frankus, author of the book, *The Palestinians,* spread the slogan in the name of the Palestinian revolution in several articles. I am certain, however, that this is a distortion of the expression of democracy we proclaim".[23]

The term "democratic state" was much used by the PLO. It should be noted that it means an Arab state named Palestine, established on the territory of all of Palestine, after the *destruction* of the State of Israel. The slogans promise equal rights to its citizens, but to Jews it means only rights of a religious minority to individuals and not of a national entity — and only to those Jews who "will be considered Palestinians" — and not to a people.[24] It says nothing about the right of Jews to self-determination or any minimal national rights.

- ## • "The Legitimate Rights of the Palestinian People"

The notion of "the legitimate rights of the Palestinian people" owes its existence to the PLO — but all Arab states are committed to whatever substance the PLO may choose to endow on the term. Secret resolutions passed by the Algiers Summit Conference (1973) included a commitment by all the Arab states, except Jordan "to the restoration of the national rights of the Palestinian people in the manner decided by the PLO".[25] In the secret resolutions of the Rabat Summit Conference (1974), which still hold good and which were leaked by Syria following Sadat's visit to Jerusalem, all Arab states, including Jordan, reaffirmed this commitment "for the restoration of the national rights of the Palestinian people in conformity with the resolutions passed by the PLO, as the sole representative of the Palestinian people. The Palestine problem is the problem of all Arabs and no Arab party is at liberty to withdraw from this commitment".[26] In other words — defining the Palestinian rights is the exclusive province of the PLO.

What are "the rights of the Palestinian people"? The political declaration of the 13th PNC (March 1977) defined them as the rights "of return, self-determination and establishing their national state on their national soil". (Article 11) These had to be achieved "without any conciliation[sulh] or recognition" of Israel (Article 9).[27]

The first "legitimate right" is "the right of return". The PLO's reply to the question "where to" is — "to their homes". As most of the 1948 refugees fled from the coastal plain area of Palestine, it would mean a return to the territory of Israel before June 1967 and not to the West Bank.

The second "legitimate right" is that of self-determination, to which the PLO attaches great importance. It is demanded without specifying any particular territory to which it will apply. It is done so deliberately, with an aim to make it refer to the entire Palestinian dispersion. Were that right to be granted, the Arab minority of Israel of about half a million and about 1.5 million Arabs of Palestinian origin who are living in Jordan, would be considered Palestinians and the PLO would appear as their sole legitimate representative.

A frank comment on the purpose behind that demand appeared in an organ of the Syrian Ba'th party:

"The right of self-determination of the Palestinian people means the libera-tion of Palestine and hence the end of the Zionist existence on Palestinian soil ... the reason is that when a people is called upon to determine its fate, this generally happens after it has gained a victory in the struggle against imperialism to the point where the latter has no choice but to pack its bags and go home. The latest example of this is Djibouti. As regards the Palestinian people the situation is different. Israel has no 'motherland' like France or Britain, that she can go to. In this situation, Palestinian self-determination in its fullest sense means the destruction of the Zionist idea and the Zionist institutions".[28]

The third "legitimate right" is that of founding "an independent state on the national soil". The official ideology as presented in the National Covenant defined the PLO aims to establish that state in the whole area of both Israel and Jordan.

The seemingly innocent slogan — "legitimate rights of the Palestinian people" — serves in fact as a cover and code word for the aim of annihilating Israel.

● Integration in the Negotiations — Without Recognition

Its decision to enter the political process at the same time as it retains its official ideology as expressed in the Covenant required the PLO to devise a complicated structure of apologetics and manoevres.

The first and the simplest employed by the PLO, was the decision "to cross the bridge when we will reach it", to delay the adoption of positions until an urgent need will force it to do so. Arab states were unanimous that there would be no Geneva conference without PLO participation in it. The PLO has never gone on record whether it agreed or refused to join the Geneva Conference. Agreement would be contrary to its ideology and refusal would be against its interests. The PLO therefore chose an intermediate way, saying that it had not yet been invited to the Conference and had therefore no need to adopt a position on it.

It was clear, however, that the PLO would be unable to hold such positions in the long run. Proposals were mooted that the PLO should be represented at the peace conference by another Arab element, which will be exposed to blame for negotiating with Israel, while the PLO would provisionally remain in the wings and enter the arena only to receive "trophies". Among the candidates to represent the PLO in the negotiations were Jordan, Syria and the Arab League. There was also a proposal that there would be at the Geneva Conference a united all-Arab delegation which would include PLO members. Israel agreed that Pales-tinian personalities identified with the PLO may be included among the members of one Arab delegation, but did not agree to one united Arab delegation. Nothing came of such proposals, not because of Israel's position but because of PLO reservations. The PLO had received from Arab states, just a short time previously, the right of exclusive representation of the Palestinian people, and feared that its merging in an Arab delegation might open the way for a revision of its right to represent Palestinians and to a renewed transfer of that right to Arab states.

The more time passed, the greater was the pressure on the PLO to define its position on political negotiations. PLO spokesmen had no choice but to say that they favoured entering the talks. It became the PLO official position and was included in the Political Declaration (Article 15A) of the 13th PNC convened in Cairo in March 1977. It stated that "the PLO declared its right to participate in an independent manner and on an equal footing in all conferences and international forums concerned with the Palestinian issue and the Arab-Zionist conflict".[29]

On the face of it, this resolution seemed to indicate a major moderation of the PLO attitude. The readiness to negotiate, "independently" with Israel could be regarded as a readiness to recognize its existence and right to live in the Middle East. It was, however, not so. Mahmud Abbas (Abu Ma'zin) put it plainly enough:

"Our participation in the Geneva Conference does not mean mutual recognition, since we shall relate to Geneva as to an international conference, just like the other conferences in which we and Israel participate, such as the United Nations, UNESCO and so forth".[30]

The PLO thus found a way which enabled it to conduct negotiations with Israel, in Geneva or anywhere else, without thereby according Israel any recognition and without having to alter its ideology. Israel refused to accept such a proposal.

● **Government-in-exile**

In its attempts to integrate the political process, the PLO considered another way. A government-in-exile composed of Palestinians not belonging to the PLO would be set up and it would conduct negotiations with Israel while the PLO would stay in the wings awaiting results. Such a government would probably receive wide international recognition and strengthen pressure on Israel to agree to PLO participation in negotiations.

For a number of reasons, the idea was shelved provisionally. A government, even if it governs from a place of exile, must define its territory. Such a definition would have promptly belied the moderate image the organization sought to project, as it would quickly be apparent that the PLO's final goal remained the liquidation of Israel. The PLO toyed with the possibility of declaring the government-in-exile to be "a caretaker government". The body so designated could meantime lay claim to part of the territory demanded by it, namely the West Bank and Gaza, and would only later, once it had managed to gain control over the whole of Palestine, declare itself a regular government in every way.

Another difficulty was that the PLO was not prepared to transfer the reins of leadership and representation of the Palestinian people into the hands of another body, and did not relish the prospect of the internal struggles that were likely to arise over influential positions and titles. There was, of course, a possibility, that instead of nominating Palestinians who are not PLO members to the government-in-exile, the PLO would declare its own leadership as the government-in-exile. But then the PLO would be forced to enter into negotiations with Israel. Other ways had therefore to be chosen for achieving the goal of being integrated into the negotiations.

● Meetings With Israelis

The PLO entered a series of secret meetings with unofficial Israeli personalities who did openly declare themselves Zionists.

As reported by the Beirut-based journal *Events,* the Fath Central Committee decided after the Algiers November 1973 Arab summit, to form a team of Fath members to be responsible for "keeping in touch with current events in Israel". Mahmud Abbas (Abu Ma'zin) and Khalil Al Wazir (Abu Jihad), both members of the Central Committee, were appointed Chairmen. The team also included Habib Kahwaji, editor of the Damascus paper *Al-Ard*, Sabri Jiryis, Issam Sartawi and some Fath representatives in Europe.

The first moves were made in London. PLO's official representative, Sa'id Hamami, wrote two articles for the *Times* in November and December 1973. It was the first time that a PLO official spoke about a willingness to accept, as part of a comprehensive settlement, a Palestinian state on the West Bank, and including Gaza. In March 1975, Hamami presented in London a paper on a "Palestinian strategy for peaceful co-existence", that was met with bitter protest and opposition from the Rejection Front [Hamami was assassinated on January 4, 1978. See CHAPTER ONE on assassinations and terror against those who advocated talks with Israelis.]

A Council for Israel-Palestine Peace, with Reserve-General Professor Mattityahu Peled, as its President, was founded in Israel in July 1975. Meetings between members of that council and the Fath team referred to in the preceding paragraph were conducted during 1975. At one of them, according to *Events,* Sartawi asked Peled to convey a message to Israel's Premier stating that "the PLO would agree to suspend all military operations against the State of Israel, on condition that the Israeli government dropped its veto on the presence of an independent PLO delegation at the Geneva conference".[31]

It might be doubted if there was such a proposal at all. If it was, it had a private non-obligatory character and nothing came of it. The meetings between Israeli "doves" and PLO officials became more frequent early in 1977 — and much less frequent thereafter. The Israeli Council for Israel-Palestine Peace issued a statement at a press conference in Tel-Aviv on January 2, 1977, to the effect that the Council and the PLO had agreed to sign a joint statement in which the PLO accepts the Council's Zionist principles and that the Council awaits ratification of that statement in the next few days.[32] The PLO reply was, however, different. A PLO statement published in Damascus included personal attacks on

Gen. (Res.) Mattityahu Peled, the principal spokesman at the press conference. "The Palestinian people," it said, "will cut off the hands of anyone who will renounce one grain of its national and historical rights and will struggle with all means till the day of liberation.[33]

Some PLO personalities who participated in the talks were assassinated by Rejectionists during 1978 (see CHAPTER ONE).

• Strategy of "Phased Stages"

In the period between 1967 and 1973 the slogan of "removing the consequences of aggression" was dominant in the Arab world. There was some ambiguity as to whether the term "aggression" was understood to mean the results of the 1967 war, to remove Israel from the territories she was administering as a result of that war, or to bring about Israel's annihilation, as Israel's mere existence was considered to be an aggression. While the aims were intentionally left unclear and defined in a way to enable more than one interpretation, there were no doubts with regard to the ways to achieve such aims. The Khartoum Arab Summit of August 29–September 1, 1967, announced clearly that there will be no negotiations with Israel, no recognition of Israel and no peace with her.

A comment in the leading Cairo daily said clearly that "the Palestinian Resistance opposition to Israel is actually opposition to the latter's right to existence and not to the extent of this existence".[34] "The hoped for state in Palestine", said Shafiq Al-Hut, the head of the PLO office in Beirut, "can only be created on the ruins of the Zionist entity and the destruction of the State of Israel."[35]

A change in this Arab strategy appeared after the October 1973 war. The secret resolutions of the Algiers Arab summit adopted a staged strategy, opening with the heading "the temporary objective of the Arab nation" and stating:

"The Conference resolves that the objectives of the current stage of the joint Arab struggle are:
1) The complete liberation of all the Arab territories occupied in the June 1967 aggression . . .
2) The liberation of the Arab city of Jerusalem . . . "[36]

The Algiers resolutions stated that "political activities complement the military battle and are considered as its continuation". The resolutions included a series of recommendations on how to act against Israel all over the world. They called for actions to bring about changes in US policy of supporting Israel and to warn her that such a policy endangers her interests in the Arab world.[37]

The changing Arab strategy required the PLO to make ideological-political adaptations. Its ideology, as expressed in the National Covenant and PNC resolutions, considered the armed struggle but not political methods and defined final aims, but not stages on the way to them. It was, however, not difficult for the PLO to adapt itself to the situation as it had faced similar problems before.

The President of Tunisia, Habib Bourguiba, visited the region in winter 1965, proposing a negotiated settlement and a solution of the Palestine problem based on the 1947 UN resolutions. He stated that the correct method of safeguarding Arab interests would have been to take realities into account "in order to change them into different realities". Later "another step forward" could have been taken. The Arabs should have adopted a long-term strategy of "pressures and concessions in order to break the opponent's morale". Bourguiba proposed a staged negotiated settlement and the use of political and not military methods. Bourguiba argued that if Israel rejected such a settlement, the Arabs' position would then be strengthened and their use of force would be understood abroad.[38]

Fa'iz Sayegh, who established the PLO Centre for Palestinian Studies in Beirut in 1965, attacked the Bourguiba proposals, defining them in a long article to be no more than a "handful of vagueness". Sayegh introduced on that occasion the PLO position on the strategy of stages, distinguishing between two different forms of this strategy:

> "There are two forms of stages . . . The theory of stages that might reach its aim is the theory of escalating stages, which builds each stage on the basis of what had been built in the earlier stage and prepares in each stage towards building of the next stage. But the theory of stages that was currently published is a closed theory of stages. Its first stage contradicts the next stages and cancels them . . . It is satisfied with only the first stage and does not continue to advance later towards the final aim . . . The slogan of this alleged theory of stages is not 'take whatever you can take and be prepared to take the rest tomorrow', but its slogan is 'be satisfied with what you can take . . . and leave the rest to your adversary' . . . It is not a theory of stages of development, but of a deadlock . . . it is not a theory of stages of struggle but a theiry of stages of surrender".[39]

The 12th PNC conference, the first convened after the 1973 war and Algiers summit provided a solution to that problem. Article 4 of its resolutions said:

> "Any liberation step that is achieved constitutes a step for continuing [the efforts] to achieve the PLO strategy for the establishment of the Palestinian democratic state . . ."[40]

The PLO continues to advocate the strategy of stages. This strategy is also closely connected with its intermediate aim — an establishment of a Palestinian state "on every part of Palestinian land to be liberated".

• A Palestinian "Authority" Or State

The idea of the establishment of a Palestinian state requiring recognition of Israel was another difficulty confronting the PLO. Moreover, the concept would require a state which would have fixed boundaries, sign international conventions, join the United Nations and deal with prosaic matters, such as education, welfare, etc. All this would be at the expense of continuing the struggle against Israel. By adopting a "stage by stage" strategy, the PLO may have found a partial answer.

The resolutions of the 12th PNC were evasive about agreeing to the founding of a state [dawla] and spoke about the founding of an authority [sulta]. The latter was to be "national, independent and fighting".[41] An authority could have no recognized boundaries and would not be obliged to sign international conventions. It would in time become a "state", but only after taking control of all and undivided Palestine.

Some observers viewed the very readiness of the PLO to accept any territory of Palestine as a sign of a tendency to moderation. The inclusion of the term "fighting" and another clause saying that "the PLO will struggle against any plan . . . the price of which is recognition, conciliation or secure borders" showed that it was not so. But the camouflage of moderation succeeded and the PLO found itself able to retain its extreme ideology and declared aims, while earning in the Western information media an image of growing moderation.

At the 13th PNC in March 1977, when PLO self-confidence became stronger, the notion of "authority" had given place to "state". The final statement of this PNC session said:

"The Council also affirmed its adherence to the PLO's strategic objective, the liberation of Palestine from the racist-Zionist occupation, so that it can become a homeland to the people of Palestine in which a democratic state of Palestine can be established".[42]

The Palestinian state as a stage on the way to liquidate Israel was reaffirmed, however, after the peace initiative of President Sadat. The six point programme agreed on by all Palestinian organizations, as announced in Tripoli on December 4, 1977, included the following:

"Fifth: To strive for the realization of the Palestinian people's rights to return and self-determination within the context of an independent Palestinian national state on any part of Palestinian land without reconciliation or negotiations, as an interim aim of the Palestinian revolution".[43]

● Palestinian State and After

In the period 1978−1979, several PLO spokesmen were asserting that if only Israel would consent to the founding of a Palestinian state in the West Bank and Gaza, they for their part would be prepared to undertake to end the armed struggle against Israel. Some went as far as to state that peace would then prevail between the two states.[44] The official PLO position, however, continued to be that even when they will stop armed struggle, they will continue to fight Israel by all other possible means − economic, political, cultural, etc.

Faruq Al-Qadumi, in charge of PLO foreign relations, explained the nature of peace that is to prevail between Israel and the Palestinian state:

"There is a state of interim peace [salam marhali] and a state of permanent peace [salam da'imi]. The permanent peace will not come about except through the upbuilding of a democratic Palestinian state . . . and that is a remote aim. Whereas the interim peace is the founding of a Palestinian state on *part* of our soil. And there can arise in the region none but one of these two kinds of peace".[45]

Qadumi spoke about it more clearly in an interview with *Newsweek*. He said that the PLO was ready to accept "at this stage" a Palestinian state "on only part of our territory". It did not mean, however, "giving up the rest of our rights". Qadumi spoke about "two phases of our return. The first phase to the 1967 lines and the second to the 1948 lines . . . The third stage is the democratic state of Palestine. So we are fighting for these three stages".

Asked if the PLO was willing "to rely on political and diplomatic means for the ultimate solution" he replied: "well, if they can be effective, we will do it . . . if not, then we will continue to resume our armed struggle". The PLO had said in the past that it must have all of Palestine. "Now we say that this can be implemented by stages".[46]

These positions were not modified over the years. Late in 1979, Mahmud Abbas (Abu Mazin), a member of the Fath Central Committee said that "any settlement leading to the establishment of an independent Palestinian state on Palestinian soil will be considered as the natural beginning and a genuine step towards solving the Middle East crisis". However, he added, "the ultimate issue is Arab-Jewish co-existence within the framework of a democratic state". He considered that if "the Jewish people in occupied Palestine and the Palestinian people would be asked for their opinions, our people would choose to go back to their homeland whereas the Jews who originally came from outside Palestine, would also choose to return to the countries from which they came".

As to the status of "a future Palestinian state", he said that "what is important now is to force Israel to withdraw from the occupied territories and to establish an independent Palestinian state. Only then will the Palestinian people determine their relations with Jordan or any other Arab country, taking into consideration the Palestinian people's interests and those of the Arab nation at the same time". He stressed that "the Palestinian people are unionist by nature". He considered that if Palestinians would be given a choice between repatriation or compensation, "our people would definitely choose to return to the home-land".[47]

*   *   *   *

To sum up: PLO official ideology aims to bring an end to the existence of the State of Israel — and probably also of Jordan and to establish a Palestinian state in their place. The essence of this ideology is included in the Palestinian National Covenant first defined in 1964, amended in 1968, and still in force.

This official ideology is an impediment to the PLO itself, as it prevents it from achieving its main aims: to integrate in the political process and establish a Palestinian state. The PLO tries to overcome this obstacle in three principal ways:

● by belittling the Covenant, presenting it as a ritual, as a dream that has little to do with the present;

● by expressing a readiness to enter the political process but without any recognition of Israel;

• by adopting the strategy of stages, according to which the PLO agrees to establish a Palestinian state in a part of Palestine, considering it to be a *first stage* on the way to establishing such a state in all of Palestine.

All those three ways have one common characteristic: to retain the official ideology which calls for the complete destruction of Israel and for an establishment of an Arab Palestinian state in its place.

NOTES TO CHAPTER THREE

1. An Al-Fath publication "Studies and Experiments in the Revolutionary Field" stated that liberation required not only the liquidation of a political entity but of a society as well. This objective demanded the use of violence of various forms, all with the purpose of destroying those areas, industrial, agricultural and financial, which sustained the life of the Zionist society. (Quoted by *Ruz al-Yusuf*, Cairo, July 1, 1968).

2. The Palestinian Covenant was carefully defined but has in this case an internal contradiction. Article 2 states that the boundaries of the British Mandate are the boundaries of Palestine, while Article 20 says: "The Balfour Declaration, the Mandate documents, and what has been based upon them are considered null and void." Arafat said in his speech to the UN General Assembly on November 13, 1974, that "in the guise of a League of Nations Mandate British imperialism was imposed on the Palestinian people". (*UN Monthly Chronicle*, vol. XI, no. 11, December 1974, p. 80). The Covenant and Arafat himself rejected the British Mandate but considered the Mandate's boundaries to be *the* boundaries of Palestine. They could not be otherwise as no Palestinian political entity had existed for a long time, the last being in the time of the Crusades.

3. *Al Nahar*, (Beirut), March 5, 1971. For 8th PNC resolutions see: MENA, (Cairo), March 4, 1971.

4. Isam Sakhanini, "First Experience for the Thesis: the Palestinian Trans-Jordan", *Shu'un Filastiniyya*, (Beirut), September 1975, pp. 22–26.

5. Voice of Palestine, (Cairo), June 8, 1974. In: BBC, ME 4622/A/2, June 11, 1974.

6. Arafat in his 1974 UN speech considered "the beginning of the Jewish invasion" to be much earlier, saying "the Jewish invasion of Palestine began in 1881". (*Journal of Palestine Studies*, Beirut, vol. IV, no. 2, Winter 1975, p. 185). Full text of address, *ibid.*, pp. 181–192. For a description of Fourth PNC session see: *Al-Majlis al Watani al-Filastini al Mun'aqad fil-Cahira min 10–17 Tamus 1968*, (no place, no date). See also MER, 1968, pp. 427–431.

7. Sabri Jiryis "The Palestinian Problem – The Other Side of the Coin", *Al-Nahar*, (Beirut), May 13–15, 1975.

8. "Palestine will not be liberated without armed struggle", *Filastin Al-Thawra*, (Beirut), June 29, 1975, pp. 28–32.

9. Somalia was faced, when achieving independence in July 1960, with similar problems of claims to the Ethiopian Ogaden area, north of Kenya and Djibouti. To acquire the area she received considerable military aid from the USSR and entered into a series of local wars with Ethiopia, the last of them ending in 1978 with Somalia's defeat. Ethiopia has demanded that Somalia renounces all her territorial claims which Somalian leadership finds impossible to do – to renounce what they have long proclaimed and to abandon the idea that all Somalis are to be united in one State. They prefer, therefore, a policy of "neither war, nor peace". The same might happen with the PLO.

10. *Le Monde*, (Paris), January 6, 1976

11. The resolutions of the 8th PNC, that convened in Cairo in February–March 1971, said, inter alia:

   "The PLO is the only representative of the Palestinian Arab masses and their various combat and political organizations, bodies, unions and societies, regardless of their inclinations and ideologies, provided they fully abide by the principles of the Palestinian National Covenant" (MENA, Cairo, March 4, 1971).

12. MENA, March 20, 1977.
13. *Al Nahar*, May 13–15, 1975
14. Walid Khalidi "Thinking the Unthinkable: a Sovereign Palestinian State", *Foreign Affairs*, vol. 56, no. 4, (July 1978), pp. 695 – 713.
15. *Al Munadil*, as quoted by *Al Ba'th* (Damascus), February 1, 1977.
16. DPA, Cairo, in Arabic, March 19, 1977, as quoted in FBIS, ME, March 21, 1977, p. A4.
17. "Democratic State" proposals were presented in a PDFLP publication: *Nahwa Hall Dimuqrati lil Qadiya al-Filastiniyya* (Towards a Democratic Solution of the Palestine Problem), Beirut, 1970.
18. MENA, September 7, 1969.
19. *ibid.*, March 4, 1971.
20. *Al Anwar*, (Beirut), March 15, 1970
21. Bernard Lewis "The Return of Islam", *Commentary*, (New York) vol. 61, no. 1. (January 1976), p. 43.
22. *Al-Ray Al-Amm*, March 16, 1969.
23. Arafat to *Al-Jumhuriyya*, (Cairo), January 6, 1970. Arafat referred here to Anna Frankus (Ania Francos) the author of *Les Palestiniens*, (Paris, Juillard, 1968), who had done much to popularize Palestinian organizations in European Leftist publications.
24. "Jews as a group have no historical, religious or political right to Palestine, but the democratic state of Palestine will guarantee the rights of the Jews as individual citizens of the State". (*Al-Ahram*, Cairo, September 14, 1969, in a comment on the 6th PNC.)
25. *Al Nahar*, (Beirut), December 12, 1973.
26. *Al Safir*, (Beirut), November 30, 1977.
27. MENA, March 20, 1977.
28. *Sawt Al-Tali'a*, (Damascus), February 1978.
29. MENA, March 20, 1977.
30. Qatar News Agency, January 1, 1977.
31. *Events*, (published by Al-Hawadith, Beirut) no. 10, February 11, 1977, pp. 7, 10–11.
32. *Ha'aretz*, (Tel-Aviv), January 3, 1977.
33. Published in the Sa'iqa organ *Al Tala'i* and broadcast by Voice of Palestine, Damascus, January 11, 1977.
34. *Al Ahram*, (Cairo), September 14, 1969.
35. *Al-Anwar* (Beirut), March 15, 1970.
36. Al Nahar, (Beirut), December 4, 1973.
37. ibid., ibid.
38. Quoted from MER, 1967, p. 260.
39. Fa'iz Sayegh, *A handful of vagueness. A research on the meaning of Bourguiba'ism and its Slogans*, Beirut, Center for Palestinian Studies, May 1965, second edition – July 1966. Quoted from Y. Harkabi, *Arav ve-Israel*, vol. 5, p. 26 (Hebrew)
The excerpt reprinted here was fully quoted by Fa'iz Sayegh seven years later when he attacked those in the Arab world who called on acceptance of the UN Security Council resolution 242, saying that they will activate in this way against Israel a strategy of stages and force her in the first stage to withdraw from the territories that she had occupied in 1967. Sayegh said that what he had written in 1965 applied also to the situation in 1972. (Fa'iz Sayegh, "Remarks on the Security Council resolution 242", *Shu'un Filastiniyya*, vol. 15, November 1972. Quoted from *ibid.*, vol. 1, pp. 62–63.
40. Voice of Palestine, Cairo, June 8, 1974. BBC Monitoring Service ME/4622/A/2, June 11, 1974.
41. *ibid.*, ibid.
42. MENA, March 20, 1977, in FBIS, ME, March 21, 1977, p. A11.
43. "The Document of Union" (Al-Wuthqa Al Wahdawiyya) that was ratified by the PLO, Fath, PFLP, DFLP, PFLP-GC, Sa'iqa, ALF, PLF. WAFA, Voice of Palestine, Damascus, December 5, 1977; *Journal of Palestine Studies*, vol. VII, no. 3, (Spring 1978). p. 188.

44.   Al-Sa'iqa head, Zuhayr Muhsin, when asked if he wants the destruction of Israel, said: "If we were in a position to do so we would do it today and not wait until tomorrow. But . . . we cannot do it . . . Israel is not legal in our eyes, it will never be legal and therefore we will never recognize it". After obtaining an Israeli withdrawal behind the June 1967 borders, the right of the refugees to return, the right of Palestinians to self-determination", "we are ready to end the state of war with Israel and conclude peace, but we will never recognize Israel", (*Die Presse,* Vienna, November 16, 1977.

45.   An interview with Faruq Al-Qadumi, *Shu'un Filastiniyya,* June 1977, p. 40.

46.   Faruq Al-Qadumi interview with William E. Schmidt, *Newsweek,* March 14, 1977, p. 56; *AP,* March 7, 1977; *International Herald Tribune,* March 8, 1977.

47.   Qatar News Agency, Doha, September 26, 1979, in FBIS, ME, September 27, 1979, pp. A1–A2.

CHAPTER FOUR

SOCIAL BACKGROUND OF POLITICAL AND IDEOLOGICAL PROBLEMS

Political and ideological aspects of the Palestinian problem are closely related to the social structure of Palestinian society. Its division between the people of the uplands, hills and mountains and those of the lowlands, coastal plain and the larger interior valleys, might at first glance be seen as having no political significance. A closer examination of that division is necessary in order to understand the political and ideological complexities of the Palestinian problem. These include the emergence of the PLO and the thrust of its ideology, the prospects for a Palestinian state in the West Bank and other issues.

A deep gap developed over generations between the Palestinians of the mountains (which came to be known as the West Bank) and those of the coastal plain.

While those Palestinians who did not abandon their land and continue to keep it (and this refers primarily to the West Bank population) might, as other Palestinians, be satisfied with the establishment of a Palestinian state in the places in which they live, the PLO is committed to "the liberation of all of Palestine" according to its ideology and social origin. People from the coastal plain are unwelcome in the mountain area — even the poorest fellahin have reservations about a marriage of a daughter to an inhabitant of a refugee camp.

A Palestinian state to the inhabitant of a refugee camp means a state in the areas of the coastal plain. As the leadership of the PLO and most Palestinian organizations has been in the hands of exiles — they would probably lead the Palestinian state, if established. Despite the slogans, it is doubtful if they would be willingly accepted by the West Bank population, who regard them as strangers. The leaders of the state — coastal people — would see it a base for the "liberation" of what they regard as their homeland — Haifa, Lydda, Jaffa, Ramla, etc. — and in pursuit of this "liberation", they would perpetuate and increase the instability and tension in the whole area.

The coastal plain of Palestine was for the most part sparsely inhabited since the Crusades. Travellers who visited the country told a continuing tale of uncultivated lands and villages in ruins. The disappearance of settled fellahin encouraged a continuous infiltration by nomadic Bedouin tribes from the deserts and semi-deserts of the east and south into what was once fertile plains and valleys.[1]

The Bedouin tribes turned primarily to the coastal plain and internal valleys. Relations between them and the local population were in accordance with the old patterns of struggle between nomads and permanent settlers and with the emergence of areas in which no strong central authority existed, the Bedouin held the upper hand. The villagers were expelled into the hills of the east which were easier to defend. Those who did remain suffered much from sporadic raids and plunder, crop burning and the demand for heavy ransoms. Much of the coastal plain was not cultivated, and became "dead land" (mawat).[2] River mouths filled up, the waters swamping the land of the plains. Roads of necessity ran east to the hills and even to the mountains.[3]

Changes in this situation came about only from the late 19th century. The Ottoman land law of 1858 was enforced by the central and regional authorities in order to facilitate the appropriation of tracts of land in Palestine by influential and rich families from Beirut, Damascus and, to a smaller extent, Jerusalem, Jaffa and other sub-district capitals of the Ottoman Empire.

Modernisation followed in the wake of both European interest in Palestine and with Jewish immigration to Palestine. Gradually, agriculture was introduced successfully, where corn crops had failed, due to a thick layer of sand covering the soil.

Relative security for the settlers replaced the wild conditions prevalent in the area for the centuries of desolation. In the course of time, settlements dotted the whole area, roads connected them to the towns, railways further improved communications and law and order came to the land.

The Bedouin had to adapt themselves to the new situation. While some adjusted themselves to permanent settlement, others returned to the desert.

Thus a settled population developed in the villages in the coastal plain parallel to the growth of urban population in towns like Haifa, which in the course of two generations, rose from a village into a city. This growth of the population in a relatively short time was, however, too rapid to bring in its wake a developed hierarchy of leaders from extended families or clans (hamulas) as had happened over many generations in the upland areas. The coastal plain hamulas were relative newcomers, of only decades, generally lacking any tradition of leadership, or a distinguished origin. Their social status was determined primarily in accordance with their wealth. This induced mountain dwellers to regard with contempt the coastal people, with whom they preferred not to mix.

Palestinian refugees of 1948–1949 were mainly from the coastal plain. Few left the mountain area and except a few places, as in the area between Jerusalem and the coast, the original population remains to the present day.

Hence the Palestinian dispersion in the Middle East comes from the coastal plain. As the bulk of the PLO membership comes from refugee camps and as a result of Palestinian dispersion, it means that the PLO is primarily composed of people whose origin is the coastal plain.[4]

This has far-reaching political implications. The first is related to the demand that Israel enables refugees to return ("the right of return", Arabic Haq Al-Awda). The PLO has demanded a return not to the West Bank, but to the places which they left, i.e. to the coastal plain, to the territory of Israel before June 1967 — and nowadays demands a return to places in Israeli territory which were defined as Jewish, before 1948.

PLO spokesmen have declared consistently that they oppose any solution of the refugee problem which would settle them outside of Palestine, or in the West Bank, and that they want to realize the "right of return" to lands they occupied before June 1967. George Habash declared:

> "The Palestinians in the East Bank [i.e. in Jordan] and those who live in Lebanon, are not from the West Bank and Gaza Strip. They came from the place that is called actual Israel. The only solution for these people is to return to their country and not to the West Bank".[5]

In hundreds of interviews, addresses and statements, PLO personalities repeat the same demand — to return to Jaffa, Haifa, etc. in the coastal plain. Almost every request to apply "the right of return" has been to the coastal or other areas of pre-1967 Israel and not to any place in the mountain areas, such as Hebron, Nablus or Ramallah.[6]

Arabs who lived permanently in the mountain area of Palestine, later named "the West Bank", consider themselves to be the elite of Palestinian society. The area can be compared to a mountain fortress, comparatively easy to defend. Past conquerors of Palestine usually failed to subdue it and those who succeeded maintained only a nominal control over the area. Even in the last centuries of Ottoman rule, the area retained a measure of autonomy. Bedouin tribes also encountered difficulties in entering the interior of the mountain area. In the few places where they succeeded as in the areas of Hebron and Bethlehem, they failed to integrate among the local population and for the most part were driven back to the desert areas. The result was that the Arab population of what became the West Bank was much more homogenous than that of the coastal plain.

With time there developed among that population a uniform and hierarchic organization of extended families — *hamulas,* accepted by all. This structure pertains still today. Ties of marriage, livelihood and economy, political affiliations, taxation, defense, legacies, blood vengeance and compensation, of the division of land plots and even the marketing of products were conducted through the wider family and not on an individual basis.[7]

Power struggles among *hamulas* determined the face and character of Palestinian society. Before urbanisation in the 19th century the power centers and domiciles of the most distinguished families were in the villages. In the second half of the 19th century these power centres moved to the towns in the control of strong *hamulas* who lived there. The latter became owners of much of the land in the villages around those towns, turning the fellahin who lived there into share-croppers.

Palestinian society was built, as any other society in the form of a pyramid, the lower strata at the base, the elite on top. The Palestinian social pyramid, however, had no real vertex. There was not one single leading family on the top, but a number of *hamulas* more or less equally distinguished in lineage, equally strong in manpower, equally rich, having an equal influence and control over centres of power and equally close ties with the authorities. The result was that one restrained the other and prevented a situation in which all could be equal, but one would be more equal than the other! The political implication of a leadership vacuum existed, and still exists.

In Jerusalem the most important and distinguished *hamula* since the 18th century was that of Al-Husseini. It was great in terms of numbers, owned much property and held many positions of power. Its hegemony survived the end of the Ottoman rule and persisted into the period of the British Mandate. Its role in the Supreme Muslim Council gave it control over the religious affairs of the Muslim population. In order to extend its influence over all of Palestine, the family organized groups of supporters named *Al-Majlisiyyun* (The People of the Council), in most parts of the country.

The power of the Husseinis was challenged by the rival Jerusalem family of Al-Nashashibi. It was great too in the terms of numbers, it also owned extensive property, it also held positions of power to the end of the Ottoman period and at the beginning of the Mandate. Its base of power was in the municipality of Jerusalem, which gave it control over the city's local affairs. The Nashashibis established all over the country a rival to the Al-Majlisiyyun camp, named Al-Mu'aridun (The People of the Opposition) which too succeeded in spreading everywhere.

The Husseinis and Nashashibis were rivalled by the family of Al-Khalidi, smaller in numbers but very rich and distinguished, being related to Khalid Ibn Al-Walid, the Arab commander who conquered Palestine at the time of the early conquests of Islam. The Al-Khalidis controlled most educational institutions of Jerusalem and in particular, the great Al-Kahlidiyya library.

A fourth family, Al-Dajani held an important religious site — according to Islam, the place of burial of King David. It refused to concede this site to the Husseinis who controlled all other Muslim holy places in the country.

The rivalry between these families resulted in a situation of checks and balances on the one hand and of sharp internal struggles on the other in which there were no winners.

In Nablus, the struggle at the beginning of the 19th century was between the families of Nimr and Tuqan both with distinguished and strong urban connections. An additional family, Abd Al-Hadi which came from the rural area[8] challenged openly the hegemony of the Tuqans, and in this struggle, which reached its peak in the middle of the 19th century there were also no winners. New families appeared, mainly of merchants such as Shak'a, Masri, Nabulsi.

Their wealth enabled them, by the end of the 19th and during the 20th centuries, to wield considerable power, to accumulate capital, to invest in immovable property in the towns and in lands outside it, and to develop a wide net of trade relations, etc. They did not, however, succeed in dominating the Abd Al-Hadi and Tuqan families with the consequence that the leading Nablus families still rival each other and struggle among themselves.

The same situation pertains in Hebron between the families of Qawasma, Tamimi and Ja'bari, and in Jenin between the families of Abushi, Jarar and a branch of the Abd Al-Hadi family. It is so in other places too — a number of *hamulas* on the top, fighting each other, but with no domination achieved by any of them. Rivalries without any one family achieving distinction appears throughout the West Bank and even more so in the whole upland area.

West Bank families wield much power today. Their economic situation might be described as excellent, as a result of the considerable economic advance of the West Bank as a whole and of their accumulating wealth from property, business and incomes derived from working in the West Bank itself, in Israel and in Jordan. Since 1967 all *hamulas* whose sons serve as civil servants (teachers, judges, employees, etc.) have been earning double salaries from the Israeli administration and from Jordan. Many of them have close political ties both with Israel and with Jordan. The pending struggle for leadership will probably be hard and prolonged.

This *hamula* pattern applied not only to Palestinian society but also existed in other Middle East countries, in Syria, Egypt, and Iraq. In the 1950's those countries underwent military coups after which the military filled the positions at the top of the pyramid, and achieved a dominant position in their societies. As there were no military cadres in Palestinian society, the leadership vacuum still exists.

● **The Exiles vs Upland Notables**

The PLO, comprising organisations of exiled Palestinians tries to emulate the military cadres in several Arab countries by seeking to monopolise the top echelons of Palestinians society. It aspires to leadership and aims at establishing an independent Palestinian state under its leadership. It claims to be "the sole legitimate representative of the Arab people of Palestine" and much of its power flows from the by now almost universal acceptance given to that claim. Among the people of the West Bank, many see the PLO as their sole representative and declare that they will transfer leadership to it when this will be possible.

On what is this recognition based? There is no doubt that it is based on the image of the PLO as revolutionaries dedicated to the Palestinian cause — an image greatly enhanced by the international recognition of the PLO, the resolutions of the Algiers and Rabat Arab summits which decided to transfer to the PLO the right to represent Palestinians, and no less due to a fear of internal terror. The tendency to accept the PLO appears in any interview, address or declaration of West Bank personalities. But do they actually want it? Are there other, less visible tendencies which are accepted by many but do not appear to surface?

When examining the dominant family record of the West Bank population, it emerges that this population in no way conforms to the criteria which characterises Palestinian organisations associated in the PLO.

While the West Bank population lives in that part of Palestine which they had never abandoned, the PLO membership is drawn from the exiles and refugees who had left their land in 1948. Land is a key element in conservative Arab society, and refugees being landless are considered to belong to a lower social status than the fellahin in the West Bank.

It has been said by West Bank Arabs that "we survived the Turks, British, Jordanians and Israelis, and have continued to live on our land while they, the refugees, left their land and escaped in 1948 to the hotels of Beirut". Absorption of the landless Arab refugees by the indigenous West Bank Arab population was notoriously difficult: will the West Bank Arabs willingly absorb exiles and refugees who had fled to Lebanon, Syria and Jordan? Will "landed Arab gentry" accept domination by a "landless Arab invader?"

Will the established West Bank population willingly accept domination by Palestinian organisations, associated in the PLO, who proclaim radical left wing and communist slogans? They fear that if those who proclaim such slogans will come to power, one of their first steps will be the nationalisation of land and confiscation of private property.

The elite *hamulas* which dominate the West Bank are jealous of their past. Most PLO leaders, however, come from the coastal plain, where the population was heterogenous. A traditional Arab from Nablus asserted, "Do you think that I will agree to transfer *my* Nablus to the rule of George Habash? Who is George Habash? He is from the mobs of Lyssa."

However, even among the settled Arab population of the coastal plain, there are those who have looked askance at "interlopers" who came to Palestine within the past century, and whose sons are to be found in the PLO today.

It would be mistaken to interpret these tendencies in conventional western terms as manifestations of "a class struggle", between "the haves and the have-nots". It goes deeper than that, since even among the Arabs on the West Bank, there are poor fellahin and share-croppers who consider themselves superior to the refugees from the coastal plain who had abandoned their land.

Jordan's connection with the West Bank goes beyond the continuity of Jordanian law in the area, of the educational system, of parliamentary representation in Amman, of citizenship rights and obligations and of currency arrangements.

Many West Bank *hamulas* have relatives and *hamula*-branches in Jordan. Many Palestinians hold key positions in the Jordanian economy and administration. Jordanian reluctance to "hand the West Bank over" to the PLO is based not only on this continued connection, but even more strongly on the mutually acknowledged fact by Jordanians and the PLO that such a transfer would be only a stage in the domination of Jordan itself by the PLO.

In the event that Israel would transfer the administration of the West Bank to the PLO, radical Palestinian organizations will try to establish an Arab People's Democratic Republic of Palestine on the pattern of the People's Democratic Republic of the Yemen [both George Habash and Naif Hawatmah, on the one hand, and present South Yemen leaders on the other, came from the same Arab Nationalists Movement. Al-Qawmiyyun Al-Arab], but this time in a much more sensitive region. Organizations that represent interests of particular Arab countries like Sa'iqa and the ALF, will try to direct developments to the advantage of their sponsoring countries.

Present evidence leads to the conclusion that PLO domination of the West Bank and the Gaza Strip will vouchsafe neither tranquility nor stability in the region itself, let alone in the Middle East as a whole.

NOTES TO CHAPTER FOUR

1. D. K. H. Amiran, "The Pattern of Settlement in Palestine", *Israel Exploration Journal (Jerusalem)*, vol. III, (1953), No. 2, pp. 65 – 78; No. 3, pp. 192 – 209; No. 4, pp. 250 – 260; Amnon Cohen, *Palestine Since 18th Century: Patterns of Government and Administration*, Jerusalem, Magnes Press, Hebrew University, 1973; A. Reifenberg, *The Struggle Between the Desert and the Sown: the rise and fall of agriculture in the Levant*, Jerusalem, Government Press, 1958.

2. Most of those lands were owned by rich effendis, a great part of them non-Palestinian, who lived in Beirut or Damascus. With the arrival of Jewish settlers in the area, they tried to purchase land in the mountains, but owners of the land there had no wish to sell, with the result that Jews bought non-cultivated "dead lands". This led to a concentration of Jewish settlement in the lowlands and very few settlements in the mountains.

3. The Survey of Palestine directed by Conder and Kitchener in 1871–1877 showed that most of the settlements and population were in the uplands and only a small number in the plains. Large areas of the plains were malarial swamplands. There were relatively few coastal towns. (C. R. Conder and H. H. Kitchener, *The Survey of Palestine*, London, 1881–1883).

4. An examination of PLO leadership presents this situation:

Personality	Organization	Origin
Yasir Arafat	Fath	El Arish
George Habash	PFLP	Lydda
Wadi Haddad	PFLP	Lydda
Zuhayr Muhsin	Sa'iqa	Tulkarm
Ali Hassan Salama	Fath (Black September)	Qula, near Lydda
Sa'id Hamami	Fath	Jaffa
Na'if Hawatimah	Democratic Front	Jordan (no Palestinian)
Ahmad Jibril	PFLP-GC	Syria (no Palestinian)

5. George Habash to *Stern*, according to DPA as reported by MENA, February 15, 1977.

6. The UN General Assembly resolutions concerning the refugees, beginning with resolution No. 194 of December 11, 1948, and including No. 3236 of November 1974, accepted that PLO demand. Resolution 194 speaks about the need of the return of refugees that will want it "to their homes". Resolution 3236 (Article 2) reaffirms "the inalienable right of the Palestinians [i.e. all Palestinians and not only refugees] to return to their homes and property from which they have been displaced and uprooted, and calls for their return".

7. See A. Cohen, "Hamula", *The Encyclopaedia of Islam*, vol. 3, (Leiden, E. J. Brill and London, Luzac, 1971), pp. 149–150.

8. The origin of the Abd Al-Hadi family is from the village Aruba in the district of Jenin. The family owns plots in the districts of Nablus and Jenin to this day.

THE GREAT POWERS AND THE PLO

CHAPTER FIVE

THE PEOPLE'S REPUBLIC OF CHINA AND PALESTINIAN ORGANIZATIONS

The People's Republic of China was the first foreign power to establish ties with the PLO. Shortly after the establishment of the PLO, its Chairman, Ahmad Al-Shuqayri, visited China, met leading personalities and was promised Chinese support. In June 1965, Shuqayri stated that his organization had obtained unconditional military help from the PRC and that an Arab Palestinian military personality was in Beijing (Peking)[1] to organize military cooperation.[2]

A PLO office was opened in Beijing and the PRC granted the PLO qualified recognition, as representing the Palestinian people. The PLO representative was invited to official receptions at which he proclaimed pro-Chinese sentiments and publicly attacked the US. Limited amounts of small arms were given to the PLO and tens of its members underwent training in guerrilla warfare and augmented by studies of the thought of Mao Zedong (Mao Tse-tung). Praise was frequently showered in PLO statements and publications by leading PLO personalities on the PRC, and its great leader, Mao. Public recognition was given by the PLO leadership to efforts by the PLO to apply the Chinese methods of struggle to the Middle East situation.

The Arab-Israeli Six Day War in June 1967 was widely covered in China's information media, with attacks both on the US and the USSR. The latter was presented as a "paper tiger" which had failed to help her friends when they were in need of help.

This was the period of the "Great Cultural Revolution" in China, of the doctrine of the armed struggle by the people and of PRC support of revolutionaries as a means to play a leading role in "Third World" countries. But the Chinese also preached "self-reliance" and told their friends that they had to do the fighting by themselves.[3] Even if the PRC were to decide to provide more aid, they explained it would be unable to supply what Arab leaders expected from it and could in no circumstances compete with the Soviet Union in supplying military, financial and other aid. At the request of the USSR, pro-Soviet Arab states pressed Palestinian organizations dependent on them, to break off their ties with the PRC.[4] Conservative Arab oil producing states – from which major Palestinian organizations and Al-Fath in particular received most of their aid – apprehensive of Chinese penetration into the Middle East put even stronger pressure on the PLO to break off even the most tenuous ties with the PRC.

Nevertheless, Al-Fath succeeded in maintaining good relations both with conservative Arab states and the PRC. PLO relations with China seemed to have cooled when Shuqayri was removed from leadership towards the end of 1967, were strengthened again in 1969, when Al-Fath took control of the PLO. Al-Fath tried to exploit USSR-PRC competition to gain support from both. After a PLO delegation headed by Yasir Arafat, achieved little from a visit to Moscow in February 1970, a delegation headed by him went to Beijing the very next month.[5] The visit was planned to reassure the PRC leadership that the Moscow talks had not meant a change in PLO orientation – and also to ensure further PRC military aid.

PRC information media gave a relatively wide coverage to the activities and struggle of Palestinian organisations. As its small scale was not likely to impress Chinese readers who were used to the great size and the ramifications of their country, the descriptions tended to exaggerate, to make the PLO's arena and efforts appear larger and more impressive. They, of course, made frequent allusions to the attention given by the PLO to *The Thoughts of Mao*.[6]

On the eve of the September 1970 civil war in Jordan, arms intended for Palestinians reached Jordan, mainly through Syria or Iraq, from the PRC. Chinese diplomats in Damascus served as instructors and supplied arms to the Palestinians. Due to the great distances involved, and to the limited Chinese production capacities, such supplies did not include heavy arms but were generally limited to rifles, grenades, mortars, explosives, anti-tank guns and automatic weapons up to medium machine guns. Chinese arms and instructors were not only supplied and assigned to the PLO but also to the more radical PFLP and PDFLP,[7] whose leaders had criticised the USSR for advocating a political settlement of the Arab-Israeli conflict and upheld PRC theories on people's war and guerilla strategy and tactics. The PRC, however, preferred at that time to give wide publicity to her ties with the PLO and Al-Fath and to play down links with the radical organizations.

Arms and training continued to be provided by the PRC to Palestinian organizations throughout the early 1970's. "More than 75% of the arms used by Palestinian revolutionary groups have been given to us from China," the head of the PLO mission in Beijing admitted at the close of 1972. China, he added, was "the only major power which has considered the head of the Palestinian mission as an ambassador, has accorded him full protocol, and has given him a building in the embassies quarter – the building and the Ambassador's diplomatic car fly the Palestinian flag". Members of the command of Al Fath, when visiting Beijing were given more attention than visiting foreign ministers. "They are accorded official and public welcome and are received by the Foreign Minister, senior army officers and Chinese experts on Middle East affairs, and housed in one of the grand guest palaces where the Palestinian flag is raised".[8] Abu Al-Raid acclaimed PLO ties with China in a Palestinian radio station broadcast early in 1973. "When you visit one of the Palestinian revolution bases or training camps, you will find that the rifle is Chinese-made and that the fighter might have received his training in China," he said.[9]

In the later 1970's, however, more emphasis was given by the PRC to ties with existing governments and those with revolutionaries were abandoned (with a few exceptions). Diplomatic relations were established between the PRC and a great number of Arab countries and such relations assumed greater importance than those with the PLO. PRC support for the Palestinians was mainly restricted to political aid. In propaganda, however, the change was more muted. A gap thus developed between Chinese words and actions, between high sounding, revolutionary declarations and a more cautious implementation of policy.[10]

Rivalry with the Soviet Union overshadowed many other considerations. The principal and urgent aim of the PRC in the Middle East was to weaken the USSR positions in that area and whatever contributed to that was evaluated in terms of PRC self-interest. This in turn led to closer relations with Egypt and the Sudan, to an establishment of relations with Oman.[11] It even led to a reassessment of Israel's role in the Middle East. Israel was still subject to sharp attacks in PRC media — but there were indications that the Chinese favoured an independent Israel to stand up against the USSR and its allies in the Middle East.[12]

Gradually, but steadily, Chinese interest in Palestinian organizations weakened, not only as a result of changing PRC foreign policy priorities, but also because of the PLO's orientation towards the Soviet Union.

President Anwar Al-Sadat's initiative to conduct direct talks with Israel placed the PRC in a dilemma. She had an interest in strengthening Sadat and his role in the Arab world but an open support of his initiative would damage her ties with the PLO, Syria, Iraq, the PDRY and Algeria which opposed Sadat's initiative. Chinese spokesmen tried therefore to express support of Sadat in general but to avoid an expression of position on this specific subject, to present facts, to quote others but not to give their own views.

A PLO delegation visited China between October 29—November 3, 1978, with an aim to persuade PRC leaders to oppose Egypt's negotiations with Israel. The delegation brought with it a message from Yasir Arafat to Chairman Hua Guofeng (Hua Kuo-feng) just at a time when Arafat visited the USSR and spoke about friendship with the Soviet Union. The Chinese were ready to express support for the Palestinians and to condemn Israel, but refused to criticise Egypt. They tried to manoeuvre between friendship for Egypt and the PLO but giving preference to the struggle against "Soviet hegemonism", they left themselves with a narrow margin.[13]

Chinese policy aims at avoidance of taking sides on disputed controversial problems in the Arab world. It enables them to keep ties with the greatest possible number of Arab states. The Palestinian problem is seen to be paramount in the Arab world and thus their commitment to support the Palestinian cause at least in words, is seen to contribute to their position in that world.

NOTES TO CHAPTER FIVE

1. Chinese names and places are given here according to the system adopted by the PRC State Council since January 1, 1979: Chinese phonetic spelling (Pinyin), with the conventional spelling given in parentheses, e.g. Beijing (Peking), Hua Guofeng (Hua Kuo-feng), Deng Xiaoping (Teng Hsiao-ping).

2. The visit was considered to be on a "people-to-people" level, the delegation being invited by the Chinese People's Institute of Foreign Affairs (CPIFA). The joint statement on the visit was signed in Beijing on March 22, 1965, by Zhou Enlai (Chou En-lai) as Honorary President of the CPIFA and not as Premier. Text of statement was given by NCNA on March 22, 1965. (*Survey of China Mainland Press*, US Consulate General, Hong Kong, No. 3425, March 26, 1965, pp. 35–37)
Details on the visit were given in the PLO publication: *Munazzamat Al-Tahrir Al-Filastiniyya wa-Jumhuriyyat Sin ash-Sha'biyya* (The PLO and the PRC), no place, no date [Cairo, PLO, 1966]
A description of his talks with Zhou Enlai was given by Shuqayri in his memoirs (Ahmad Al-Shuqayri, *Min Al-Qummah ila Al-Hazimah: Ma'a Al-Mulok wa Al-Rosaa* (From the Summit to the Defeat: With Kings and Presidents), Beirut, Da'ar Al 'Awden, 1971, pp. 229–232.

3. The PRC position of "people's war" at that time was summed up by Lin Biao (Lin Piao) in 1965 when he served as Vice-Chairman of the Chinese CP Central Committee, Vice-Premier and Minister of Defense. Such a war, he said, has to rely "on the strength of the masses in their own country and prepare them to carry on the fight independently even when all material aid from outside is cut off". Those who lean wholly on foreign aid cannot achieve a victory or consolidate it. In this sense, "revolution cannot be imported". It does not exclude "mutual sympathy and support on the part of revolutionary peoples" to such struggles. Chinese "support and aid to other revolutionary peoples serves precisely to help their self-reliant struggle". (Lin Piao, "Long Live the Victory of People's War", *Peking Review*, No. 36, September 3, 1965, pp. 9–30).

4. When a Chinese ship carrying arms for Palestinians arrived at the Iraqi port of Basrah in April 1969, the Soviets warned the Iraqis that permitting the off-loading of that ship would lead to an end to all Soviet arms supplies to Iraq. After behind-the-scenes negotiations conducted over a long period Iraq allowed the ship to unload but promised the Soviets that it would not happen again. (*Al-Risalla*, Kuwait, May 3, 1969).

5. *Peking Review*, No. 14, April 3, 1970, pp. 4–5.

6. *ibid.*, No. 21, May 23, 1969, pp. 28–30.

7. *The Times*, (London) August 19, 1970; *Sunday Times*, August 23, 1970; *Daily Telegraph* (London), August 26, 1970; *Sunday Telegraph*, August 30, 1970; *Christian Science Monitor* (Boston), October 1, 1970.

8. Mamduh Rida, *Al-Jummuriyah* (Cairo), December 28, 1972.

9. Cairo Voice of Palestine, January 15, 1973, in FBIS, ME, January 16, 1973, pp. A1–A2. See also: John K. Cooley, "China and the Palestinians", *Journal of Palestine Studies*, (Beirut), vol. 1, No. 2, (winter 1972), pp. 19–34; R. Medzini, "China and the Palestinians – a developing relationship", *New Middle East*, (London), No. 32, May 1971, pp. 34–37.

10. Aryeh Yodfat, "The PRC and the Middle East", *Asia Quarterly*, (Bruxelles), 1977/3, pp. 223–236; 1978/1, pp. 67–78, 1978/4 pp. 295–308; Lilian Craig Haris, "China's Relations with the PLO", *Journal of Palestine Studies*, (Washington, D.C.), vol. 7, No. 1 (issue 25, Autumn 1977) pp. 123–154.

11. PRC support was provided in the later 1960's to the Popular Front for the Liberation of Oman (then named Popular Front for the Liberation of Oman and the Arabian Gulf, PFLOAG).

12. PRC Foreign Minister Chiao Kuan-hua was reported to have said in a "secret speech" in Tientsin on May 20, 1975: "Israel . . . is a fait accompli. We cannot repatriate the expelled Palestinians, thereby creating an Israeli refugee problem". China, however, did not think of normalizing her relations with Israel. "Israel's continued existence would be advantageous to China, even if no diplomatic relations are established with Israel . . . the mere existence of Israel is enough to perpetuate the confrontation between the 'Soviet revisionists and the US imperialists'. Therefore, it is better to pursue a policy of a bystander". (*Frankfurter Allgemeine*, October 14, 1975, p. 6)

13. NCNA in English, October 30, 1978, in FBIS, PRC, October 31, 1978, p. A25; Alain Jacob, *Le Monde* (Paris), November 1, 1978.

CHAPTER SIX

THE USSR, THE PLO AND "THE PALESTINE PROBLEM"

The USSR has consistently determined its position on the "Palestinian problem", not on merit but as a function of changing USSR interests in the Middle East. The Soviets have since 1947 spoken about the existence in Palestine of two peoples, Arabs and Jews, both deserving, as other peoples, a recognition of their national rights.[1]   The USSR voted in the UN General Assembly on November 29, 1947, for the resolution calling for a partition of Palestine and for establishing there a Jewish and Arab state and an economic union between both states.[2]

The State of Israel established on May 15, 1948 was recognized by the USSR three days later, on May 18, 1948.[3]   The war proclaimed by Arab states against Israel was condemned by the USSR. As a result of that war, most of Arab Palestine came under Egyptian and Trans-Jordan administration. In April 1950 Trans-Jordan decided to annex the territories she had occupied and to change the name of the state to the Hashemite Kingdom of Jordan. It was not recognized by the USSR which saw in that step a violation of the UN General Assembly decision of November 29, 1947 to establish an Arab Palestinian state.[4]

Following that unilateral action by Jordan, for two decades the Soviets in referring to Palestinian Arabs distinguished between:

— the Arab population of the State of Israel, which deserved equal rights with all other Israeli citizens and whose future was to be linked with that state;

— Arab refugees who had left Palestine in 1947–1948. The USSR saw their problem as a humanitarian, rather than a political problem, advocating that those who wished to return to their homes should be allowed to do so and that those who did not wish to return should be compensated for their property;

— Arabs from the West Bank of the Jordan River and from the Gaza Strip, who were under Jordanian and Egyptian administration respectively, were generally regarded by the Soviets as an integral part of the Jordanian or Egyptian populations. In the aftermath of the June 1967 war, the USSR advocated a return to the situation which prevailed before that war, i.e. a return of those territories to Jordan and to Egypt.

The USSR preferred at that time not to express a clear opinion about the status and rights of Palestinian Arabs and what was said (and very little was in fact said about it) could be interpreted in more than one way. The Soviet aim was to attract Arab nationalism and to shape it as a tool to remove any Western, particularly American presence, and interests in the Middle East.[5] Soviet spokesmen generally did not speak about an "Arab nation" (though Soviet information media directed to Arabs sometimes used this term), but about "Arab peoples", which may become in the future one nation, but had not yet reached that stage. The USSR saw an analogy in the situation in Anglo-Saxon countries or in Spanish speaking peoples in Latin America which have a common past, a common language and culture but belong to different nations. It was in that framework of Arab peoples − Egyptians, Syrians or Jordanians, etc. − that they saw the Palestinian Arabs and for years they preferred not to commit themselves to a firm opinion on their fate.[6]

A clear position on this subject was taken towards the close of the 60's by the Communist Party of the Soviet Union (CPSU) in comments on a draft political programme of the Syrian Communist Party (CP).[7] The Soviets advised the Syrians to accept the existence of Israel and that while resisting Israeli policy "there must be no talk about eliminating the Israeli state". The return of Palestinian Arab refugees who wish to do so and compensation for those who do not wish to return would be a solution to the Palestinian problem. Israel has to withdraw from all territories occupied in June 1967 and from then on, "the struggle must continue and must be directed against Zionism".

"The slogan of the right to return [of Arab refugees to Israel] must be maintained. After the return, there will be the right to self-determination, meaning: determining for themselves the administration and the form and character of the state . . . The demand for a unitary state is also one of the rights of self-determination. The right of self-determination does not necessarily mean a separate state".[8]

The Soviets called for a stage by stage change in the pattern of the State of Israel. Arab refugees would come back and constituting a majority would determine Israel's future. Israel will then turn from a "Zionist" (i.e. a Jewish) state into a bi-national Arab-Jewish state and may in due course become an Arab Palestinian state.

However, in open expressions of opinion, USSR spokesmen did not go that far, and generally spoke about both the right to existence of Israel and "ensuring the legitimate national rights of the Arab people of Palestine", without defining what those rights were. Since the end of 1974, the USSR line shifted towards supporting the rights of the Palestinian Arabs to self-determination, to a "national home" and to their own state.

Palestinian organizations which declared themselves to be struggling for the rights of the Palestinian people and a Palestinian state in place of Israel met initially with Soviet reservations. The USSR gradually came to recognize them and to give them support.

● Negative Soviet Attitudes Before June 1967 War

The USSR established in the late 1950's and early 1960's close ties with a number of Arab countries, provided them with military and economic aid, expressed support for the Arab struggle against Israel, but seldom referred to the Palestinian problem; and when doing so, only in generalizations and more in terms of a humanitarian rather than a political problem.

A joint Soviet-Egyptian communique on President Nasir's USSR visit in August 1965 spoke about the Soviet support "for the inalienable legal rights of Palestine Arabs",[9] i.e. the Arabs of that country, and not a separate entity. During the visit to Egypt of USSR Premier A. Kosygin, he said on May 17, 1966, that the Soviet Union understands "the ardent interest of the Arabs" in the Palestine problem and "we favour its settlement on a just basis. As before, the Soviet Union has a sympathetic attitude towards the struggle for the restoration of the inalienable, legal rights of the Palestine refugees."[10] The problem was seen by him in an humanitarian and not a political light, a problem of refugees and not of a people.

This Soviet position was, inter alia, an expression of their negative attitude to the PLO and to its leader Ahmad Shuqayri, since this organization's establishment in 1964. Generally, the Soviets ignored its existence, declined its requests for arms and instructors and refused to invite its leader to visit the USSR. The fact that the Peoples' Republic of China supported the PLO and that the PLO was consistently proclaiming pro-Chinese slogans served to increase Soviet reserve towards the PLO and Shuqayri.

Al-Fath activities were completely ignored in the USSR apart from Soviet condemnations of Israeli retaliations against Al-Fath terrorism in Israel, representing those acts as "the activity of mythical diversionary groups".[11] In cases in which they could not completely deny that such acts had been perpetrated, they claimed that they might have been organized by intelligence services of Western powers with an aim to undermine Syria's "progressive" regime. A Soviet note to Israel on November 6, 1966, said that "it is possible that these incidents were organized by well-known services or by agencies of these services expressly for provocation purposes".[12] Statements of Arab leaders including pro-Soviet ones, expressing support for the PLO or Al-Fath, were not mentioned in the Soviet Press and broadcasts, which customarily omitted those references as a mark of USSR displeasure.

● Aftermath of Six Day War (1967–1969)

The USSR promised the Arabs, in the aftermath of the June 1967 Six Day War, to bring about by way of a political solution, Israeli withdrawal from the

territories she had occupied.   Pressure "to do something and not just wait"
increased among the Arabs and a guerrilla struggle against Israel in the occupied
territories seemed to many Arabs to be the only way still open to them. The
USSR called for restraint and expressed opinions against involvement in what
might cause a new war.   Instead, the USSR supported efforts to strengthen
existing Arab regimes and their military forces with USSR aid and support. The
USSR advised the Arab states to distinguish between the aim "of liquidating the
consequences" of the Six Day War and the Palestine problem in general. The
USSR advised making the former the first priority and then finding a solution to
the latter. Priority to the Palestine problem was seen by the USSR as "placing
the cart before the horse", as harming and making more difficult a political solution of the Middle East conflict, at a time when Arab countries were not yet
ready for a military solution.[13] Soviet advice to this effect was proffered on the
diplomatic level. But on the propaganda level Palestinian organizations and their
actions were honoured and praised, were termed national liberation organizations
or "partisans" with all the glamour that the description carried from World War II
resistance to the Nazis. This was a function of Soviet anti-Israeli propaganda and
also of the Soviet image of sympathy with Arab aspirations which the Soviets
desired to build up.

PLO leader, Ahmad Shuqayri's extreme calls and flirtations with Chinese
were given a chilly reception in the Soviet Union and his enforced resignation
was given favourable comment in the Soviet press. Soviet condemnation of
Shuqayri became more frequent and explicit after his removal. His "throw all
the Jews into the sea" and "destroy Israel" slogans were said to have damaged
Arab interests.[14] In fact, Shuqayri had formed a useful foil for Soviet criticism
indirectly aimed at other Arab "extremists" who still held important positions
and proclaimed slogans similar to his.

But Al Fath continued to consider, as did Shuqayri, that even if a political
solution of the conflict were achieved, it would itself continue to struggle until
the "liberation of Palestine", i.e. the end of the State of Israel. The matter came
to the fore during Egypt's President Nasir's visit to Moscow in July 1968. It
would appear that by this time, the Soviet Union had realised that the PLO and
other Palestinian organizations, however useful for propaganda purposes, were
an impediment to Soviet policies.[15] It seems that no definite promises were
given by Nasir that guerilla activities would stop after the achievement of a political solution. Perhaps the Soviets understood that Nasir could no longer control
such activities and that he had to support them if he was to continue to retain
any influence over them.

Nasir was accompanied in his Moscow visit by Al Fath leader, Yasir
Arafat. Arafat's first Moscow visit, even if unofficial, went unannounced at that
time.[16] The Soviet position in relation to Palestinian organizations seemed to
be similar to that of Nasir: to continue to support them in the hope that such
support would bring with it a measure of influence and control. Another Soviet
consideration was to turn those organizations away from the PRC. This could

)e achieved by adopting more extreme revolutionary phraseology. No substan-
:ial material assistance was then involved as the PLO or Al Fath received
ibundant aid from Arab governments — much of it in the form of Soviet made
irms.[17]

● USSR Reappraisals of Palestinian Organizations (1969–1970)

Changes in the Soviet attitude to Palestinian organizations began to appear
it the end of 1969. While the earlier caution and reserve still remained, some re-
ippraisals of the role and potential of the Palestinians when kept under pressure
)y Arab leaders — and a desire to reduce Chinese influence on the Palestinian
)rganizations were factors. The principal factor, however, was that the Soviets
)egan to see an element which might influence developments in the Middle East
ind that it would therefore be worthwhile to attract them into the Soviet orbit.

The first statement of support for the Palestinians from a leading Soviet
)ersonality was made by CPSU Politburo member and USSR Trade Union head,
A. N. Shelepin in Budapest on October 17, 1969.[18] It came just at a time when
the Leftists, including the Communists, in Lebanon supported Palestinian
demands for unrestricted freedom on Lebanese territory. The Soviet press gave
full support to those demands, but at the same time called for compromises,
expressing Soviet anxiety that a deepening of the crisis might result in the
Lebanese Right calling for American assistance. Americans might land military
forces as they had done in 1958, Israel might occupy Lebanese territory and the
'reactionaries" at home would have an opportunity to suppress the Left. The
US, however, played a passive role, stayed in the background and showed that it
1ad no plans to intervene. That enabled the USSR to play a more active role.
She issued warnings at a time when American intentions were already clear, so
that strong-worded declarations could bring the USSR propaganda gains and
prestige without having to run the risk of being called upon to back up verbal
threats with deeds. The USSR was, however, not completely sure that an
American intervention might not come at a later stage and therefore advised
Egypt and Syria to prevent a further exacerbation of the situation that could
make the US change her position.[19]

The crisis in Lebanon contributed to making the Soviets change their attitude to Palestinian organisations, Al-Fath in particular. The Soviets began to
see in them a power in Arab politics which had to be taken into account and was
therefore worthy of direct Soviet contacts, a factor which could be used by
them to change the pro-Western regimes in Lebanon and Jordan and as a means
of pressing the US to accept USSR proposed solutions of the Middle East crisis.

A delegation of representatives of Palestinian organizations headed by
Yasir Arafat visited the USSR on February 10–20, 1970, at the invitation of the
"unofficial" Soviet Committee of Solidarity with Asian and African countries.
The visit was given much publicity in Arab countries and was described in the
Arab press as a sign of Soviet recognition of the PLO and of its aims and of sig-
nalling the beginning of direct Soviet support. In the USSR, the visit was almost

completely ignored. The official Soviet news agency TASS published only short notices about the arrival of the mission and then at the end of the visit.[20] The delegation asked for official Soviet recognition and military aid and attempted to persuade the Soviet leadership to abandon a political solution. No positive replies were given. Small arms were promised to be provided not directly, but through Arab states. No official recognition was given. The Soviets also failed to achieve what they wished: to reverse the PLO's flirtation with the PRC, to increase coordination between different Palestinian organizations and to end terror activities outside of Israel while increasing activities in Israeli occupied territories. The USSR failed to convince the PLO that its interests lay in strengthening ties with Arab Leftist forces, in more coordination with pro-Soviet Arab states, Egypt in particular. But the mere fact of the visit amounted to a Soviet de facto recognition of the PLO. The USSR would have been embarrassed to deny what Arab publicists wrote or said on the success of that visit and its many achievements. Instead the USSR ignored it and their silence could be interpreted as tacit agreement to the Arab claims for it.

The acceptance by Egypt and Jordan of the American proposals for a ceasefire along the Suez Canal was endorsed by the USSR but opposed by Palestinian organizations. This led to Soviet criticism of the latter's position. A Soviet weekly distinguished then between Israel's "ruling circles" and her "toiling people", who "want to live in peace with their neighbours". The author expressed preference for the establishment of an Arab Palestinian state in accordance with the UN resolution of November 29, 1947, but was opposed to turn the question into a "struggle to liquidate the state of Israel". The implementation of the "just national rights of the Arab Palestine people" can be assured without infringing "the rights of the Israeli people", he wrote.[21]

Such views, however, rarely appeared in the Soviet press. Generally, there were only repetitive slogans which were intentionally ambiguous, with references to "Palestinian people's rights" and about the USSR support of their "just struggle", without saying what those rights were and without obligating themselves to providing aid.

● From August 1970 Ceasefire to October 1973 War

The Soviet attitude to Palestinian organisations continued to be inconsistent up to the October 1973 war. In Soviet propaganda media, "full" support was promised for "the struggle of the Arab people of Palestine", but the USSR was careful not to obligate itself to anything specific. The attitude adopted appeared to be approval for a revolutionary organization which struggled for a "just cause" but disapproval of what were, in USSR terms, wrong methods. There were indications that the USSR disapproved of the fact that the PLO was not controlled by the USSR or by any other "responsible" element, that it was "hot headed", "adventurist", "irresponsible" and even that it was dangerous for the USSR to identify itself with the PLO and its activities. "Unofficial" Soviet recognition was however given and the USSR acted in the belief that by providing aid, arms, training, other services and political support, it might also increase its influence over the PLO.

In the civil war which broke out in Jordan between the regime and Palestinian organizations in September 1970, the USSR opted for a neutral position. The Soviet press tried, at least in the initial stages of the civil war, not to express opinions and to present only facts. It clearly reflected the USSR wish to stop the chaos in Jordan and the hijacking of planes by Palestinians. Soviet policy was to diminish the influence of the PRC-oriented factions and to weaken those Palestinian organisations which opposed a political solution of the Arab-Israeli conflict. But on the other hand, the USSR was committed, at least in its propaganda, to the Palestinians.

The developments in Jordan in September 1970 brought an end to PLO activities in Jordan and from Jordanian bases. The USSR provided the PLO with limited quantities of arms, some military training in the Soviet Union (that could be used by the USSR for political indoctrination) and political support. As a first step the USSR agreed to compensate Palestinians for most of the arms that they had lost in the fighting in Jordan.

A PLO delegation headed by Arafat visited the USSR between October 20–29, 1971.[22] This visit, like the earlier one, was treated on the "popular" level and not as official – and Soviet information media gave scant coverage to it. It took place after abortive attempts by Sudan's pro-Communist elements to seize power. This failure led to an anti-Communist, and indirectly, also an anti-Soviet campaign in Arab countries and the visit was used by the USSR to recover its ground.

Arafat visited Moscow again at the head of a PLO delegation on July 17–27, 1972, as a guest of the Soviet Committee for Solidarity with Afro-Asian countries. It was in the days in which Egypt's President Anwar Al-Sadat ordered Soviet military forces to leave Egypt. The USSR began then to pay more attention to the Palestinians and to increase aid to them, seeing in them a factor whose significance was growing in the Arab world. The Soviet statement on the visit said that the delegation had talks with "representatives of the Soviet public", – that they spoke about "continuing cooperation and solidarity" and that the "Soviet people" will continue "to provide aid in the future too to the Palestinian resistance movement".[23] Palestinian sources, however, claimed more than that: meetings of Arafat and members of his delegation with senior Soviet officials, their visit to a military academy near Moscow in which they met Palestinians, which implied that Palestinian officers underwent a training in the USSR similar to that given to officers from Arab armies. Arafat claimed further that promises had been made to him of aid including food, medical aid, blankets, grants for study in the USSR and also political assistance.[24]

The assassination of 11 Israeli sportsmen at the Olympic Games in Munich on September 5, 1972, by what Soviet media named "the extremist Palestinian organization Black September" met with expressions of disapproval by the USSR. However, Soviet criticism was mild and restrained, suggesting that neither

Arab countries and governments, nor Palestinian organisations, have any responsibility for what was done by a few extremists in Munich. Soviet reporters wrote more on Israel's retaliatory raids, asserting that there was no connection between the latter and what had happened in Munich.[25] There were similar Soviet reactions to other activities of this kind, by Palestinian organisations.

Soviet interest in Palestinian organisations increased and the USSR was ready to provide limited aid. The USSR, however, continued to see the PLO as only a secondary and auxiliary element. The USSR continued to rely on Arab states in the Middle East and regarded their relations with Palestinians as a means to influence Arab governments. Palestinian importance was seen at this stage to be more potential than actual, as a possible option for the future which they considered to be worthwhile to cultivate.

● Aftermath of October 1973 War

The 1973 war did not lead to immediate changes in the Soviet attitude to Palestinian organisations. The USSR was concerned to prove that it was impartial and could thus perform a mediating role, sponsoring a political settlement.

In November 1973, a few weeks after the war, Arafat went once more to Moscow at the invitation of the Soviet Afro-Asian Solidarity Committee.[26] As subsequently reported by a member of the Palestinian delegation which had accompanied Arafat, the USSR advised the PLO to participate in the Geneva Peace Conference for the Middle East, to establish a state regardless of size but without abandoning their long-term aims. The USSR promised to continue its support for Palestinian rights and described the PLO as "the only legitimate representative of the Palestinian people".[27] [Official recognition of such status for the PLO came only a few years later.]

At the opening of the Geneva Peace Conference on December 21, 1973, USSR Foreign Minister, Andrey Gromyko (who served with US Secretary of State, Henry Kissinger as Co-Chairman of that conference) spoke about the need to ensure the existence and rights of the State of Israel. With regard to the Palestinians, Gromyko said that "it is naturally assumed that justice will be assured for the Arab people of Palestine" and that "the problem of Palestine cannot be considered and solved without the participation of the representatives of the Arab people of Palestine".[28] Gromyko, as did other Soviet speakers, spoke in general and even ambiguous terms.

● Ties Become Official

A PLO delegation headed by Arafat visited the USSR from July 30–August 4, 1974, for the first time not only as guests of the "unofficial" Soviet Afro-Asian Committee, but of the CPSU and USSR Government. The delegation held meetings with CPSU Politburo member, Central Committee Secretary and Head of CPSU International Department, Boris Ponomarev and others. A TASS communique on this meeting said, *inter alia:*

"The sides noted with satisfaction the importance of the decisions taken at the conference of heads of Arab states in Algiers (November 1973) and the conference of Moslem States in Lahore (February 1974) on the recognition of the PLO as the sole legitimate representative of the Arab people of Palestine.

"The Soviet side reaffirmed the invariability of the Soviet Union's stand in support of the struggle of the Arab people for the full liberation of the Arab territories occupied by Israel in 1967 . . . the attainment by the Arab people of Palestine of their legitimate national rights in compliance with the charter and decisions of the United Nations organization . . . meets the interests of all states and peoples.

"The Soviet Union expressed support for the participation of the Palestine Liberation Organization in the Geneva Peace Conference and exercising equal rights with other participants . . . "[29]

Moscow radio in an Arabic broadcast (August 4, 1974) added the following: ". . . so that they can submit their programme for a solution of the Palestine question within the framework of the international efforts designed to achieve a settlement of the Middle East issue".

The TASS communique, quoted earlier, had added that the Soviet side, in answer to the PLO request, "gave consent to the opening of a PLO representation in Moscow".[30]

Arab publications reported Soviet promises to supply the PLO with modern equipment,[31] and to support the establishment of a Palestinian administration in the West Bank and Gaza Strip.

The Soviet statement was still far from an acceptance of PLO positions but what was important was the beginning of open official and declared Soviet-PLO ties.

● "Statehood" and "National Home"

An address by the Chairman of the USSR Supreme Soviet, Podgorny, in Sofia, Bulgaria, on September 8, 1976, included, *inter alia*, a summing-up of Soviet proposals to regulate the Arab-Israeli conflict:

"The Arab territories are still occupied by Israeli troops. There is no agreement on ensuring the legitimate national rights of the Arab people of Palestine, including their sovereign right to their own statehood in one form or another. There is no agreement on guarantees of security of the Middle East states – either the Arab states or Israel".[32]

Podgorny introduced here a term "statehood" that was to be frequently repeated in Soviet references to the Palestinians. It was not clearly defined and could be interpreted to mean many things – an independent state, autonomy or even a federation with Syria or Jordan. This "statehood" was to come about not in the place of Israel which he did not attack in his address as Soviet leaders generally used to do – Podgorny here even confirmed Israeli right to security. It was intended to make clear how far the USSR would be ready to go in support of the Palestinians.

An address by Brezhnev in Kishinev on October 11, 1974, spoke about the need to "satisfy the legitimate rights of the Arab people of Palestine and their right to their national home".[33]   Brezhnev used the term "national home" — which could be interpreted in different ways. It recalled the Balfour Declaration of November 2, 1917, which had also referred ambiguously to a "national home" for Jews in Palestine.

The decisions of the Rabat Arab summit conference at the end of October 1974 recognising the PLO as "the sole representative of the Palestinian people" were welcomed by Soviet spokesmen. The USSR promised to support moves to place "the Palestine problem" as a separate item on the UN General Assembly agenda in November 1974, and to move UN resolutions on Palestinians' rights. Arafat's UN address received official Soviet blessing.[34]

Soviet commentators took to repetitions of PLO slogans, altering an emphasis, introducing an innuendo, but Arab readers or listeners were given the impression that the USSR had accepted PLO statements at face value or at least had not questioned them.

Continued terror activities like that in Beit Shean, Israel, on November 14, 1974, flagrantly contradicted Soviet assertions that the PLO "had matured, was showing realism and had abandoned terror". Soviet embarrassment over the Beit Shean attack was more acute, since it had been perpetrated by the PDFLP (with PLO leadership approval), ideologically closer to the USSR than other Palestinian organisations.

The Soviet position on this matter was indicated a few months later, in a Moscow radio broadcast in Arabic:

"A PLO spokesman once again denounced resorting to any means of terrorism ... the PLO proceeds, in its just struggle, from a position of maturity and reality. It is well-known that terrorist actions in no way belong to the means of revolutionary struggle; rather they greatly harm such a struggle.

"Those operations to which some irresponsible Palestinian elements still resort do not bring the victory of their just cause one step closer. On the contrary, the Zionist and imperialist propaganda use them to degrade the PLO's growing reputation on the international scene".[35]

The Soviets could, however, not prevent the PLO, and organizations affiliated to it, from further terror acts. They repeatedly but in vain advised the PLO to desist from terror.[36]   The USSR was under no illusion, recognizing that the PLO was not an homogenous disciplined body and that even vulnerable to internal pressures, the PLO was not likely to abide by commitments.

● USSR Fails to Realise Arab Solidarity

Kissinger's failure in March 1975 to achieve a US mediated Egyptian-Israeli agreement — successful six months later — raised USSR hopes that they might succeed where the Americans had failed. They had been, on the whole, reacting to American initiatives, but they were now anxious to initiate their own plans for a political solution. They wanted to reconvene the Geneva conference with the participation of the PLO. They invited Egyptian, Syrian, Iraqi and PLO representatives to Moscow to work out a jointly coordinated position.

Speaking on April 23, 1978 at a dinner in Moscow in honour of Syrian Deputy Prime Minister and Foreign Minister, Abd al-Halim Khaddam, Gromyko said that the Geneva Conference should be attended by the PLO with equal rights to those of the other participants. He added that it would be necessary to make "serious preparations" so that the reconvened conference could take up "concrete questions of settlement". The Conference should lead to agreements that will bring about an Israeli withdrawal, "to ensure the legitimate rights of the Arab people of Palestine up to the establishment of their own statehood" and to ensure the rights of all states of the Middle East, including Israel. "Israel may get, if it wishes, the strictest guarantees, with the participation under an appropriate agreement of the Soviet Union too," he said.[37]

A PLO delegation headed by Arafat went to the USSR a few days later — from April 28–May 5, 1975.[38] Zuhayr Muhsin, head of the PLO's military department and of Al-Sa'iqa reflecting Syria's position, decided not to go to Moscow, saying that "the Soviets committed a new blunder by offering strictest guarantees for Israel's independent existence" and that there was "no important issue" on the agenda of the PLO delegations in Moscow.[39] During the visit, the USSR pressed for a formal declaration by the PLO to support a Palestinian state including the West Bank and Gaza, and a public declaration by the PLO of its acceptance and recognition of Israel within its pre-June 1967 borders.[40] It was implicit in the official Soviet statement on that visit that no agreement was reached.

The USSR then reappraised its Middle East policy and re-examined its own chances of solving the Arab-Israeli conflict. Talks were held in Moscow with Iraq's "strong man" Saddam Husayn, Egypt's Foreign Minister Fahmi, Syrian Foreign Minister Khaddam, Arafat and others. This was followed by a visit by Soviet representatives to several Arab countries. But the USSR did not succeed in co-ordinating the Arab position, nor was there anything sufficiently definite to serve as a basis to reconvene the Geneva conference. Instead, they found a widening gap, not only between the Arabs and Israel, but between different Arab positions.

● "Friendly Contacts" with PLO

The USSR bitterly attacked the Egyptian-Israeli agreement signed, with US mediation, at the beginning of September 1975. Soviet efforts in the Middle East concentrated on preventing a similar agreement between Israel and Syria. The agreement was also sharply criticised by Syria and exploited to increase Syria's role in the Arab world. Palestinian organizations, over which Syria increased her patronage, were encouraged by both Moscow and Damascus to do everything possible to undermine the agreement by promoting tension between Arab countries and Israel which would involve Egypt too.

In the USSR, the leadership was pre-occupied with preparation for the 25th CPSU Congress convened at the end of February through early March 1976. Soviet media stressed more strongly its support for "national liberation movements". It came, in part, as an attempt to divert attention inside the Soviet Union from its own failures: in Soviet economy, agriculture, in particular, and in foreign affairs (as in Egypt). That tendency expressed itself in a Soviet-Cuban military involvement in Angola and increasing Soviet publicity for its relations with the PLO.

The report of L. I. Brezhnev to the CPSU Congress (February 24, 1976) included the PLO in the list of Arab countries friendly to the USSR. He referred to the strengthening of "friendly contacts" with the PLO: "in the Middle East", he said, "the danger of war will continue until Israel withdraws from "the occupied territories"; and he went on to say: ". . . as long as hundreds of thousands of Palestinians driven from their land are deprived of their legitimate rights and live in appalling conditions and as long as the Arab people of Palestine are denied the possibility to create their national state;" and added that: ". . . the security of all the states of the region, their right to independent existence and development must also be guaranteed". Brezhnev declared that: ". . . the USSR was prepared to participate in international guarantees of the security and inviolability of the frontiers of all Middle East countries either in the UN framework or on some other basis".[41]

Brezhnev distinguished between Palestinians' "legitimate rights" − a solution of the refugees' problems − and "national rights" − the right to establish a Palestinian state. He referred to the right to establish such a state but did not call for its establishment, inferring, perhaps, that Palestinians might decide not to use that right or to transfer it to others, e.g. to Syria. No mention was made of USSR aid, support, recognition, co-operation, etc. with the PLO.

● PLO Office in Moscow

The PLO opened an office in Moscow on June 22, 1976. The opening of such an office was agreed upon in August 1974 but was delayed, among other reasons because of the difficulties in defining the official status of that office.[42] Offices of foreign representatives in Moscow can be on an inter-party, government or popular level. The PLO office in Moscow is on the lowest, that is to say "unofficial" level, accredited to the Soviet Committee of Solidarity with the countries of Asia and Africa (SCSAA) and not to the USSR Foreign Ministry. The Committee became a sort of "Palestinian lobby" in the USSR. Its deputy head, V. Kudryavtsev, is an *Izvestia* senior commentator and occasionally writes pro-PLO articles in which he indirectly argues with those in the USSR who consider that the Soviet Union had overdone its commitments to Palestinians and that the latter had not yet proved that they were worthy of such support.

The opening of the office came at the time of the visit of King Hussein of Jordan to the USSR (June 17−28, 1976).[43] The Soviets had an interest in strengthening ties with Jordan, even if that would mean a weakening of ties with the PLO. In fact, the risk was not great as the Soviets believed since the PLO had no other choice but to accept it. And opening a PLO office in Moscow was something of a sop.

The responsibilities of the PLO office in Moscow included the handling of Palestinian students in the USSR at universities, military and vocational schools. The PLO office, like Arab communist parties, received a number of grants for studies in the USSR.[44]

The PLO office in Moscow also processed financial and direct aid, officially for Palestinian refugees, but channeled in fact to fighting organizations in Lebanon and elsewhere. The PLO Moscow office also supervised medical aid, food, blankets, tents, etc., treatment in the USSR of wounded Palestinians. The PLO office was also responsible for processing direct and indirect military aid in the form of arms and other military equipment and training in the USSR, a need aggravated by the role of Palestinian organizations in the civil war in Lebanon.

● **Civil War in Lebanon – 1975–1976**

The USSR long felt the need of a center for her activities in the Middle East, to propagate ideas and to be a base for revolutionary organisations, a "listening point" and an information center. Egypt had provided the USSR with all this at the time of Jamal Abd al-Nasir.

After the vacuum created by Sadat's expulsion of the Soviet presence in Egypt, the USSR saw Lebanon as a potential replacement.

Relatively centrally located it also had developed a sophisticated network of local information media, and there were large numbers of educated people ideologically close to the Soviet Union and ready to serve it. To achieve its ends, the Soviets preferred that power be in the hands of a regime that would be dependent on USSR aid and protection. The first precondition for that was the destruction, or at least, the enfeeblement of the existing order. In the early stages of the civil war in Lebanon in 1975, it looked as if things were not going the Soviets' way. Soviet media stressed in particular the role of the Palestinian organisations in that war.[45]

Syria, however much it had supported the Palestinians and the Left in the early stages of the war in Lebanon, turned against them in 1976. The USSR was placed in a delicate position, with allies fighting each other. Palestinians, the Lebanese Left, Communists, Syrians, Iraqis, Libyans, all had received Soviet aid directly or indirectly but they were finding themselves on conflicting sides, fighting among themselves. The USSR elected to pose as not being involved in an internal Lebanese affair which the Lebanese themselves had to solve.

The Soviets expected and hoped for a "hotting up" of the Israeli-Lebanese border and the entry of Israeli forces into Lebanon. Their media spoke day after day about Israeli preparations, the concentration of Israeli forces, penetrations by Israeli units, etc. Such Soviet warnings in the past had provoked the Arabs but not this time. The USSR was calculating on an Israeli diversion and US support for Israel, deflecting the Arabs still closer to the USSR. But this did not happen and the Soviets continued to be faced with a complicated situation in which whatever they would do would be to their disadvantage. They wanted the Leftists and Palestinians to win but they also did not want to lose their influence over Syria.

Palestinians appealed to the Soviets for help but the latter were in no hurry to commit themselves. They therefore elected to supply military aid to the Palestinians via Libya and Iraq. A few hundred Palestinians studying in the USSR and East Europe were "permitted" to participate in the Lebanese fighting. The Soviets, however, were not ready to jeopardise their relations with Syria because of direct aid to the Palestinians.

Arab summit conferences convened in Riyadh and Cairo in October 1976 decided to bring an end to the fighting. The Soviets were not pleased, seeing in the decisions signs of increasing Saudi Arabian and Egyptian influence in the Arab world.[46]   But they also wanted to see an end to the fighting and were ready to accept Syria's peace keeping role, even if it meant Syrian control over Lebanon and to a large extent over the Palestinian organizations. The Soviets wanted the Palestinians to be strengthened but on the other hand, did not want them to be completely independent, dictating to Arab governments, complicating USSR relations with Arab states and provoking another Arab-Israeli war, from which the USSR would gain nothing.

● USSR solutions for the Arab-Israeli conflict

The USSR gave general approval to the idea of the establishment of a Palestinian state in the West Bank and Gaza Strip after Israeli withdrawal. Israel and the Palestinian state would be required to give each other recognition and the USSR would be a guarantor of mutual existence and secure frontiers. The USSR considered the UN General Assembly decision on partition of Palestine of November 29, 1947, still to be valid. They were not insisting on Israeli withdrawal to those frontiers but that both sides would make mutual concessions: Israel to withdraw to the pre-June 1967 frontiers and the Arabs to recognize them.

A "Proposal from the Soviet Union on a settlement in the Middle East and on the Geneva Conference" was presented on October 1, 1976, to the governments of the US, Egypt, Syria, Jordan, Israel and to the PLO leadership. It included "the following proposals for the conference agenda":

the withdrawal of Israeli troops from all Arab territories occupied in 1967;
the exercise of inalienable rights by the Arab people of Palestine, including their right to self-determination and the establishment of their own state;
the ensurance of the right to independent existence and security for all states directly participating in the conflict, the Arab states — neighbouring with Israel, on the one side, and the State of Israel, on the other — with appropriate international guarantees offered to them; stoppage of the state of war between the concerned Arab countries and Israel.

The Soviets proposed to convene the Geneva conference in two stages: preparations and then the concentration of efforts "towards hammering out essential accords". The conference was to end in the adoption of a final document (or documents) of the nature of an agreement. The PLO must take part in the work of the conference "on an equal footing from the very outset".[47]

Israel replied she was ready to participate in the Geneva conference – but without the PLO; that she was ready to sign a peace treaty, but only with existing governments – Egypt, Jordan and Syria, – and not with any organization.[48] The Soviets hinted that they might agree to PLO participation only in the committees but not at the plenary meetings.[49]

A joint Soviet-Egyptian statement of June 1977 referred to the right of the Palestinians "to establish their own independent state, to return to their homes and to receive compensation in accordance with the UN decisions".[50] The inclusion of the latter two recommendations was unusual in a Soviet communique but may have been included as a result of President Carter's declaration two weeks earlier, on May 26, 1977, that Palestinians had a right "to be compensated for losses that they have suffered".[51] The Soviets did not want to appear to be lagging behind the Americans on this matter.

A joint Soviet-Yugoslav communique of August 1977 referred to the "appropriate resolutions" of the UN Security Council and General Assembly. It did not mention resolution 242. It called for the convening of the Geneva Conferences without delay, "with the participation of all interested parties" stipulating precisely that "the PLO has to participate from the very beginning and with equal rights in the conference as the sole legitimate representative of the Arab people of Palestine".[52]

Here the PLO figured "as the sole representative" of the Palestinians, something Soviet spokesmen generally avoided, being ready to quote others at the UN or at other international forums and Arab states – as having recognized the PLO as the sole representative of the Palestinians but without their own commitment.

Soviet leaders promised to give the PLO a right of veto at the Geneva conference. USSR Premier Kosygin at a Kremlin reception for Iraqi leader Saddam Hussein, on February 1, 1977, called for the renewal of the Geneva conference, and for PLO participation in its work with equal rights. The USSR position was unchanged, that "no decision concerning the fate of the Arab people of Palestine will be accepted without (the approval of the) Palestinians or against their wishes".[53]

It was repeated by Brezhnev at a dinner in honour of President Hafiz Al-Asad on April 18, 1977. He said that the PLO "the lawful representative of the Palestinian Arabs" (he did not say the "sole" representative) must take part in the Geneva conference proceedings "on an equal footing. We firmly advocate that not a single decision, concerning the Arab people of Palestine be taken without the Palestinians and against their will".[54]

Proposals to establish ties between the Palestinian state and Jordan, made by President Sadat at the end of 1976, were opposed by the USSR.[55] They wanted a "truly independent" Palestinian state, having close ties with them and not with conservative US-oriented Arab states. The Egyptian proposal was considered in Moscow as a continuation of a tendency, which they saw in the civil war in Lebanon, to bring an end to the independent status of the Palestinians and to make them dependent on "Arab reaction" and the US.[56] Calls by President Sadat on July 1977 to establish a Jordanian-Palestinian confederation led once again to Soviet reaction against it.[57]

Soviet preference was that there should be no solution to the Palestinian problem. They wanted a prolonged struggle which would mean that Soviet aid would be needed indefinitely. A struggle would also lead to an increasing radicalization, while a political settlement would lead to the rise of more moderate elements, according to the Soviet analysts.

● Winning Over PLO From Within

The PLO received considerable Soviet support. The Soviets were, however, not sure if they could rely on it and if there would not be a repetition of what happened to them with Egypt — after the extensive aid that had been given to her by the Soviet Union. Hence Soviet contacts tried to influence the PLO from within to strengthen ties with those who were closer to them ideologically, to strengthen such forces and to see in them an alternative to the current PLO leadership, to whom Soviet support would be shifted, if the leadership would turn away from the Soviet Union.

One such group favoured by the Soviets was the "moderate extremist" (sic) PDFLP headed by Na'if Hawatimah. It was ideologically close to the USSR, adopted USSR positions, advocated an independent Palestinian authority in the West Bank and Gaza Strip, but also advocated terrorism and was active in that, in spite of USSR advice against it.[58]

A "Palestine National Front" (PNF) delegation visited the USSR between April 5–12, 1976, at the invitation of the Soviet Afro-Asian Solidarity Committee. The delegation spoke about the "brave struggle of the population of Palestinian terroritories" and "the Front's activities to organize the resistance movement". It condemned the policy of "Arab reaction" and its cooperation with "international imperialism" saying that "their activities which are directed to undermine Arab-Soviet friendship, contradict the basic interests of Arab peoples".[59] It was an indirect warning to Arafat that the Soviet might shift its support from him to other Palestinian forces and organizations.

The PNF was in fact a communist front organization. A Moscow radio broadcast referred to "the big role played by communists in the front. The Jordanian Communist Party — the party of the Jordanian and Palestinian communists — has directed scores of officials, active and experienced in the class struggle, to the front".[60]

The West Bank Communist Party, for years a part of the Jordanian Communist Party, began to act independently as a Palestinian Communist Party and to identify with the PNF-Soviet efforts to give the PNF a larger role in the PLO and to make it appear as representing the West Bank "masses".

● **Palestinian Organizations as a Revolutionary Force**

In the Soviet view, Palestinian organizations were a revolutionary element contributing to fermentation and unstability, around which could be consolidated all those who oppose the US and a *Pax Americana,* would want to undermine it, and lead to the downfall of existing regimes — a role that theoretically communist parties had to play but seldom did. The PLO, and still more the radical Palestinian organizations did so in Jordan and Lebanon and could do the same in other countries with a large Palestinian community.[61]

Such a situation was seen in Soviet circles to exist in the Persian Gulf and the countries of the Arabian Peninsula. They saw the situation in Kuwait to be similar to that in Lebanon. There, too, Palestinians constituted a big percentage of the population, dissatisfied with the existing situation, regarding themselves as discriminated against and treated as if they were inferior, in spite of their generally higher educational and professional level. This situation corresponded in the USSR terminology to "a class struggle" between an archaic, medieval feudal regime and a proletariat with the latter in need of a vanguard, a small group of dedicated revolutionaries to lead them — to rally them to fight not only Israel but also imperialism and reaction. In Soviet terms the Palestinian organizations represented that vanguard.

● **Soviet-American Statement of October 1977**

The Arab world considered the USSR as able to contribute in its struggle against Israel, but not to bring about an Israeli withdrawal through negotiations and agreements. Those elements in Arab leadership who sought that direction turned increasingly to the US. But the suspicion continued in the region and still more in the US, that the USSR is able to prevent any political settlement that would be made without its participation and that conversely the USSR might contribute extensively towards any settlement by influencing Syria and the PLO towards more moderation and even to encourage them to join in the political process.

Such considerations were behind the Soviet-American statement on the Middle East of October 1, 1977. The statement called for a comprehensive Middle East settlement "incorporating all parties concerned and all questions", including issues such as "withdrawal of Israeli armed forces from territories occupied in the 1967 conflict, the resolution of the Palestinian question including ensuring the legitimate rights of the Palestinian people, termination of the state of war and establishment of normal peaceful relations". They called for the convening of the Geneva conference, not later than December 1977, "with participation in its work of the representatives of all the parties involved in the conflict, including those of the Palestinian people".[62]

It soon became clear that the USSR either had not used her influence or having used it, had failed to get results. The chances for convening the Geneva conference were small, and if it was convened, there was no chance for an agreement there.

● **Soviet Reactions to Sadat Initiative**

Egypt saw that there was a chance for a political settlement in which she could regain the Sinai. As the PLO stood in the way and the US and the USSR gave priority to the PLO's role, leading to a deadlock in the political process, Egypt decided to turn directly to Israel.

Sadat's visit to Israel on November 19–21, 1977, restored a central role to Egypt and Israel. The US continued in the role of mediator while the USSR was shunted again to a marginal position.

The Sadat initiative and the Egyptian-Israeli negotiations and subsequent agreements were sharply criticised by Moscow. The USSR stressed in particular the Palestinian problem, its central role in the Arab-Israeli conflict and the fact that without a solution to it, there would be no end to the conflict. In contrast to past practice in which the USSR focused attention on the Arab states and its relations with the PLO were subservient to this, the Soviets gave to the PLO and to the Palestinian problem in general a central role which they had not given them earlier. This came about in no small way as a result of the deteriorating USSR position in those states directly confronting Israel. While the USSR continued to have close ties with Syria, its influence over her had been reduced. The PLO alone continued to be dependent on the USSR, and to be manipulated by the USSR.

Arab opposition to the Sadat initiative was used by the USSR to strengthen its ties with Arab countries opposing the initiative. The USSR conducted consultations and high level contacts with leading representatives from Iraq, Syria and Libya and with the PLO leadership.

Arafat visited the USSR at the head of a PLO delegation and was received by Brezhnev on March 9, 1978. The official Soviet news agency TASS, reported that "Yasir Arafat spoke about the struggle conducted by the Palestinian resistance movement in the present aggravated situation in the Middle East for the implementation of its national aspirations, against intrigues by imperialism and reaction". Brezhnev emphasized that "the Soviet Union invariably sides and always will side with the just cause of the Arab people of Palestine who staunchly struggle for their freedom and independence. In this just struggle the Palestinian people headed by the Palestine Liberation Organization achieved considerable successes and turned into one of the leading detachments of the Arab national liberation movement ... " Brezhnev went on to ". . . wish the courageous Palestinian people further successes in its just struggle and in rallying its ranks. In this cause, the Palestinian people can always count on the support of the Soviet Union".[63]

This statement coincided with preparations for a raid in Israel on March 11, 1978, for which the PLO took responsibility, in which civilians were killed.

It can be assumed that Arafat's hosts in Moscow had not been informed and that in accordance with their position on terrorism, that they would have advised against it.

TASS confined its reporting to the PLO news agency WAFA's version — "an armed clash between a detachment of Palestinian partisans and Israeli army units". According to TASS "Israeli propaganda is trying to use this incident to discredit the PLO, and the Begin government openly regards it as a pretext for a major military provocation against neighbouring Arab countries".[64]

The USSR could do little to change the situation. They criticised the Sadat initiative but had nothing different to offer.[65] All that they could do was to follow "rejectionist" Arab states' calls and slogans. They advocated a political settlement and called to convene the Geneva conference but that was opposed by even those Arab states in their political orbit, who were against any agreements and hostile to the concept of peace on any terms.

● Camp David Agreements and After

USSR recognition of the PLO was even more forthright after the Egyptian-Israeli Camp David Agreements of September 17, 1978. A statement on a USSR visit by a PLO delegation headed by Arafat on October 29—November 1, 1978, was termed — for the first time — "a joint communique". It did not say by whom the delegation had been invited.

The communique "firmly condemned" the Camp David agreements and welcomed the convening of the Baghdad conference against those agreements. Arafat "expressed profound gratitude . . . for the fraternal aid . . . and for the consistent, selfless all-round support". The communique favoured:

". . . the implementation of the legitimate national rights of the Palestinian Arab people, including the right to self-determination and for the creation of a state of its own, and also its right to return to its hearths in conformity with existing UN resolutions. This requires the collective efforts of all the interested parties with the equal participation in them of the PLO as the sole legitimate representative of the Arab people of Palestine", and supported "the observation of the legitimate interests of the Palestine resistance movement in Lebanon".[66]

The USSR sharply criticised the Egyptian-Israeli peace treaty signed on March 26, 1979, and the negotiations to establish an autonomy for the people of the West Bank and Gaza.

Aware that in spite of the extensive aid they had provided to the PLO, they had only a limited measure of control over it and its activities, they attempted direct contacts with various Palestinian organizations and personalities and invited them to visit the USSR.

Thus from May 9—19, 1979, there was a visit of West Bank mayors, who were described as "representatives of the public" of the West Bank.[67] The visitors "declared full support for the PLO as the sole legitimate representative of the Palestinian people".[68] But the invitation in itself indicated that the USSR preferred not to put all its eggs in one basket. Its policy was to consolidate its ties with the official PLO leadership but also to seek and maintain contacts with other Palestinians.

At the summit meeting of Brezhnev and Carter in Vienna on June 15—18, 1979, the Middle East situation was discussed but no agreement was reached. USSR Foreign Minister, A. Gromyko said on June 25, 1979:

"The positions of the Soviet Union and the USA on this matter are different. The American side tried to prove that the Soviet Union would be better off supporting the separate treaty between Egypt and Israel . . . the Soviet Union could not agree with such a view . . . the positions of the sides on this matter were and remain different.

". . . the Soviet Union's principled position on Middle East affairs was and remains the same . . . All the lands captured by Israel from the Arabs must be returned; the Palestine Arab people must be granted the opportunity to create its own, if only small, independent state . . . All the countries of that region, including Israel . . . should have the possibility to exist and develop in the Middle East as independent sovereign states".[69]

● Is USSR In Favour of a "Staged Solution"?

The USSR gave public support in Gromyko's statement as on other occasions to the concept of two states, Israel and a Palestinian state, that have to co-exist and recognize each other. There is reason to believe in the opinion of some Palestinians that if an opportunity would arise for the Palestinians to destroy Israel, the Soviet Union would do nothing to prevent it. On the other hand, no Soviet promises were given to them, at least not on public record, in which their right to all of Palestine was recognized. Soviet media sometimes said, rarely and indirectly, that the slogan of a "secular Palestinian state" of Muslims, Christians and Jews might perhaps be a good idea but could not be implemented in the existing situation.

In talks with PLO representatives, USSR leaders may have said that recognition of Israel's existence does not mean abandoning the vision of an Arab Palestinian state in the whole region. They may have propounded that argument that even while they recognize capitalist regimes and states they have not abandoned the Marxist-Leninist belief that a day will come in which communism will rule all over the world, but that in the existing situation, one has to be realistic, to know when to retreat, to accept the situation as it is, to establish a national state, regardless of its size and limitations.

Thus, in talks with those ideologically close to them, (Arab communists or the PDFLP) USSR leaders may be talking more about "future visions": "progressive" regimes in most Arab countries, a union or at least close ties between them, perhaps also a "progressive" regime (or support for those who advocate it) in Israel. They may be manipulating slogans and ideas like "internal contradictions" in Israel, "the end of imperialism", "mass departures by Jews from Israel" – all these factors leading to a greater Israeli integration in the Arab world, of her own volition or forced by a struggle. They may be suggesting another possibility: the return of many Arab refugees to Israel, an increase of Israel's Arab population and a decrease of the Jewish population leading to an Arab majority which will then be able to act for a united Arab Palestinian state in all of Palestine.

One should however distinguish between Soviet promises of arms and training, financial aid, UN votes, etc. that oblige the USSR to implement them, and vague plans about the future which do not oblige them to action in the present or near future.

• Expectations, Wishes and Hopes

It is clear that the USSR sustains more than one position on the Palestinian problem. The CPSU International Department and Soviet Committee of Solidarity with Afro-Asian countries responsible for relations with the Palestinian organizations constitute a "Palestinian lobby" of sorts and have an interest to attach considerable importance to the subject of the Palestinians. But the Soviet leadership has other priorities, global and regional interests, in which the Palestinians do not loom large. They are only a tool, sometimes quite useful, but their use is tactical, for immediate needs.

USSR interest in the PLO and other Palestinian organizations rests on seeing in them:

— a political force in the Middle East that influences what is going on in the region and might influence, directly or indirectly, positions and activities of Arab states. It is to a certain extent a unifying factor whose slogans most Arab countries are ready to accept;

— an element that perpetuates the Arab-Israeli conflict and by that Arab reliance on the USSR;

— a revolutionary element in the Middle East that introduces chaos and instability which the USSR might use to her advantage.

The USSR wishes to maintain ties with all, or most Palestinian organisations and not to be involved in conflicts among them. They tend to ignore the fact that the PLO is not a homogeneous and disciplined organization that can be directed from above and that Arafat was unable to enforce "discipline" on it, or to implement all his undertakings on its behalf. The USSR thus sees the PLO as an element which might be used for short term needs but not as a partner with which a long-term strategy can be planned and which can maintain a particular policy and line over the long haul.

The Soviets, aware of the inherent difficulties in their ties with an irresponsible and unpredictable element such as the PLO may be working on the supposition that the PLO may become "more mature" and more responsible. They frequently quote Arafat and other PLO leaders when condemning terrorist activities.

The real questions confronting Soviet leadership include:
- will the PLO turn to become an organization in which the leadership can enforce its decisions on all its factions?
- does Arafat actually lead the PLO and will agreements with him be kept? what is the PLO's ideological context?
- what will be the character of the Palestinian State and who will constitute the government that will be established by it and what will their political orientation be?
- will it be headed by "bourgeoisie" that will cooperate with Western powers and "Arab reaction" or by pro-Soviet forces?

- who can ensure that after helping the PLO to establish a state, the latter will not "betray" the USSR and not turn in an orientation to the US?

The USSR has sought in vain from the PLO a clear definition of aims and means, and even of boundaries of a Palestinian state — a clear political programme from the PLO involving close ties with the Arab left and communists and co-operating with them:

- a greater integration of the PLO into USSR policy in the Middle East and in Soviet proposals to solve the Arab-Israeli conflict; more adaptation by the PLO to changing USSR relations with Middle East States;
- more "resistance" activities in Israel-controlled territories, accompanied by an end to terrorist activities in other places;
- more cooperation and coordination between Palestinian organisations.

USSR policy aims to keep the Palestinians fighting and therefore in need of Soviet aid so that they can be useful in furtherance of Soviet policies. Soviet policy aims at preventing American-sponsored agreements without Soviet participation in negotiations and guarantees to them. The latter is extremely important in Soviet eyes as it would legitimise their presence in the area and give them a pretext for intervening. The main Soviet target in the Middle East is not, however, the PLO, but the Arab states. For the Soviet leadership, relations with the PLO are a means of influencing Arab states and their leaders rather than an aim in itself.

NOTES TO CHAPTER SIX

1. Andrey Gromyko, then USSR representative to the UN, said to the UN General Assembly on May 14, 1947, that "it is essential to bear in mind the indisputable fact that the population of Palestine consists of two peoples, the Arabs and the Jews. Both have historical roots in Palestine. Palestine has become the homeland of both these peoples, each of which plays an important part in the economy and the cultural life of the country". He supported the plan for the partition of Palestine into two states, one Jewish and one Arab. (UN, Official Records of the First Special Session of the General Assembly, Vol. I, *Plenary Meetings of the General Assembly* . . . 28 April–15 May, 1947 (A/307), pp. 127–135).
2. UN, Official Records of the Second Session of the General Assembly, *Plenary Meetings* . . . 16 September–29 November, 1947, Vol. II, 128th Plenary Meeting, 29 November, 1947, pp. 1422–1425.
3. *Pravda* (Moscow), May 18, 1948.
4. *Izvestia* (Moscow), May 11, 1950.
5. Jaan Pennar, *The USSR and the Arabs: The Ideological Dimension*, N.Y., Crane, Russak, 1973.

6. For Soviet positions on this subject, see: Aryeh Yodfat, *Arab Politics in the Soviet Mirror*, N.Y. and Toronto, Halsted Press, John Wiley and Sons, 1973.

7. It was intended for Syrian Communist Party internal use, "leaked" out and published in the journal of the Syrian Ba'th party left-wing (that ruled in Syria in February 1966—November 1970), *Al-Rayah*, Beirut, June 26, 1972.

8. *ibid.*, ibid.

9. *Pravda*, September 2, 1965.

10. *ibid.*, May 18, 1966.

11. *Izvestia*, May 8, 1966.

12. Israel, Ministry of Foreign Affairs, *The USSR and Arab Belligerency*, (Jerusalem, 1967), p. 37.

13. According to a Soviet Middle East expert: "all the attempts of imperialist propaganda to maintain that the centre of gravity in the Arab-Israeli conflict has moved into the struggle of the Palestinian partisans are, all the same, naked demagoguery: the main sides of the conflict can only be Israel and the Arab states". (Georgi Mirsky, Moscow Radio Home Service, January 21, 1969).
"The resistance movement did not have any serious military effect. Israel could have ignored it" was said by the CPSU to the Syrian Communist Party (See Note No. 7).

14. *Pravda*, December 22, 1967; *Izvestia*, December 28, 1967. According to Soviet Middle East expert, Igor Belyaev, "it transpires that Shuqayri is not a man who expresses the views of the Arabs, but rather one who, by his ultra-extremist activity, has served the CIA more than anyone else". (Moscow Radio, March 17, 1968).
See also the memoirs of Ahmad Shuqayri, *Min-al-Qummah ila al-Hazimah: Ma'a al Mulok Wa al-Rosaa* (From the Summit to the Defeat: With Kings and Presidents). (Beirut, Da'ar al Awden, 1971).

15. According to the Egyptian Ambassador to the Soviet Union, Soviet officials on that occasion expressed reservations in regard to "the armed resistance movement". (*Al Akhbar*, Cairo, July 14, 1968).

16. Al Nahar, (Beirut), July 19, 1968; *Al-Hawadith* (Beirut), July 12, 1968.

17. A comment by Georgy Dadyants in Sovetskaya Rossiya (April 15, 1969), described the aims of the Palestinian organizations as "unrealistic" and as receiving their main support from "reactionary" Arab states. It said: "It is clear that the aims of the Al-Fath and certain other organizations, which boil down to the liquidation of the state of Israel and the creation of a 'Palestinian Democratic State', are not realistic. It is doubtful whether history can be turned back and whether one Palestinian people made up of Jews and Arabs can be recreated".
"Saudi Arabia and Kuwait", he said further, "generally support the organizations of the Palestinian resistance. But the aims of this support are not entirely clear. Is it a matter of Arab solidarity, or of a desire to prolong the conflict and make the situation more complicated so as to deliver a blow against the progressive regimes?"
See also: Aryeh Yodfat, "Moscow reconsiders Fatah", *New Middle East*, (London) No. 15, December 1969, pp. 15—18, idem. "The Soviet Union and the Palestine Guerrillas", *Mizan*, (London), January—February 1969, pp. 8—17.

18. *Trud*, (Moscow), October 29, 1969.

19. *Pravda*, October 26, 1969.

20. Statement on visit, *ibid.*, February 29, 1970.

21. *Za Rubezhom* (Moscow), No. 31, July 31—August 6, 1970. p. 8.

22. *Pravda*, October 30, 1971.

23. *ibid.*, July 28, 1972.

24. Tel-Aviv Israeli military forces radio, July 23, 1972; *Davar* (Tel-Aviv), July 31, 1972.

25. *Pravda*, September 10, 1972; *Sovetskaya Rossiya*, September 12, 1972.

26. *Pravda*, November 27, 1973.

27. *Afrique-Asie* (Paris), December 10—23, 1973, p. 13.

28. *Pravda*, December 22, 1973.

29. TASS, August 3, 1974. Quoted from FBIS, DR, Vol. III, SU, August 5, 1974, pp. F3—F4.

30. *ibid.*, ibid.
31. According to *Al-Liwa* (Beirut, August 3, 1974), Arafat was promised in Moscow ultra modern arms, anti-tank and anti-aircraft in particular.
32. *Pravda,* September 9, 1974.
33. *ibid.,* October 12, 1974.
34. *Izvestia,* October 19, November 14, 1974; *Pravda,* November 15, 25, 1974.
35. Moscow Radio in Arabic, August 16, 1975, FBIS, DR, Vol. III, SU, August 19, 1975, p. F5.
36. PFLP head, George Habash, said in reply to Soviet calls to Palestinians to desist from terror and to participate in the Geneva Conference that "the Soviet Union is mistaken to believe that the peaceful solution is the way to settle the Middle East conflict . . . The PFLP considers the socialist camp states as its strategic allies, yet this does not prevent differences within the same camp". The PFLP "strongly rejects the proposed Palestinian mini-state" and will continue to denounce all those who "are trying to drag some of the resistance groups to the Geneva Conference" (*Al-Nahar*, Beirut, August 18, 1974).
George Habash was attacked a few days earlier in the Moscow *Literaturnaya Gazeta* (August 14, 1974). It said that "George Habash's irresponsible actions, his extremism and pseudo-revolutionary tendencies, larded with Maoist demagoguery only play into the hands of the enemies of the Arab people of Palestine".
37. *Pravda,* April 24, 1975.
38. *ibid.,* May 5, 1975.
39. *Daily Star,* (Beirut), May 4, 1975.
40. *Afro-Asian Affairs,* (London), No. 11, June 16, 1975.
41. *Pravda,* February 25, 1976.
42. According to *Reuters* (November 24, 1975) quoting "Arab sources", Kremlin officials told Palestinians that they were not interested in offices but in embassies.
43. Joint Soviet-Jordanian Communique, *Pravda,* June 29, 1976.
44. According to the head of the PLO Moscow office, Muhammad Ibrahim Al-Sha'ir "more than 600 Palestinian students are studying in Soviet universities and institutes, in addition to the male and female students who come to the Soviet Union to complete intermediate and advanced courses in first aid, nursing, mechanics, administration and other fields". (Moscow in Arabic, December 29, 1976, In: FBIS, DR, III, December 30, 1976, p. F4).
45. "It was to the Lebanon that the nerve center of the Palestinian Resistance Movement moved after the 1970 September bloodbath in Jordan . . . It would hardly be an exaggeration to say that the Palestinian movement has . . . become in a sense, a catalyst in the political processes, occurring in the Lebanon. Chief among these processes, is the gradual, but continuous, consolidation of progressive forces ∴. Left forces in the Lebanon have been working hard to prevent local reactionaries and bourgeois extremists from providing a Jordan-type solution for the Palestinian question". (Alexander Ignatov, "Why the Shooting in Beirut", *New Times*, No. 30, July 1975, pp. 25–27.
46. *Izvestia* (October 19, 1976), quoted the Iraqi communist *Tariq ash-Sha'b* expressing reservations of the Riyadh Summit. Reservations on the Cairo summit appeared in a comment in *Pravda,* October 30, 1976.
Brezhnev said on October 25, 1976, that in Lebanon, "forces of internal reaction, armed and encouraged by Western powers with the support of Israel and Saudi Arabia, attacked the local Leftists and Palestinians. Unfortunately, Syria has found itself drawn into the orbit of military action". Referring to the Riyadh agreement, he said that the USSR had a positive attitude "to the mere fact of an agreement to end the war in Lebanon," but he expressed doubts about its results. Hopes were expressed by him that "the process of normalization of the situation would take place . . . without detriment" to the leftists and Palestinians. (*Pravda,* October 26, 1976).
47. TASS in English, October 1, 1976; *Pravda,* October 2, 1976.
48. *Ma'ariv* (Tel-Aviv), October 11, 1976.
49. *Ha'aretz* (Tel-Aviv), October 28, 1976.

50. *Pravda* June 12, 1977.

51. *Department of State Bulletin,* April 11, 1977, p. 335.

52. *Pravda* August 20, 1977.

53. *ibid.* February 2, 1977.

54. *ibid.* April 19, 1977.

55. *Izvestia* January 1, 1977.

56. Moscow in Arabic, January 12 and 26, 1977; Moscow Peace and Progress in Arabic, February 17 and March 14, 1977.

57. *Pravda,* August 3 and 4, 1977.

58. A PDFLP delegation headed by Hawatimah visited the USSR on December 12–19, 1975, at the invitation of the Soviet Committee of Solidarity with Asian and African countries, "had meetings with representatives of the Soviet public" and talks in the CPSU Central Committee's International Department. (*Pravda,* December 20, 1975).

59. *Pravda,* April 14, 1976.

60. Moscow in Arabic, August 11, 1976. In: FBIS, DR, III, August 16, 1976, p. F4.

An August 1977 Soviet comment on the 4th anniversary of the establishment of the PNF on August 15, 1973 said that the front "includes communists, resistance organizations operating in the occupied territories and some independent personalities". It is a part of the PLO and "a link between the PLO leadership and the Palestinian masses in the West Bank and Gaza". (Moscow in Arabic, August 14, 1977, In: FBIS, DR, III. August 19, 1977, p. F3).

61. "The Palestinian Resistance Movement . . . objectively . . . serves as a connecting link of the progressive layers of different Arab countries". (V. Kudryavtsev, *Izvestia,* July 31, 1976).

"Today the Palestinian question is the main link in the Arab people's struggle against imperialism's intrigues in the Near East . . . the Palestinian problem creates a definite basis for united action by the revolutionary forces for the purpose of defending the Palestinian resistance movement and exposing all the plans to liquidate it". (Aziz Mohammad, First Secretary of the Iraqi Communist Party, *Pravda,* November 3, 1976).

62. *Pravda* October 2, 1977.

63. *ibid.* March 10, 1978.

64. *ibid.* March 13, 1978.

65. The fact is that the proposals presented by Sadat in Jerusalem on November 21, 1977, heavily criticised by the USSR were not much different from those outlined by Brezhnev on March 21, 1977. (*Pravda,* March 22, 1977). When Sadat met in Knesseth members in Jerusalem on November 21, 1977, he was told by the pro-Soviet General Secretary of the Israeli Communist Party, Meir Vilner, that his proposals were similar to Soviet positions.

66. *Pravda,* November 2, 1978.

The right "to return to their homes in conformity with the UN decisions" appeared in the Soviet-Syrian communique on the Asad October 5–6, 1978, USSR visit, after the Camp David Agreements (*ibid.,* October 7, 1978) and after Gromyko's March 24–26, 1979 visit in Syria. (*ibid.,* March 27, 1979).

67. *Izvestia,* May 16, 1979.

68. *Pravda,* May 20, 1979.

69. *ibid.* June 26, 1979.

CHAPTER SEVEN

US–PLO: INDIRECT DIALOGUE

The US held no clear position in relation to Palestinian organizations and Palestine Arabs in general before the June 1967 war. References to it were generally made on an humanitarian basis and the problem was seen to be more one of refugees than of a particular national entity.

A reference to Palestinians as a people appeared in the joint USSR-US communique issued at the conclusion of Brezhnev's visit ot the US between June 18–25, 1973. "A Middle East settlement", it said, "should take into due account the legitimate interests of the Palestinian people".[1] The reference was to "interests" and not "rights". It could still be seen more as a humanitarian than a political problem, but the mere reference to the subject represented a change – it was no longer ignored.

As stated by Secretary of State, Henry Kissinger in September 1975: "The US preference prior to Rabàt [October 1974 Arab Summit] had been that the [Palestinian] issue should be settled in a negotiation between Jordan and Israel. That is still basically our preference".[2]

No official ties existed between the US and the PLO and contacts – such as there were – were unofficial and on at a low level, without announcing or even admitting their existence. With the signing on September 1, 1975, of a Kissinger-mediated Israeli-Egyptian interim agreement, an American commitment was made to Israel that the US would continue to adhere to its policy with regard to the PLO. It would neither recognize the PLO nor negotiate with it as long as the PLO refused to recognize Israel's right to exist and refused to accept Security Council resolutions 242 and 338. The commitment was since then re-affirmed many times by the Ford and Carter administrations.

Kissinger said about it on September 17, 1975:

"With respect to the PLO, until the PLO accepts the existence of the State of Israel and accepts Security Council Resolutions 242 and 338, the United

States has no decision to make, because we cannot encourage a negotiating process between parties, one of which wants to destroy the other and has as its avowed policy, the destruction of the other. But a settlement of the Palestinians and a settlement of the West Bank will have to be a part of an overall settlement.[3]

A distinction was made here between the PLO, and the problem of the Palestinians. The first official extensive US reference to Palestinians was made by Assistant Secretary of State for Near East and South Asian Affairs, Harold H. Saunders on November 12, 1975. In a statement to a sub-committee of the US House of Representatives Committee on International Relations, Saunders said that "the legitimate interests of the Palestinian Arabs must be taken into account in the negotiation of an Arab-Israeli peace. In many ways, the Palestinian dimension of the Arab-Israeli conflict is the heart of that conflict".[4]

The Saunders statement differs little from subsequent statements emanating from the Carter administration. Its importance in 1975 was that it broke new ground.

A report by a study group published about that time by the Brookings Institution in Washington, D.C., went much further. It assessed that "for a peace settlement to be viable ... " Palestinians' right to self-determination ". . . will have to be recognized in principle and, as a part of the settlement, given satisfaction in practice". The report presented two possibilities:

"(1) an independent Palestinian state accepting the obligations and commitments of the peace agreements, or

"(2) a Palestine entity voluntarily federated with Jordan but exercising the extensive political autonomy King Hussein has offered."

"Either of these agreements might be supplemented by close economic cooperation with Israel and Jordan, possibly evolving into a wider regional common market", it stated.

No position was expressed "as to who can negotiate authoritatively on behalf of the Palestinians ... It is not clear to what extent the PLO can negotiate on behalf of the Palestinians on the West Bank, in Gaza, or in Jordan, to whom it does not have ready access ... Nevertheless it can certainly be said that a solution to the Palestinian dimension of the conflict will require the participation of credible Palestinian representatives who are prepared to accept the existence of Israel".[5]

The Brookings Study Group included Zbigniew Brzezinski of Columbia University who later became President Carter's National Security advisor. Its report served, even if it was not officially acknowledged as such, as a basis of the Carter administration's policy on this subject after taking office at the beginning of 1977.

● Carter Administration – First Stage

The Nixon-Ford administrations tried to avoid dealing with the Palestinian problem. They preferred a stage-by-stage approach, dealing first with the problems that could more easily be solved, leaving the more difficult ones for a later stage. The Carter administration wanted a comprehensive settlement and this forced it to deal with all problems – including those that were seen as problematic and difficult to solve where the gap between the positions of the two sides seemed to be almost unbridgeable.

President Carter's remarks on March 16, 1977, at Clinton, Mass., included the term "homeland" for the first time. He said:

"The Palestinians claim up till this moment that Israel has no right to be there, that the land belongs to the Palestinians, and they've never yet given up their publicly professed commitment to destroy Israel. This has to be overcome.

"There has to be a homeland provided for the Palestinian refugees who have suffered for many, many years".[6]

On May 26, 1977, President Carter went further, saying that the US was bound by a policy of supporting United Nations resolutions which "do include the rights of the Palestinians to have a homeland, to be compensated for losses that they have suffered".[7]

The existence of a Palestinian entity was recognized but that entity, President Carter said on July 12, 1977, "whatever form it might take and whatever area it might occupy, should be tied in to Jordan and not be independent".[8]

The official US position was to have no direct contacts with the PLO, "as long as they remain committed to the destruction of Israel". Contacts existed indirectly through Arab states. They would become direct, President Carter said on August 8, 1977, when Palestinians ". . . will recognize UN resolution 242 in its entirety".[9]

A State Department statement released on September 12, 1977, said that "the status of Palestinians must be settled in a comprehensive Arab-Israeli agreement. This issue cannot be ignored if the others have to be solved". It went on:

"Moreover, to be lasting, a peace agreement must be positively supported by all the parties to the conflict, including the Palestinians. This means that the Palestinians must be involved in the peacemaking process. Their representatives will have to be at Geneva for the Palestinian question to be solved.

"With respect to UN resolution 242, all of the participants in the peace conference should adhere to the terms of that resolution . . ."[10]

It meant that Palestinian representatives – it did not specify which representatives – will have to participate in Geneva – but only after they declare recognition by them of Resolution 242.

It was extended a few weeks later by President Carter. He said that "it is obvious that there can be no Middle Eastern peace settlement without adequate Palestinian representation. The PLO "don't represent a nation. It is a group that represents a substantial part of Palestinians. I certainly do not think that they are the exclusive representatives of the Palestinians". As to ties with the PLO – "we will begin to meet with them and to search for some accommodation and some reasonable approach to the Palestinian question if they adopt 242 and recognize publicly the right of Israel to exist".[11]

The Carter administration assessed that without PLO cooperation, it would be difficult, perhaps impossible to solve problems of the region. They also calculated that Saudi Arabian and American financial aid would woo the PLO away from the USSR and that a Palestinian state with ties with Jordan could not become a Soviet base and a source of trouble in the region.

US appeals were rejected by the PLO. One of the principal reasons behind this rejection was the fear by its leadership that acquiescence to American approaches would hand over control of the Palestinians to Jordan and to moderate traditional leaders and not to the PLO leadership. Arafat went to Moscow to warn that if changes were to come about in the PLO leadership, the USSR would lose their last friends in the Middle East.

The US-USSR statement of October 1, 1977, on the Middle East went further. The statement spoke about Palestinians' "legitimate rights" while earlier American statements spoke about "legitimate interests". It called for a comprehensive settlement of the Arab-Israeli conflict " ... including ensuring the legitimate rights of the Palestinian people" and it called for convening the Geneva conference, with the participation of representatives "of the Palestinian people".[12]

The US was gradually turning closer to recognition of the PLO, asking only for a non-committal but conciliatory statement to facilitate talks between US officials and the PLO. But PLO leaders would not budge.

• Aftermath of Sadat Initiative

President Sadat's visit to Jerusalem in November 1977, and the subsequent peace initiative, culminating in Israel-Egyptian negotiations, compelled the US to retreat from the Soviet-American statement. Egypt and Israel were now playing the primary roles. The US had to adapt itself to this new situation.

The US has not engineered Sadat's moves which initially were counter to US recognition of the interests of the USSR, Syria and the Palestinians over that of Egypt. But the PLO, and all the Arab "rejectionists", as well as the USSR, sharply attack the US as the guilty party. It contributed to a brief slow-down in the process of US and PLO reconciliation.[13]

The "Aswan formula" marked a return by the US to an emphasis on the Palestinian problem. President Carter said on January 4, 1978, in Aswan, that "there must be a resolution of the Palestinian problem in all its aspects. The problem must recognize the legitimate rights of the Palestinian people and enable the Palestinians to participate in the determination of their own future".[14]

There was an almost unanimous American view that the Arab-Israeli conflict ran against American interests and that its solution and end would facilitate US relations with the Arab world and prevent the return of the USSR to the region, and specifically avert the dilemma of the October 1973 war when the US was presented as supporting Israel and sacrificing its interests in the Arab world.

According to generally accepted US administration positions, Arab-Israeli agreements had to include:

Israeli withdrawal to the 1967 lines with "minor changes" that will be dealt within the negotiations

a political and territorial, not only humanitarian solution of the Palestine problem providing Palestinians with the right to participate in talks on their future, without finally defining the way how this problem would be solved or who would represent the Palestinians

security arrangements, demilitarized areas, location of limited forces and arrangements for international forces, to supervise the security arrangements. (It presupposed separation of the question of sovereignty over territories from the question of security arrangements in those territories).

These principles determine American positions on ways to solve the Arab-Israeli conflict in general and in particular the future of the West Bank and Gaza and the role of Palestinians.[15]

● From Camp David to the Israeli-Egyptian Peace Treaty

At a meeting at Camp David on September 5—17, 1978, between President Carter, President Sadat and Prime Minister Begin, a framework agreement was reached "on the resolution of the Palestinian problem in all its aspects", "full autonomy to the inhabitants" of the West Bank and Gaza and the recognition of "the legitimate rights of the Palestinian people and their just requirements".[16]

In March 1979 President Carter visited the Middle East. On March 19, addressing the Egyptian People's Assembly, he pledged that he would remain personally committed to move on to negotiation concerning the West Bank and the Gaza Strip and other issues of concern to Palestinians. He said he felt "a personal obligation in this regard". The negotiations that were proposed in the Camp David agreements were to provide the Palestinian people "with an opportunity to participate in the determination of their own future". He urged "representative Palestinians" to participate in those negotiations.[17]

President Carter was asked by Israel TV to define on March 22 "the exact American attitude towards the PLO". His reply was:

"Our attitude these days is the same as it has been for a long time. The PLO has not been willing to recognize the applicability of UN resolution 242, and the PLO has not been willing to accept the right of Israel to exist. Until the PLO is willing to do these things, we will not deal with the PLO".[18]

President Carter reiterated this statement but in more detail on the same day for Egyptian TV:

"We would like to have direct relations with the Palestinians and we will, as part of the negotiating process in the future. The Palestinians who live in Gaza and the West Bank will be invited and encouraged to participate in these discussions, the mayors of the cities and other representatives to be chosen by the Palestinians themselves.

"We have a problem with the PLO. The PLO has never yet been willing to accept the applicability of UN resolution 242 . . . Also the PLO has never recognized Israel's right to exist. And as soon as the PLO itself, as an organization, is willing to accept these bases, then we'll immediately start working directly with that organization as such.

"But in the meantime, the Palestinians who reside in the West Bank–Gaza area, the Palestinians who reside in Egypt and Jordan, and even others who don't reside in either of these countries, if they're mutually acceptable, will participate in the negotiations".

In reply to a question if it would not be useful for the US to take the first step and explain her positions to Palestinians, President Carter said:

"We have not only sent representatives to meet with Palestinian leaders in the West Bank and Gaza areas, both from the Administration and the State Department — and also, for instance, the majority leader of the Democratic Party in the US Senate met with a representative group — but when I've met with President Asad of Syria and King Hussein of Jordan and with King Khalid and Crown Prince Fahd in Saudi Arabia, I have encouraged them to do everything they could possibly do to involve the Palestinians in the peace process".

"As you know, there are threats and there are demonstrations of terrorism which tend to prevent the Palestinians who want to have full autonomy from participating in these processes. And I think the threats of terrorism and the hatred that presently exists, the threat of war, the threat of economic boycotts and punishment against Egypt are certainly not conducive of realising the hopes of the Palestinian people".[19]

In Washington D.C., on March 26, 1979, the Israeli-Egyptian peace treaty was signed. A joint letter from President Sadat and Prime Minister Begin to President Carter of the same date said that Egypt and Israel had agreed to start negotiations with the objective of establishing "a self-governing authority in the West Bank and Gaza in order to provide full autonomy to the inhabitants".[20]

● Indirect Dialogue Between US and PLO

President Carter was asked a few days after the signing of the Israel-Egyptian peace treaty to "redefine" his "Palestinian policy" and "the current position" on this matter. He replied:

"Well, I wouldn't want to redefine it because it's been very consistent from the beginning (laughter). And I wouldn't change one part of it.

"As far as direct relations or consultations or negotiations with the PLO is concerned, we will not do this unless the PLO endorses the United Nations Resolution 242 . . . As long as the PLO and its constitution and commitment is dedicated to the destruction of Israel, we will not negotiate with them.

"As far as the Palestinian people themselves are concerned, we are eager to see them join in the discussions and negotiations . . . "

President Carter expressed the hope that Palestinians will "escape from the unwarranted constraint of the threat of terrorism against them if they negotiate to get full autonomy".[21]

On May 18, 1979, asked if there were changes in US policy towards the PLO, President Carter replied:

"No, there's been no change. I don't contemplate any change. Our nation is pledged again, on its word of honour, which I have corroborated since I've been in office, that we will not deal with the PLO until they accept UN Resolution 242 as a basis for negotiations, which all the other Arab entities have done and until they recognize the right of Israel to exist.

"And I think that any such meeting as that on any kind of an official basis, would be counter-productive. And we're not doing it surreptitiously. We're not cheating on our commitment. Obviously, as is well known by Israel, there are members of the PLO, individual members* who are mayors of major cities, for instance, in the West Bank and in the Gaza Strip, and both we and the Israelis deal with them as Palestinians, not, however, in their capacity as members of the PLO. So there has been and there will be no change in this policy".[22]

A distinction was made here between a dialogue with Palestinians, including PLO supporters and even members, in "their capacity as members of the PLO", and as "individuals or representatives of West Bank and Gaza residents" (mayors of cities or others).

Changes came, however slow and tentative. A situation developed as defined by a PLO official: "The US realized that the PLO is becoming an important political factor and that if they want to tackle the Palestine question they cannot do so without consulting the PLO". He noted that while a dialogue between the PLO and the US might be in the offing, the time for it had not arrived.[23] No formal dialogue took place between US officials and the PLO, but they pursued contacts with non-PLO Palestinians, as with Palestinian professors, sympathetic to the PLO. Non-official US personalities had talks with PLO leaders, including Arafat.[24]

"There is clearly an exploratory process going on", said a 'prominent Palestinian political analyst'. "A formal dialogue would be very tricky. Both sides see both dangers and advantages in the process . . . the Americans seem to be feeling the question out in order better to plan options in case of a breakdown in the autonomy talks".[25] The immediate US aim was with PLO approval to lead moderate Palestinian leaders of the West Bank and Gaza to the autonomy talks, and at a later stage to direct PLO-US ties.

● **Arafat's Vienna Meeting**

PLO tactics were to bring about changes in the US attitude to it, through direct appeals to the American public and particular sections with an interest in

---

* The President intended to say "supporters" of the PLO (Printed in the transcript).

close American-Arab ties. Arab oil-producing states and American oil interests also began to press through Washington's West European allies, still more dependent than the US on Arab oil supplies.

The Administration too had an interest in a greater West European involvement that would put pressure on Israel, influence the PLO to become more moderate and weaken its ties with the USSR. It seemed that the contacts that the Socialist International was maintaining with the PLO were in consultation with the United States. President Carter was reported to have asked the chairman of the Socialist International Executive and former Chancellor of the Federal German Republic, Willy Brandt, to "sound out the PLO".[26] The US appears also to have been at least well informed about the meeting between Chancellor Bruno Kreisky of Austria and former Chancellor, Willy Brandt with Arafat in Vienna on July 6–8, 1979.

Kreisky said he did not get the impression that the PLO had an intention to destroy Israel and that he did not think "that such ideas are realistic".[27]

Was the US behind this meeting? Al-Sa'iqa and PLO military department head Zuhayr Muhsin said it was within the framework of their agreement with the US and not independent of it.[28] Kreisky said he had informed the US Ambassador in Vienna, Milton A. Wolf, a day before Arafat's arrival about the proposed meeting. Asked if the United States was involved in the preparations for the Arafat visit, US Embassy officials said that Kreisky and Brandt were not "unaware of US importance in the Middle East and Europe. They would not do something which would make the US in the long run unhappy".[29]

Ambassador Wolf was reported to have met three times with PLO official, Dr. Issam Sartawi, one meeting on the latter's initiative and two initiated by Kreisky. The Ambassador presented the US position that there will be no contacts with the PLO as long as it does not recognize resolution 242 and Israel's existence.[30] Dr. Sartawi denied that the US had either encouraged the Vienna meeting or participated in it. He said the meeting had resulted from PLO-Socialist International contacts in which the US had played no role.[31]

The importance of the Vienna meeting for the PLO was not in what was said or concluded there, but in the fact that it had happened. The major Western European countries, not only Austria, but Britain, France and West Germany were dealing openly with the PLO. It was convenient for the US that the talks had been initiated by West Europeans. This would create precedents and in that way blunt some of the criticism anticipated to come from the American public, if the US were to conduct talks with the PLO.

The Arafat-Brandt-Kreisky meeting early in July was followed by a meeting on July 26 in the apartment of Kuwait's UN Ambassador between US Ambassador to the UN, Andrew Young and the PLO observer at the UN, Labib Tarazi. Young reported to Washington that he had not talked business with Tarazi, but when it became known that it was not so, he resigned from his office.[32]

In Israel, worries were expressed regarding shifts in US policy. Foreign Minister, Moshe Dayan, said on August 7, 1979:

"The United States, anxious over its economic ills, its problems of energy, oil and prices, is seeking an understanding with Saudi Arabia. The Saudi price is American recognition for the Palestine Liberation Organization and a solution for Jerusalem. The Saudis live in fear of a PLO instigated coup. The result — the US has agreed to help carry through the Security Council a new resolution that will supercede 242 and contradict it . . ."[33]

The Administration tried to assure Israel and her friends in the US that American policy had not changed. On August 8, 1979, President Carter reiterated to Israel's Ambassador to Washington, Evron, US opposition to the creation of a fully independent Palestinian state. He did not say that the US would never deal with the PLO. Asked if oil is not "being used as a political weapon to spur the Middle East peace talks", President Carter denied it. He said: "I have never met an Arab leader that in private expressed a desire for an independent Palestinian state. Publicly, they all espoused an independent Palestinian state, almost all of them, because that is what they committed themselves to do at Rabat. But the private diplomatic tone of conversations is much more proper than is often alleged by the press and others . . ."[34] "If a credible PLO spokesman walked in and said, 'We accept 242 and Israel's right to exist', then the US might have to open contact with the PLO", a State Department official said.[35]

Disagreements between the US and Israel now appeared on a wide range of issues. The US, criticising Israeli raids on Palestinian bases in Southern Lebanon, said that Israel "may have" broken the US law by using American supplied weapons for other than defensive purposes. Dissatisfaction was expressed about Israeli settlements in the West Bank and the slow progress of autonomy talks. President Carter compared Palestinian organizations with the US civil rights movement.

If US policy had indeed not changed towards the PLO, at least outwardly, it was not because of Israeli influence but because of the PLO's "all or nothing" position in the belief that time was in its favour. Whatever Tarazi, Sartawi, or other PLO officials might say in private talks indicating a readiness to accept Israel's existence, nothing of the kind emerged from official PLO quarters — no readiness to drop those sections of the PLO Covenant which committed it to bring an end to the existence of Israel, no clear statement about a readiness to co-exist with Israel, or to stop terror activities against the civilian population. Even if there were some leading PLO personalities seeking such changes, none were able to introduce them. They could not do it without the agreement of those Arab states on which they depended and without splitting the PLO, with those opposed to changes, being able to establish with the aid of "rejectionist" states, a rival organization to the PLO which could be built around already existing organizations enjoying the support of a particular Arab state (as Al-Sa'iqa by Syria or the ALF by Iraq).[36]

A stalemate in the autonomy talks might bring Washington, under Saudi Arabian and some West European pressure, to try to bring Palestinians and eventually the PLO into the negotiating process. It may also lead to an opposite development — a tacit PLO go-ahead for Palestinians to run in autonomy elections and vote for PLO approved candidates.

Israel warned that it may withdraw from the autonomy negotiations if the US pressed too hard for a rapproachement with the PLO. A senior Israeli Foreign Ministry official was quoted as saying: "The problem facing Americans is how to involve the Palestinians in the autonomy talks without losing Israel as a participant".[37]

NOTES TO CHAPTER SEVEN

1. *Pravda* June 26, 1973.
2. Secretary of State, Henry Kissinger News Conference at Cincinnati, September 17, 1974. *Department of State Bulletin,* October 6, 1974, p. 510.
3. *ibid.*
4. *ibid.* December 1, 1975, p. 797.
5. *Toward Peace in the Middle East.* Report of a Study Group (Washington, D.C., The Brookings Institution, December 1975), pp. 10–11.
6. *Department of State Bulletin,* April 11, 1977, p. 335
7. *ibid.,* June 20, 1977, p. 654.
In answer to requests for clarification of President Carter's statements, US State Department spokesman, Hodding Carter said the President was referring to the UN General Assembly resolutions 181 (of November 1947 providing for a Jewish and Arab state in Palestine) and 194 (of December 1948 endorsing the right of Palestinians to return to their homes or to choose compensation for their lost property).
8. *ibid.,* August 8, 1977, p. 176.
This was repeated by President Carter on September 16, 1977. He said:
> "I've never called for an independent Palestinian country. We have used the word 'entity' . . . we think that if there is a Palestinian entity established on the West Bank, that it ought to be associated with Jordan . . . "
(*ibid.* Ocotber 24, 1977, p. 571).
9. *ibid.,* September 19, 1977, pp. 379–380.
10. *ibid.,* October 10, 1977, p. 463.
11. President Carter's televised press conference, September 29, 1977, *ibid.,* October 31, 1977. p. 585.
12. *Pravda,* October 2, 1977.
13. Zbigniew Brzezinski, the President's National Security Advisor, said that US efforts to persuade the PLO to moderate its positions had failed. As a result it was "bye-bye PLO". (*Paris Match,* December 29, 1977)
14. *Department of State Bulletin,* February 1978, p. 12.
15. See statement by Harold H. Saunders, Assistant Secretary of State for Near Eastern and South Asian Affairs, June 12, 1978, *ibid.,* August 1978, p. 32.
16. For texts of the Camp David frameworks, see *ibid.* October 1978.
A review "What the Camp David framework calls for on the Palestinian issues" was made in an address in Pittsburgh on April 3, 1979, by Alfred L. Atherton, Ambassador-at-large with special responsibility for Middle East negotiations. Ambassador Atherton listed the following:
> "A Palestinian self-governing authority will be established in the West Bank and Gaza for a 5-year transitional period, during which negotiations will take place to determine the final status of these areas.
> "At the start of the transitional period, the Israeli military government and its civilian administration will be withdrawn and replaced by the self-governing authority freely elected by the inhabitants of these areas . . .

"Elected Palestinian representatives and the Government of Jordan are invited to participate, along with Egypt and Israel, in negotiations based on all the provisions and principles of Security Council Resolution 242 ... Thereby the Palestinians can participate, as they have every right to do, in determining their own future ... The agreement on the final status of the West Bank and Gaza will be submitted to a vote by the elected Palestinian representatives. These elected representatives will, by themselves decide how they shall govern themselves, after the 5-year transitional period, consistent with the terms of their agreement on the final status of the area.

"Representatives of Palestinians not now living in the West Bank and Gaza, as mutually agreed, may join the negotiations on establishing the elected self-governing authority in those areas ... "

(*Department of State Bulletin*, May 1979, p. 63)

17. *ibid.* p. 21. For President Carter's address to the Israel Knesseth, see *ibid.*, p. 28.

18. *ibid.* p. 31.

19. *ibid.* pp. 31–32.

20. *ibid.* p. 14

21. President Carter's interview with Editors and News Directors, April 6, 1979. *Weekly Compilation of Presidential Documents* (Washington), vol. 15, no. 15, April 16, 1979, pp. 623–624.

22. idem., May 18, 1979, *ibid.* No. 21, May 28, 1979, pp. 907–908.

23. Shafiq Al-Hut, head of Beirut office of the PLO to the Beirut magazine, *Monday Morning,* May 7, 1979.

24. Reports appeared about "private" meetings between US Palestinian professors having close ties with the PLO and National Security Advisor, Zbigniew Brzezinski, Mideast negotiator Robert Strauss and others.

Arab diplomatic sources in Amman were quoted saying that former US Under Secretary of State, Joseph Sisco, had held several meetings with Arafat (*Al-Qabas,* Kuwait, July 7, 1979). "A senior Arab diplomat" maintained that "a ranking Carter administration official" met with Basil Aql, PLO delegate-designate to the UN. PLO and US officials have denied the report (*Christian Science Monitor*, weekly international edition, July 16, 1979).

In mid-August 1979, a five man delegation led by former Attorney General, Ramsey Clark, held meetings in Beirut and saw Palestinian refugee camps. The meeting was arranged by Congressman Paul Findley (Rep., Illinois), who met Arafat in Damascus, in November 1978. (*Time,* August 29, 1979).

25. *Christian Science Monitor*, weekly international edition, July 16, 1979.

26. *ibid.*, July 23, 1979.

27. Voice of Palestine in Arabic, July 12, 1979, in FBIS, ME, July 13, 1979, pp. A1–A5.

28. *Al Liwa* (Beirut), July 16, 1979.

29. *Christian Science Monitor*, weekly international edition, July 23, 1979.

30. *Ha'aretz,* August 16, 1979; *Time,* August 27, 1979.

31. Le Monde, (Paris), July 23, 1979.

32. *Newsweek,* August 20 and 27, 1979; *IHT,* August 18–19, 1979; *US News and World Report,* August 27, 1979; *Time,* August 27, 1979.

33. *Economist,* August 11, 1979, p. 49

34. President Carter at Tampa, Florida, August 30, 1979 – Weekly Compilation of Presidential Documents, September 10, 1979, Vol. XV, No. 36/1585.

35. *Newsweek,* August 20, 1979.

36. Considerations of this kind were behind the decision of PLO Central Council in Damascus on August 12, 1979, to adhere to the PLO National Covenant and not to accept resolution 242. It said that the dialogue with international factors, including Western Europe, had to be based on PNC Decisions and the Covenant. (Voice of Palestine, August 12, 1979; SANA Damascus, August 12, 1979. Cited in: FBIS, ME, August 13, 1979, pp. A1–A2.

37. *Time,* August 13, 1979.

Epilogue

A number of developments and changes have occurred betwen the completion of the original manuscript and its going to the press, hence the purpose of this epilogue is to update the text wherever necessary.

By the beginning of 1980, the first stage of the peace process between Israel and Egypt had been completed. Israel gave back to Egypt about two-thirds of Sinai, including all the oil fields. Egypt opened an embassy in Tel Aviv and started a normalization process in its relations with Israel. The whole process was, however, slowed down in the course of the first half of 1980 and the expected difficulties in the autonomy talks did in fact arise.

The PLO exerted itself to make the most of this situation[1]. The organization improved its position in the international arena: Europe moved towards the PLO, the UN accepted more pro-PLO resolutions. These developments gave the PLO more self-confidence to reiterate more frequently the demand to destroy Israel. On the other hand, the PLO seemed somehow to be losing ground in the inter-Arab arena. For the fist time, open reservations were expressed against the Rabat resolutions. Libyan leader, Col. Mu'ammar Al-Qadhdhafi, questioned whether the PLO was the sole representative of the Palestinian people. King Hassan of Morocco on April 28, 1980, called upon the PLO to retreat from the Rabat resolutions. Jordan considerably improved her inter-Arab position and — though with PLO cooperation — extended her influence in the West Bank.

In the internal arena there was more polarization. The pro-Syrian organizations and the PDFLP, which formerly had supported Arafat's political methods, on Syrian instructions, turned to the "rejectionist" camp. It left Al-Fath the only organization accepting the use of political means of struggle (in addition to military) against Israel.

● PLO and Khomeyni Regime in Iran

The blow to American interests when Ayatollah Khomeyni seized power in Iran was regarded by the PLO as an endorsement of Arafat's taunting "bye-bye to American interests in the region", in reply to US National Security Adviser, Zbigniew Brzezinski's taunt at the end of 1977 — "bye-bye PLO". Similarly, Iran's cutting off oil supplies to Israel and the radical anti-Israeli declarations of Khomeyni and his followers were received with satisfaction by the PLO. Khomeyni followed the example of Idi Amin Dada of Uganda, converting the Israeli Embassy building into a PLO office.

Even before the overthrow of the Shah, the PLO had trained hundreds of Iranians, then in opposition to the Shah, and had supplied them with arms, ammunition and publicity material. When Khomeyni took power, reports appeared about Palestinians serving as his guards. Palestinians were said to play a major role in determining new Iranian policy, to be behind the ruling issued by

Khomeyni in which he decreed the Egyptian-Israeli treaty inimical to Islam and behind the appeal to isolate Egypt at the Islamic Conference in Rabat in May 1979. Pakistan and other Islamic countries who had been hesitant to become involved in the Arab dispute on this matter, agreed to suspend Egypt's membership.[2]

After the seizure on November 4, 1979, of the American Embassy in Teheran, by Iranian students who held its personnel hostage, reports appeared that Palestinians were among those who had planned the seizing of the Embassy and among the students holding the hostages. Palestinians were said to have joined the guards over the hostages and to have given them technical assistance.[3] Some of the students were identified as having received training in Palestinian camps in South Lebanon and afterwards maintaining ties with the PLO.

The PLO attempted on the one hand to present themselves to the Iranians as supporting them, but on the other hand to present to the West an image of how they were undertaking to influence Iranians to release the hostages. Proposing to mediate on this issue, the PLO endeavoured to extort from the US recognition, or at least a dialogue in which its image in American public opinion would be improved. The Khomeyni regime saw matters differently and objected to any PLO mediation. The effort was therefore abandoned, whereupon the PLO denied having had any intention to mediate, returning rather to attacks on US policies in the region.

The PLO's representative in Iran, Hani Al-Hasan, who was reported to have been switched from political adviser to Arafat to political adviser to Khomeyni, said in Ardakan (east of Esfahan) that

". . . the era of American hegemony . . . is at an end. Brother Arafat has handed over to the Imam [Al-Khomeyni] total command of the Palestinian security forces. If we follow the Imam's policy, no enemy or aggressor will be able to crush us . . . we shall be able to prevail over our enemy America."[4]

In a meeting early in December with an Iranian delegation, a month after the seizure of the American hostages, Arafat reiterated, "the Palestinian revolution's principled and unequivocal position in support of the heroic Iranian revolution and its leader, Ayatollah Khomeyni". He declared:

"We in the Palestinian revolution place all our people's and revolution's capabilities at the disposal of the Iranian people's revolution. We consider the US threats as directed against the Palestinian revolution".[5]

Arafat said in Beirut on December 7, 1979, at a rally, "for solidarity with the Iranian revolution":

"Just as our Iranian brothers have decided to send fighters to fight with us on this front line trench, we are prepared to send our columns to fight with them there in the front line trench . . . the Iranian revolution . . . will not be frightened . . . . the Iranian people will also destroy the American planes, the American fleet, and the American threats . . . .

"We and the Iranian revolution . . . are one revolution led by one man Imam Khomeyni . . . . Tell Imam Khomeyni to give the order and we will all obey and move to strike US imperialism and US imperialist interests at any time and in any place . . ."[6]

Not that relations between the PLO and Iran were always smooth. One of the main obstacles was the heterogenous character of both Iranian and Palestinian revolutionary bodies. The warm relations between the two Muslim leaders, Khomeyni and Arafat, gave rise to concern among the two Christian leaders, George Habash of the PFLP and Na'if Hawatimah of the PDFLP, both of them having had close relationships with leftist and Marxist Iranian organizations, not all of them unquestioningly loyal to Khomeyni. There were reports that the PFLP and the PDFLP had been supporting the revolt in Khuzistan with arms and training.[7]

When asked about the PFLP attitude towards the Iranian revolution, George Habash replied that the PFLP 'welcomed it and applauded it", but also had "certain reservations".

> "These concern the revolution's attitude toward the other leftist forces that contributed to toppling the Shah . . . . the manner with which the problem of minorities in Iran is being dealt with . . . the statements being made by some Iranian figures regarding the Shah, character of Bahrain and other parts of the Arab Gulf . . ."[8]

The deterioration in relations between Iran and Iraq also influenced relations between Iran and Palestinian organizations. Most of the "Rejection Front" organizations in the PLO, including the PFLP, were traditionally supported by Iraq. The Iraq-supported ALF was naturally on the side of Iraq.

The strained relations between the PLO and the Shia' population of south Lebanon, which turned in mid-1980 to a confrontation and scattered fighting, created further problems which the Shi'ite Iranian regime could not ignore. The PLO was asked time and again to improve its relations with teh Shi'ites in South Lebanon.

Those and other considerations gave rise to ambiguities in PLO positions in relation to the Khomeyni regime.

● **Tenth Arab Summit**

Arab Summit conferences had generally taken the shape of PLO "fortresses", buttressing it against attempts by Arab states to restrict its rights and activities. But, unexpectedly, at the Arab Summit convened in Tunisia on November 20–22, 1979, there were attacks on the PLO, this time by the most "patient state" until then – Lebanon.

The Summit convened at a time when a series of Middle East developments overshadowed the Palestinian problem. It was therefore important to Arafat that the Summit would stress the centrality of the Palestine problem. He wanted full legitimacy for the continuation of PLO activities in Lebanon, more financial aid and a renewed declaration that the PLO was the sole legitimate representative of the Palestinian people. In his missions to Arab capitals, Arafat called for the use of oil as a weapon against the US and Israel and a tool to undermine the

Camp David agreements. Those aims seemed to be coordinated with Moscow which he had visited on November 12–14, 1979.

President Elias Sarkis of Lebanon exploited the opportunity of PLO weakness due to its dispute with Libya and Syria's failure to back it strongly because of her own internal problems, and presented to the Summit a number of demands calling on Arab leaders to use their influence to press the PLO for:

- ending infiltration south of the Litani River,
- no PLO concentration of armed and uniformed Palestinians in cities and towns in the south,
- no shooting across the Lebanese frontier into Israel
- no armed attacks on Isarel that are mounted from bases in Lebanon
- no claiming of credit for such actions from offices in Beirut.[9]

It seemed as though Sarkis had succeeded in persuading Arab Kings and Presidents to endorse his demands but Arafat, with the support of the radical Arab states, mainly Syria, neutralized their implementation.

Only a few of President Sarkis' demands were adopted by the Conference. It resolved that armed Palestinians would continue to stay in Lebanon, including south Lebanon, probably only nominally under joint control of the PLO and the Lebanese government. "Lebanon's full sovereignty over all of its territory" was stressed. This implied full control by Lebanon over the area of the Christian militias of Major Haddad, but it could equally mean complete Lebanese authority in the Palestinian controlled areas.[10]

● **Deterioration in PLO-Libyan Relations**

PLO-Libyan disputes at the end of 1979 led to a serious deterioration in relations between them. At the outset, these disputes took the form of regular signs of strain between the organization and an Arab country. The PLO had experienced similar disputes with Jordan, Syria, Lebanon and Iraq. Here, however, was a new element, a challenge to the most important achievement that had been gained by the PLO – its status as the sole representative of the Palestinians.

Quarrels and disputes between the PLO and Libya leader, Mu'ammar Al-Qadhdhafi were in themselves no novelty. Arafat's deputy Abu-Iyad (Salah Khalaf) conceded:

"We have had a long history of quarrels with Al-Qadhdhafi since 1975 . . . . Al-Qadhdhafi advocated the view that a Palestinian leader may move only when he orders him to . . . . He always wants us to tow his line fully. We must be the friends of his friends and the foes of his foes . . . . What he wants is a paid revolution, and he treats us like paid mercenaries. He never abided by the decisions made at the different Arab summit conferences to give us financial support. He is moody. If you do not satisfy him, you get a kick. He owes us contributions in the amount between $80 and $90 million. Yet we are not prepared to submit to any Arab capital. . . ."[11]

The deterioration in relations came after the PLO had accepted the Lebanese demand at the Tenth Arab Summit to stop all military activities across the Lebanese border and not to publish any announcements about such activities from ebanon (see above). In fact, the PLO continued to conduct such operations across the Lebanese border. However, Qadhdhafi accused the PLO of neglecting he tenets of revolution, alleging that such an orgnization could no longer represent the Palestinian people. He ordered the closure of PLO and Fath offices n Tripoli and Benghazi and established Palestinian "Revolutionary Committees" imilar to those that existed in Libya, which were to be the "real" representatives of the Palestinian people.[12]

Qadhdhafi had much earlier cut off his aid to Al-Fath and gave it instead o "rejectionist" organizations, such as the PFLP, PDFLP, ALF, PLF and to the PFLP-GC. His relations with Al-Fath had never been close and the break that occurred between them was initially not regarded by Al-Fath to be a matter of erious concern, still less by the PLO.

Differences between both sides escalated when the Libyans instructed the PLO representative in Tripoli, Sulayman Al-Shuraga, to leave Libya within 24 ours, following the PLO announcement that elements manipulated by the ibyan intelligence media had for a few days been besieging the PLO and Fath offices in Libya. Libyan authorities denied this and claimed that "those besieging he offices were Palestinians who had formed revolutionary committees in esponse to Al-Qadhdhafi's call".[13]

Palestinians living in Libya were put under pressure to accept the newly ormed "Revolutionary Committees" as their representatives.

Frequent visits of "rejectionist" organizations' leaders in Libya were used o "prove" that Qadhdhafi enjoyed considerable Palestinian support even within he PLO itself.[14]

Al-Fath tried to hit back. A *Filastin Al-Thawrah* editorial (December 11, 979) attacked Qadhdhafi, saying that it "saddened" them much that he had expelled the PLO representative and not the US Ambassador.

"It hurts our national dignity that Colonel Al-Qadhdhafi should apologize for burning Washington's embassy in Tripoli . . . Al-Qadhdhafi accused the Palestinians of having infiltrated an official demonstration, burning the US Embassy and trying to involve Libya in a clash with the United States. What he really wants is that his demonstrations should be organized and controlled movements in the streets . . .

"We would like to make it clear that Al-Qadhdhafi's accusation — that the Palestinians burned the US Embassy in Tripoli — is unfounded. Those who burned the US Embassy are . . . heroic Libyans who reject these showy demonstrations organized by Al-Qadhdhafi and his intelligence services who dare not touch the huge US interests in Libya".[15]

Efforts were made to end the dispute. Fath/PLO-Libyan talks were conducted with Abd Al-Salam Jalloud, second to Al-Qadhdhafi in the Libyan regime. The outcome of the talks was reportedly positive.[16] Syria tried to mediate and on December 20, 1979, sent her Foreign Minister, Abd Al-Halim Khaddam for alks in the Libyan capital. Kahddam said his mission had been successful and nnounced a PLO-Libyan agreement to cease the tension.[17] However, the propaganda war between them continued. Libya announced on January 8, 1980 that she had broken off all her ties with Al-Fath.

The struggle between the PLO and Libya reached its peak — and recede — at the Fourth Summit of the National Front of Steadfastness and Confrontation in Tripoli (April 13–15, 1980). Syria, eager to hold the Conference, did all she could to conciliate between the sides. After a long and intensive effort, she gained Qadhdhafi's permission to accept the PLO at the Conference. Arafat reached Tripoli in President Asad's airplane. Qadhdhafi refused to let Arafat enter the Conference hall and did not mention the PLO in his opening speech. A temporary and conditional conciliation had been reached. Arafat promised to obey the "revolutionary course" in the future. The recognition of the PLO as the sole representative of the Palestinian people was, however, repeated in the Conference resolutions, but not unconditionally, as before. The PLO was recognized as *"the leader of the armed struggle* of the Palestinian people" and its legitimate representative[18]. The hint, and the threat, were clear enough.

● Moroccan Reservations on the Rabat resolutions

Among the resolutions that were adopted at the Steadfastness Front Conference in Tripoli (April 13–15, 1980) was a recognition, under Algerian pressure, of an independent Sahara Arab Democratic Republic (SADR)[19]. Since Spain's evacuation of West Sahara, an Algerian-Moroccan confrontation emerged, the first trying to create there a pro-Algerian independent state and the second to annex the area to Morocco[20]. The PLO support of the Algerian position at the Tripoli Conference caused much anger in Morocco and King Hassan, the Second, decided to react. Asked about France's President Giscard d'Estaing's initiative on self-determination for Palestinians (see below), King Hassan said:

"The Palestinian cause reached a new level when Europe has understood two elements: that there is a Palestinian people which has the right of self determination and that the PLO became one of its spokesmen, but not the only spokesman... I have suggested the Palestinians to discharge themselves from the Rabat resolutions which oppose any partial solutions. . ."

● PLO and Jordan

An improvement emerged in PLO-Jordanian relations. Arafat visited Jordan and there were talks and agreements. However, no permission was given to re-establish militias in refugee camps and to conduct PLO military activities against Israel from Jordanian territory.

Attempts by the PLO office in Amman to reinstate their militia in refugee camps in Jordan and to foment trouble for the Hashemite regime there, led to appeals to the King by loyal senior officers and bedouins with bitter memories of the events of September 1970.

Two main issues were accepted by the two sides: Jordan agreed to enlarge the PLA units stationed on her territory. Both coordinated their efforts to transfer financial aid to the West Bank, through a Joint Committee, in order to weaken its dependence on the Israeli authorities.

● Greater Polarization Inside the PLO

The PLO tried often but not always successfully to avoid adoption of decisions that would result in splits and divisions in its ranks. In early 1980 there was a sharpened polarization inside the PLO between Al-Fath and "rejectionist" organizations. The causes were, in addition to inter-Arab and personal rivalries, differing positions on relations with Iran, Libya and Jordan; Khomeyni and Iranian leftists; on Qadhdhafi; on talks with the Jordanian regime; on the Israeli-Egyptian peace; and on relations with the US. The result was that the PDFLP, the pro-Syrian Al-Sai'qa and the PFLP-GC reversed its position and supported "Rejection Front" organizations, thus leaving Al-Fath isolated.

A new organization named the "Arab Popular Liberation Movement" was reportedly established on November 18, 1979. Its founder was said to be Naji Allush, who had been deputy head of Baghdad-based Fath dissidents of Abu Nidhal.[21] He was the Chairman of the Palestinian Writers and Journalists Union, and generally held extreme political and social positions. He was opposed to the PLO and Al-Fath, considereing them too moderate.

● PLO-USSR

The PLO continued to receive extensive Soviet aid and to repeat Soviet slogans.

Arafat visited Moscow on November 12–14, 1979, a week before the tenth Arab Summit to talk over matters which the Conference would have to deal with, and concerning other matters of mutual interest. A "joint communique" on the visit called it "friendly" (but not "official") and said that the talks were held "in an atmosphere of cordiality and understanding". Arafat expressed "deep-felt gratitude" for "disinterested support and assistance" from the Soviet. He assured Moscow "that the PLO would strengthen in every possible way friendship and cooperation with the USSR and other socialist countries . . . ."

Agreement was reaffirmed "to continue regular contacts, exchange of views and coordination of action on different levels on questions of mutual interests," but there was no report of promises of further Soviet support. Both sides called for:

- "a full and unconditional withdrawal of Israeli troops from all Arab, including Palestinian territories occupied by it in 1967,
- "the implementation of the inalienable national rights of the Arab people of Palestine, including its right to self-determination and the establishment of its own independent state,
- "and also the right of Palestinians to return to their homes."[22]

The call was for an Israeli withdrawal, not conditional on any PLO promises to recognize Israel's right to exist. The withdrawal was to be "complete" to the pre-June 1967 frontiers, (i.e. including east Jerusalem). It spoke about "Palestinian territories" to stress Palestinian rights — and not Jordanian and Egyptian — to the West Bank and Gaza Strip. The Palestinian state has to be "independent", i.e. no autonomy with ties to Israel, no federation or confederation with Jordan. Palestinians should have a right to return "to their homes", i.e. to pre-1967 Israel.

Notwithstanding the importance to Arafat of these demands, the USSR has made no overt offers to help him achieve them. For Arafat, it was no less important to receive more Soviet aid — increased military supplies in particular — but here, too, the Soviets were more restrained. Larger deliveries of sophisticated arms for the PLO would make it increasingly independent of Arab states (Syria in particular) and, paradoxically, also of the Soviet Union.

The Soviets, as well as Syria and Libya, viewed with disfavor trends by the PLO towards the US and Western Europe. They warned the PLO that it might be dangerous. A senior commentator in *Izvestia* wrote that there are "powerful pro-Israeli forces in the United States" which influence US policy. The commentator presented what he claimed to be an American plan "to promise the Palestinians that if they recognize Israel, their national rights will also be recognized and when the PLO has done this, they will withdraw their promise".

The comment included one of the rare confirmations in the Soviet press that the PLO does not recognize Israel's right to exist, does not accept UN Security Council resolutions 242 and 338 and that such positions are the reasons why the US does not have ties with it. It said that the US tries to free itself from obliging herself to act on the issue — "the US President understands the need for talks with the Palestinians . . . will seek to continue contacts with the PLO in one form or another". But, it concluded, "Americans do not want an independent Palestinian state. What they want is Near East oil. . ."[23]

According to this Soviet comment, "attempts are being made on the one hand to separate the PLO from the Arab states and to isolate it and, on the other hand, to influence the Palestinians precisely through the same Arab states or, at any rate, through certain ones."[24]

USSR military intervention in Afghanistan at the end of 1979 and persued further in 1980 attracted Muslim and Arab attention to developments in that country and around it. Such attention was not looked upon with favour, neither by the USSR nor by the PLO, both of them wishing to distract attention from Afghanistan to the Arab-Israeli conflict and the Palestinian problem as a central issue of it.

The PLO was not, however, in an easy sitaution. It had to take into consideration the positions of Saudi Arabia, its most important financial backer and also the sensitiveness of a great number of Muslim states. But it had also to consider the positions and sensitiveness of the USSR, its main arms supplier, and of Syria, on whom it became increasingly dependent. This situation led PLO officials to express contradictory positions.

It was much simpler for radical Palestinian organizations, the PFLP of George Habash and still more for the Democratic Front of Hawatimah. The latter as a Christian was less influenced by the Muslim aspect of the subject. As a leftist and a radical, he feared less that a suppoert of the regime in Afghanistan and of Soviet intervention there would jeopardize conservative Arab states' support which he did not enjoy anyway.

The visit of the USSR Foreign Minister, A. Gromyko, to Syria on January 7–29, 1980, was, in addition to its other aims, a part of Soviet efforts to turn away Arab attention from the situation in Afghanistan to the Arab-Israeli conflict and Palestine problem.

In the joint USSR-Syrian communique on the visit, the sides called to achieve "a just and all-embracing settlement" (not peace but "a settlement") in the Near East on the basis of the complete withdrawal of Israeli troops from all the Arab territories occupied by them in 1967, including the eastern part of Jerusalem, and the implementation of the inalienable national rights of the Arab people of Palestine, including their right to self-determination and the setting up of their independent state, and also of the right of the Palestinians to return to their homes in accordance with the existing UN decisions."

The statement condemned those who "under cover of an artificially whipped up hullabaloo around the events in Iran and Afghanistan. . . are striving to divert the attention of the Arab peoples" away from the struggle against Israel, "to drive a wedge" between Arabs and the Soviet Union. They were "exhibiting false concern for Islam while at the same time supporting the seizure by Israel of Islamic temples in Jerusalem."[25] Soviet utterances of this kind have been made frequently.

The Soviet image in the Arab world was of a power able to contribute to a war but less to a peace process – a thesis naturally rejected by the Soviet Union, which believed that included in negotiations for a new detente between them and the Western world, after the US elections in November 1980 will be a comprehensive settlement in the Middle East.

The references to the Middle East in the Communique of the Political Consulative Committee of the Warsaw Treaty countries in Mid-May 1980 seemed to be intended for such an eventuality. These were seemingly intended for publicity but also as proposal that was in fact not much different from similar West European ones for a Middle East settlement.

The statement called for an "all-embracing Middle East political settlement with the direct participation of all interested sides, including the Arab Palestinian people in the person of its representative – The Palestine Liberation Organization, on the basis of respect for the lawful interest of all states and peoples of the Middle East, including Israel."

"Such a settlement requires the withdrawal of Israeli troops from all Arab territories occupied in 1967, restoration of the right of the Arab people of Palestine to self-determination, including the creation of its own independent state, ensurement of the sovereignty and security of all states of that area. A political settlement in the Middle East also requires that no actions impeding the attainment of these aims be taken [as Israeli settlements] that no state should interfere in the internal affairs of the area's countries and peoples, should not try to instruct them what socio-economic system they should establish, should not make claims to encroach on their national resources."[26]

No mention was made here of a return of refugees after Israel's withdrawal,

no specific mentioning of Jerusalem. It was an attempt to say that the USSR wa
not one-sided and could play a role in a peace-making process. It was also a hin
to radical Arabs, including the PLO, that Soviet support will not automaticall
be given to them and that they could not have Soviet support and at the sam
time appear to negate Soviet interests and positions.

The USSR supports the PLO, for tactical reasons, because it sees in it a
element that undermines positions of the US and those in the Middle East tha
more or less go along with the US. The Soviets have not many friends in th
Arab world and thus there is a temporary meeting of PLO-USSR interests, bu
their aims, methods and positions are basically different.

The USSR advocates a political settlement of the Arab-Israeli conflict, i
recognizes Israel's right to exist and UN Security Council resolutions 242 an
338 (though with an interpretation differing from that of the US). It fight
Zionism but accepts the basic Zionist principle (which is generally not accepte
in the Western world and by many non-Zionist Jews) that Jews are a people an
not only a religion and therefore have, as all other peoples, a right to self-deter
mination in their own state. The PLO does not accept this. Soviet commentator
often said that Palestinians have a right to struggle "by every means" but th
Soviets were against what they call "individual terror", maintaining that the PLC
has to concentrate its struggle in "the occupied territories." Soviet commenta
tors expressed worries about the positions of the PLO and its dependence or
"reactionary Arab support" and that it might indeed become increasingly
dependent on them.

The most important Soviet consideration is that the PLO continues to ac
against Western (particularly American) interests in the Middle East. The Sovie
sees the PLO as a revolutionary force that acts to undermine established order
as it tried to do in Jordan, succeeded in doing in Lebanon and might do in
Kuwait or Saudi Arabia. By the same token, the Soviet sees the PLO in the vanguard against the US-backed Egyptian-Israeli peace agreement. In Soviet terms,
the PLO is progressive, even when preaching reactionary slogans.

• PLO-US

The Iranian-American conflict, the increasing US-USSR tension as a result
of Soviet involvement in Afghanistan and a series of other developments, regional
and global, as well as the approaching US elections, induced the US administration at the beginning of 1980 to relegate the Palestinian problem in its order of
priorities. PLO support, even if only verbal, of Iran and the USSR, contributed,
too, to a slowing up in the pace of US-PLO approaches.

There were no official US-PLO ties but indirect contacts continued. Within the PLO leadership, a small but growing number began to realize that President
Anwar Al-Sadat's contention that the key to the solution of the Arab-Israeli conflict is in Washington was valid. The PLO consequently took into consideration
steps to indirectly influence the US. Hence, in order to improve its image in
American public opinion, the PLO has tried to change its terrorist image (but

wihtout completely abandoning such activities) and to elicit as much public support as possible in the US, from blacks, churches, business interest and other groups.

A report prepared and signed by former US senior officials issued by the Atlantic Council's special working group on the Middle East can be compared to the 1975 Brookings Institution report which had much impact on the Carter administration policy. It urged:

(1) "serious negotiations under the Camp David framework for a Middle East settlement;

(2) "efforts to bring Arab parties, other than Egypt, into the negotiations, especially Jordan and Saudi Arabia; and

(3) "association of Palestinian Arabs in the process. While this is not the moment to bring the Palestine Liberation Organization (PLO) into active negotiations, the US should maintain informal contact with the PLO".[27]

Attempts to solve the Arab-Israeli conflict appeared to many in the Carter administration not only as an aim in itself but no less to serve in a much larger framework — to assist the establishment of an Arab front allied with the US and veering away from the Soviet Union.

It appeared so in particular after the Soviet military involvement in Afghanistan at the end of 1979 when the US tried to use the occasion to strengthen her position in the Muslim and Arab world. The existence of the Palestinian problem made it more difficult, turned attention away from it, forced the US administration to deal with it — in spite of a preference for delay until after the elections.

President Carter's election campaign included statements that took into consideration positions of the American Jewish Community. In a Washington address on February 25, 1980, he stressed his support for a recognition of the "legitimate rights"of Palestinians, but said further:

"I am opposed to an independent Palestinian state because in our judgment and in the judgment of many leaders in the Middle East, including many Arab leaders, this would be a destabilizing factor in the Middle East and certainly would not serve United States interests.

"I will not negotiate with or recognize the PLO unless it first recognizes Israel's right to exist and accepts United Nations Security Council Resolution 242."[28]

The Carter administration policy was however far from being consistent. It took into consideration the positions of Israel's friends in the US, but a few days after the above-cited Carter address, on March 1, 1980, the US voted in the UN Security Council, on orders of President Carter, for a resolution that called on Israel to dismantle Jewish settlements in the West Bank and Gaza Strip, including East Jerusalem.[29] Protests from Israel and her American supporters brought President Carter, two days later, to retreat and to say that the UN vote had been "a mistake" and a result of "a failure of communications".[30] It led to "Arabs feeling thoroughly disappointed without appeasing Israel."[31]

Changes in positions of this kind came not only as a result of yielding t̶ pressures from different directions and a wish to satisfy as many as possible in time of an election campaign, but also because of different positions in the U̶ administration.

There were some who considered that it was perhaps a mistake to sponso̶ the Camp David Agreements which split the Arab world and made it mor̶ difficult to turn it against the Soviet Union.

There were others who would have liked the US to initiate, as was done b̶ West Europeans, a recognition of Palestinians' rights to self-determination an̶ an amendment of UN Security Council resolution 242. They advised Washington̶ not to clash with West European initaitives but to join them and even lead them̶ using it to strengthen US positions in the Arab world.

President Carter was committed to the Israeli-Egyptian peace treaty an̶ the autonomy framework agreement and saw advantages to the US and to h̶ administration in their implementation. But he too saw the Palestinian problem̶ as a central issue of the Arab-Israeli conflict and considered that without solvin̶ it will be difficult, or perhaps impossible, to solve that conflict.

The West European initiatives might be welcomed by some in the Carte̶ administration, as bringing additional pressure on Israel, in a time when the U̶ could not do so because of election considerations. It was, however, also ̶ pressure on the US which had to choose between acting against such initiative̶ and clashing with West European countries or joining it and in that way̶ indirectly admitting failure. Officially, the newly appointed Secretary of State̶ Edmund Muskie, and other US officials urged West Europeans not to undermin̶ the autonomy talks under the Camp David accords. The differences between̶ American and West European positions seemed however to be more in the ways̶ to a settlement that in the desired outcomes. On this a growing gap develope̶ between the Carter administration and the Israeli government.

It expressed itself, inter alia, in the US vote on the June 30, 1980 Security̶ Council resolution on Jerusalem which was not vetoed by the US thus enabling̶ its passage.

The American position on this matter had in fact been all the time̶ different from that of Israel. The US position on Jerusalem "hasn't changed̶ from previous statements made by USA ambassadors at the UN", said the US̶ Ambassador to the UN, Donald McHenry, in early June 1980. He refused to̶ speak about it, "because when you get off into this you get off into delicate̶ language". He was ready to give written texts of earlier statements that were̶ still valid.[32]

A letter from President Carter to President Sadat, at the time of the Camp̶ David conference, dated September 22, 1978, a copy of which was transmitted̶ to Prime Minister Begin, said:

> "The position of the United States on Jerusalem remains as stated by Ambassador Goldberg in the United Nations General Assembly on July 14, 1967, and subsequently by Ambassador Yost in the United Nations Security Council of July 1, 1969."

The cited letter of Carter was a result of a compromise in Camp David after a failure to achieve any agreement on Jerusalem.

The statement by Ambassador Arthur J. Goldberg was that the United States "does not accept or recognize... the administrative measures" that were taken by Israel on June 28, 1967, as "altering the status of Jerusalem, considered them to be only interim and provisional, and not prejudging the final and permanent status of Jerusalem." However, the Goldberg statement did not say that Jerusalem was an "occupied territory" and UN Security Council resolution 242 adopted a few months later made no mention of Jerusalem.

The statement of Ambassador Charles W. Yost to the UN Security Council on July 1, 1969, was more detailed and explicit. He said:

"The United States considers that the part of Jerusalem that came under the control of Israel in the June [1967] war, like other areas occupied by Israel, is occupied territory and hence subject to the provisions of international law governing the rights and obligations of an occupying power. Among the provisions of international law which bind Israel, as they would bind any occupier, are the provisions that the occupier has no right to make changes in laws or in administration other than those which are temporarily necessitated by his security interest, and that an occupier may not confiscate or destroy private property... I regret to say that the actions of Israel in the occupied portion of Jerusalem present a different picture, one which gives rise to understandable concerns that the eventual disposition of East Jerusalem may be prejudiced and the rights and activities of the population are already being affected and altered."[33]

President Carter accepted the Yost statement, but added that Jerusalem should not be divided and those two are in oppostion one to the other.

This epilogue was written before the US Presidential election, but no matter what will be its outcome, it seems inevitable that the US is turning closer to the PLO, at least more insofar as the U.S. will take the PLO into consideration.

● **PLO-Western Europe**

The European community as a whole moved closer to the PLO. European leaders spoke about an urgent need to recognize Palestinians' right to self-determination without presenting clearly defined positions about the meaning of the Palestinian entity and ways to solve the problem.

The West European interest in the palestinian problem was motivated, inter alia, by economic interests in Arab countries and a wish to extend economic ties, the great dependence on oil supplies from the Middle East, the wish to prevent support by Palestinian organizations for European terrorist groups.

PLO activities in Europe were much assisted by the presence there of large and politically active Arab communities, which included Palestinian refugees of 1948, and of the Lebanese civil war of 1975–1976. Palestinian students often organized in European capitals a "Palestine Day" or "Palestine Week" which included demonstrations, lectures, movies and visits by leading PLO personalities which were widely covered in the information media.[34]

Views were expressed that West European positions on this subject are coordinated with the US and that there is in fact some kind of American-West European "division of work." It has been suggested in influential Western European circles that they actually say in public what Americans think – but do not speak out openly becuase of considerations of internal policy. Both sides are considered to supplement each other – the US acts for a success of the autonomy talks but is not against European initiatives that can promote processes in which the US has much interest.

But while some such coordination does exist, it seems as if European initiatives are more a result of attempts to lead an independent policy, of distrust of the US, of believing that they know better and might succeed where Americans did not. The US assisted those who acted to remove Western Europe from the Middle East and now Europeans want to return to it. They see themselves closer than Americans to the Arab world, not only geographically, understanding it much more, being more able to find a common language with it. It expressed itself in a series of declarations, statements and initiatives of France's President Valery Giscard d'Estaing, West German Chancellor Helmut Schmidt, British Foreign Minister Lord Carrington and others for a more active European policy on the Palestinian problem, particularly if the autonomy talks reach a deadlock and bring no results.

France

France for many years supported Arab positions in regard to Israel but hesitated to support calls for self-determination for the Palestinians, considering that it might contribute to a strengthening of nationalist separatist movements in French overseas territories, and even in France itself. French spokesmen described the PLO as representing Palestinian interests, but France did not grant an official recognition to the PLO and to its Paris office.

The visit of President Giscard d'Estaing to the Middle East in March 1980 was at a time of a deadlock in the autonomy talks and just after the US had voted in the UN against Israeli settlements in the West Bank and Gaza and had then retreated from it. Giscard used this situation to appear with an independent initiative, with an aim to present himself as supporting Arab positions more than the Americans had.

The joint communique on Giscard's visit to Kuwait said that the sides called for the "recognition of legitimate rights of the Palestine people. They expressed their conviction that the Palestine problem is not one of refugees but of a people and as such they have the right to self-determination within the framework of a just and durable peace."[35]

The joint Jordanian-French statement of March 10, 1980, spoke about a need to "find an international solution for the Middle East problem." The solution had to include a "recognition of the legitimate rights of the Palestinian people, including their right to establish a homeland on their land, and the right of every state in the area to live peacefully within secure, recognized and guaranteed borders." The Palestinian "homeland" could also be in the framework of a federation with Jordan. The rights of all states meant also of Israel, but this was not mentioned in the French-Kuwaiti communique.

President Giscard and King Hussein stressed the importance of the Palestinian problem which "is not one of refugees" but of a people that "should be enabled to practice their right to self-determination within the framework of a peaceful, just and lasting settlement." In order to achieve an "international settlement" to talks had to be concluded "with the participation of all parties concerned, including the PLO."[36] The PLO does appear here as one of the parties and not as a sole representative of Palestinians.

The staement hinted at a proposal that was introduced by Jordan for an international conference on the Middle East, under UN patronage, to replace the Geneva conference, with the participation of the US, USSR, states that had participated in the 1975 conference on security and cooperation in Europe, Arab states, Palestinian representatives and Israel. It's goal would be to establish a "homeland" for Palestinians connected with Jordan.

The references to Palestinians in the French-Kuwaiti statement received immediate support of a number of West European states. In the US, attempts were made to describe it as being no change form earlier statements. PLO spokesmen generally praised it. Faruq Qaddumi said it was "a step forward" and hoped France would take "further positive steps."[37] PLO representative in Paris, Ibrahim Sus, was more restrianed and stressed not what Giscard said, but what he should add to his statement. There was in the statement no full recognition of the PLO as the sole legitimate representative of Palestinians, the French government did not grant to PLO office in Paris a status of an embassy and Arafat still waited for an official invitation of Giscard to come to Paris. But even if the Giscard statements did not introduce new elements they included a new approach to the subject.

West Germany

West Germany was the first West European state since 1974 which introduced the formula of Palestinians' rights to self-determination. As a country that was divided and represented a people who had lived in East European countries, it spoke about a right of self-determination to Germans and extended it to others, including Palestinians. West Germany's *Ostpolitik* of reconciliation with East European countries had included giving up territories that had been German for a long time – an also surrendering the conept of the unity of German people. Therefore, Germany found iself unable to accept Israeli cliams of historical rights to all of Palestine.

The Socialist International which had for years supported the US and its policy, turned more to a neutral attitude and saw itself as standing between the USSR and the US, stressing ties with Third World countries and the Palestinian problem as a part of it. West Germany's ruling Social Democratic party established ties with the PLO and its Chairman, Willy Brandt, participated with Chancellor Kreisky in a meeting with Arafat in Vienna in July 1979 (See Chapter seven). Party representatives had meetings, on various occasions, with PLO representatives.

Chancellor Helmut Schmidt said at a press conference in March 12, 1980, that a Middle East peace treaty would have to recognize Palestinians' right to self-determination, that the Giscard declarations during his visit in Arab countries corresponded to Bonn positions and that Arab leaders see a greater danger in Zionism than in the Soviet Union. It reflected the move by Bonn away from the past, ignoring the Palestinian problem and adopting positions similar to the official French ones on this subject.

Britain

The U.K. tended to keep ties with the PLO and her Ambassador in Beirut met Arafat. Contacts were, however, restricted to officials and were not held on the ministerial level.

In early 1980 a more active British policy loomed in the Middle East, which meant taking into consideration Arab positions. British statements were made favouring PLO participation in autonomy negotiations. A Foreign Office spokesman in early March expressed support for President Giscard's call for self-determination for Palestinians in the framework of a negotiated peace settlement.

Other West European countries hold similar positions.

Venice Declaration

In Venice on June 13, 1980, the heads of state and government and the ministers of foreign affairs of the nine member states of the European Economic Community issued a declaration on the Middle East. It included recognition for the right of Palestinians to self-determination, and of the PLO to participate in the Middle East peace process.

The declaration spoke about "the right to existence and security for all the states of the region, including Israel, and justice for all people, which implies the recognition of the legitimate rights of the Palestinian people." (Article 4.) It said that "all the countries in the area are entitled to live in peace within secure, recognized and guaranteed borders" and that the nine countries were prepared to participate in a guaranteeing of it (article 5).

The Palestine problem "is not simply one of refugees" and the Palestinian people "must be placed in a position to exercise fully its right to self-determination" (art. 6). All the parties concerned, including the PLO, "will have to be associated with the negotiations" (art. 7).

The nine "will not accept any unilateral initiative designed to change the status of Jerusalem" (art. 8). They stressed "the need for Israel to put an end to the territorial occupation which it has maintained since the conflict of 1967 . . . that the Israeli settlements constitute a serious obstacle to the peace progress in the Middle East. . . that these settlements. . . are illegal. . ." (art. 9).

The nine called for "the renunciation of force or the threatened use of force by all the parties" (art. 10).[38]

The document did in fact recognize the PLO as the only spokesman of Palestinians, at least as long as there is no substantial other Palestinian organization that denies the PLO such a right. The references to Jerusalem and Israeli settlements were an indirect condemnation of Israel. The calls to the PLO to stop terror were indirect and not a condition for PLO participation in peace negotiations.

The PLO Executive Committee announced on June 16, 1980, its rejection of the Venice statement.[39] It could not be accepted by the PLO as articles 4 and 5 recognized Israel's right to existence, "to live in peace within secure, recognized and guaranteed borders." Article 8 on Jerusalem did not fully answer Arab demands. The reference to "freedom of access to everyone to the the holy places" hinted at a possibility of a special status, while the PLO sees in it an Arab city and the capital of the state that it wants to establish. Article 10 called "to put an end to violence." Arafat replied to it saying that the Palestinian people do not rely on European support but – the gun they hold, that will help them to achieve their rights.

The Venice declaration reflected a West European consideration that the Camp David process had reached a deadlock, if not failure, leaving a void in the Middle East which they wanted to fill. They argued that moderate Arab states could not fully join the West if the latter would not solve for them the Palestinian problem important to them. Even if the leadership of those Arab countries would have liked to ignore the problem, it could not do so, because nationalist circles were threatening revolutions similar to that in Iran. To appease such circles there is a need to solve the Palestinian problem on the lines that the Palestinians wish it. The west will then have allies and oil.

Arguments of this kind are far from Middle East realities. But this mattered very little to those who pressed for an even more strongly worded declaration (the one adopted was softened and moderated), whether the proposed solutions were realistic or not, did contribute or not to a settlement in the Middle East. All they wanted was to show to Arab leaders that they were with them more than others, more than Americans and other Europeans, and Arabs should therefore become more friendly with them than with others. They wanted Arab oil, to sell more to Arab countries, receive more Arab investments and they believed that statements of this kind advanced their cause.

Summing Up

The main difficulty facing the PLO in its attempt to solve the Palestinian problem is its adherence to the ideology calling for the complete destruction of Israel. Previous to 1974, the PLO stressed the final goal. Since 1974 the PLO adopted a stage-by-stage strategy, seeing as its intermediate aim the estalishment of a Palestinian state in the West Bank and Gaza Strip, as a first stage towards the the establishment of a Palestinian state in all of Palestine. From time to time, there are hints from leading PLO personalities that they might, after the estalishment of the West-Bank—Gaza State, be ready to accept — some even say to recognize — Israel's existence. But when these hints are publicly stated, they are immediately denied by offical PLO spokesmen.

The PLO has not marked up many scores in the Arab-Israeli conflict arena. Its successes have been in the inter-Arab and international arenas. Their "all or nothing" position might, in part, explain this. An unsigned comment in the *Guardian* (UK) is apt:

Beginning with a question: "If the Palestinians, why not the Kurds? The latter have been fighting for autonomy for many years and failed," the comment continued:

"They [the Kurds] kill no ambassadors. They hijack no planes. They live in the hills. Who cares?

". . . One difference between the Palestinians and the Kurds is that the former are fighting an OK enemy — Israel — whereas the latter are fighting Moslem governments which collectively speak for the Third World. Another difference is that Palestinians have a vicarious hold over the West's oil supplies, through their sponsors in the producing states . . . A meeting to advance the [Palestinian] cause will end with prolonged cheers. Justice for the Kurds is not even on the agenda and no meetings take place."[40]

At this time of writing this Epilogue, it is plain that the greater the efforts by the PLO towards achieving the first stage — a Palestinian state in the West Bank and Gaza — the more stridently it proclaims its longterm, ultimate aim — a Palestinian state in all of Palestine, with no place there for the state of Israel, of any size or shape.

In May 21—31, 1980, Al fath, the largest and dominant organization within the PLO, held its Fourth Conference in Damascus. The political program issued to sum up the Conference declared clearly:

"Fath is a revolutionary patriotic movement that aims to liberate the whole of Palestine, to establish a democratic Palestinian state on the entire Palestinian soil and the complete destruction of the Zionist entity on all the economic, political, military, cultural and ideological levels."[41]

The same "destroy Israel" motive appeared in two of Arafat's interviews to Arab newspapers.[42] The London Journal *The Middle East,* posed the question,

The Middle East, journal of the Arab lobby in London, posed the question, "Should the Palestinians Change the Charter?" early in 1980. The unanimous reply from eleven PLO leaders and officials, pro-PLO professors of Palestinian origin, teaching in Washington, New York and London and other prominent Palestinians — all described as moderate intellectuals — was: "No". There was unanimous agreement that "a change in the Covenant was not necessary for the continued pursuit of Palestinian objectives towards international recognition."[43]

It seems that as long as the PLO bases its policy on a stage-by-stage strategy, it will be difficult for it to achive any aims. How can it expect is opponents to conede that first stage, when it makes it abundantly clear that in the course of time it will persue its other stated objectives?

NOTES TO EPILOGUE

1. Mustapha Khalil, till mid-May 1980, Egyptian Prime Minister, stated that Egypt had given the PLO full reports about the autonomy talks (MENA, June, 7, 1980).

2. Huda Al-Husayni, *Al-Hawadith* (London), June 22, 1979, pp. 20–21.

3. Paris Domestic Service, December 13, 1979. Cited in FBIS, ME, supp. 039, December 13, 1979, p. 10.

4. *Keyhan* (Teheran), December 3, 1979.

5. Voice of Palestine, December 5, 1979. Cited in FBIS, ME, December 5, 1979, p. A6.

6. *ibid.*, December 7, 1979. Cited in *ibid.*, December 10, 1979, pp. A3–A5.

7. According to an unnamed Iranian official "the Palestinians transported their ideological differences to Iran. While Fath chose Imman Al-Khomeyni, the PFLP, it would appear, picked the non-religious trend, that is, the liberals, leftists and the supporters of Moscow". (*Al-Hawadith,* June 22, 1979).

8. *Al-Siyasah* (Kuwait), October 30, 1979, citing the Lebanese weekly *Al-Usbu Al-Arabi.*

9. *Economist* (London), November 17, 1979, p. 71.

10. For the Tenth Arab Summit final statement, see: QNA, Doha, November 22, 1979. Cited in FBIS, ME, November 23, 1979, pp. A11–A14.

11. *Der Spiegel* (Hamburg), December 17, 1979, pp. 26–29.

12. At the beginning of December 1979, Qadhdhafi called on Palestinians to establish "Popular Councils" and "Revolutionary Committees" on the Libyan pattern to represent Palestinians. He alleged that the PLO was no longer providing a fighting revolutionary leadership. He maintained that this was proved at the November 1979 Arab summit at which the PLO surrendered and capitulated to those insisting that it ceases to conduct further activities against Israel from the Lebanese border. Qadhdhafi argued that a revolutionary element cannot be restricted by laws and has to fight till the end. He proposed to threaten navigation in the Suez Canal and Bab 'Al-Mandab Straits, to hit vessels carrying goods to Israel, "to destroy Arab oil, if it is not used for the Liberation of Palestine". Quadhdhafi did not deny that diplomatic activities are important but said that they have to be accompanied by intensive military activities on a wide scale, with no armistice. As long as the PLO will not accept this, Qadhdhafi warned that he will continue to oppose it. (*Al-Siyasi,* Tripoli, December 7, 1979).

13. *Kuwaiti News Agency* (KUNA), December 9, 1979, cited in FBIS, ME, December 10, 1979, p. 14.

14. Major Abd Al-Salam Jallud met Ahmad Jibril, Secretary General of the PFLP-GC, Dr. George Habash, Secretary General of the PFLP, Dr. Samir Qushah, Secretary General of the Palestine Popular Struggle Front and Majid Hassan, Secretary of the Al-Sa'iqa organisation in Lebanon on December 26, 1979. (Jamahiriyah News Agency (JANA), Tripoli, December 26, 1979. Cited in FBIS, ME, December 27, 1979, p. 12). All those organizations apparently welcomed the weakening of Al-Fath. They all supported Quadhdhafi's efforts to end Al-Fath domination in the PLO. Note the presence of the Syrian controlled Al-Sa'iqa representative.

15. *Filastin Al-Thawrah* (Beirut), December 11, 1979.

16. DPA, Cairo, December 11, 1979. Cited in FBIS, ME, December 12, 1979, p. A2.
17. Radio Damascus, DPA, December 21, 1979.
18. The National Front of Steadfastness and Confrontation Summit Resolutions, Tripoli Radio, April 15, 1980.
19. *ibid.,* ibid.
20. King Hassan of Morocco interview to Radio Monte Carlo, April 28, 1980.
21. *Al-Qabas* (Kuwait), December 30, 1979.
22. *Pravda,* November 15, 1979.
23. A. Bovin, *Izvestia,* November 17, 1979.
24. *ibid.,* ibid.
25. *Pravda,* Jnaury 30, 1980.
26. TASS in English, May 15, 1980. Cited in FBIS, USSR, May 16, 1980, p. BB11.
27. "Oil and Turmoil: Western Choices in the Middle East. The Atlantic Council's Special Working Group on the Middle East", *The Atlantic Community,* (Washington, DC), Vol. 17, No. 3 (Fall 1979), pp. 293–294.
The report said, inter alia:
"27 American diplomacy should devote its best efforts to guiding the current negotiations with Egypt and Israel toward a real autonomy and self-determination for the Palestinians in the West Bank and Gaza.
"29 . . . The question of the Arab Palestinians – full autonomy, a homeland, participation in the determination of their future, national self-determinations, whatever one calls it – remains at the heart of the Arab-Israeli conflict. The United States, having involved itself to the hilt in the Camp David formula, should be prepared to face the Palestine question frankly and courageously, especially if the negotiations between Egypt and Israel fail, and indeed even if they succeed. On the level of procedure, the eventual participation of Jordan and of some representative Palestinians, as proposed in the Camp David formula, will be needed, and the re-negotiation of that formula with their agreement may be necessary. On the level of substance, we do not see any solution possible unless the negotiators take up the hard questions of Palestinian self-determination together with those relating to borders and security arrangements, aiming at an eventual total package that can reconcile Palestinian rights to self-government with Israel's right to security. Only in this context will it be possible to find, in the end, a compromise settlement for East Jerusalem. And only in this context can there be real and stable peace in the Middle East.
"30. We do not think that this is the moment to bring the PLO into active negotiations. The mutual non-recognition between the PLO and Israel, however, should not rule out informal contacts between the United States and the PLO with the purpose of ascertaining the latter's views and modifying them."
(*ibid.,* pp. 302–303).
28. *Baltimore Sun,* February 26, 1980.
29. UN Security Council resolution 465 of March 1, 1980. *N.Y. Times,* March 5, 1980.
30. *ibid.,* ibid.
31. *Economist* (London), March 8, 1980, p. 45.
32. Marian Hank interviewing Ambassador Donald McHenry, *Middle East International* (Lonodn), June 6, 1980.
33. Cited from *Los Angeles Times,* March 5, 1980.
34. At the beginning of 1980, the only PLO office in Europe with a diplomatic status was in Malta, as a result of Libyan pressure. PLO information offices had been opened in

Paris, Madrid, in Brussels and PLO representatives in the framework of Arab League offices in Rome and London. PLO local information offices had been opened in Bonn and Stockholm. PLO representatives at the UN offices in Geneva and Vienna (in accordance with the UN resolution 3237 of 1974). The latter was recognized on March 13, 1980, as a PLO official representative in all contacts with Austrian authorities.

35.   Kuwait Domestic Service, March 3, 1980. Cited in FBIS, ME, March 4, 1980, pp. C3–C5.

36.   Amman Domestic Service, March 10, 1980. Cited in FBIS, ME, March 11, 1980, pp. F4–F7.

37.   Voice of Palestine, March 4, 1980. Cited in FBIS, ME, March 5, 1980, p. A2.

38.   Official English text. AP from Venice, June 13, 1980.

39.   Voice of Palestine, June 16, 1980. Cited in FBIS, ME, June 16, 1980, pp. A3–A5.

40.   "Why the Kurds are friendless," *The Guardian Weekly* (London), October 28, 1979, p. 1.

41.   *Al-Liwa* (Lebanon), June 2, 1980.

42.   Interviews to *Shu'un Filastiniyya* (Beirut), January 1980, and to *Al-Majala* (London). Transmitted by Voice of Palestine (Beirut), July 1, 1980.

43.   "Should the Palestinians Change Their Charter?", *The Middle East* (London), January, 1980, pp. 16–24.

Appendix one

PRINCIPAL PALESTINIAN ORGANIZATIONS AND INSTITUTIONS

● PALESTINE LIBERATION ORGANIZATION (PLO)

Umbrella organization with a claimed role of Palestinian national leadership. Recognized by the Arab summit conference in Rabat on October 1974 as the sole legitimate representative of the Palestinian people.

PLO-Structured Institutions

Palestine National Council (PNC) – (Al-Majlis Al-Watani Al-Falastini). Supreme PLO authority. Includes members of organizations, representatives of PLO bodies of "popular organizations" (e.g. Trade Unions, Women's and Students' Associations), representatives of the West Bank and Gaza, Jordan, Persian Gulf states and other countries.

President: Khalid Al-Fahum

Executive Committee – (Al-Lajna Al-Tanfidhyya), structured as a PLO-Government elect by the PNC. Includes about 15 members, representatives of organizations and independents.

Chairman: Yasir Arafat.

Palestine Central Council (PCC) - (Al-Majlis Al Markazi), elected by the PNC. Serves as a link between it and Executive Committee. Convenes between the PNC sessions and its duty is to control the implementation of decisions taken by the PNC and Executive Committee. In practice, it is a weak body.

President: Kahlid Al Fahum.

Palestine Liberation Army (PLA) – established as the military arm of the PLO. PLA units are stationed in Arab states, kept by them financially, and act in coordination with these states. Theoretically, PLA units are subordinated to the PLO Executive Committee, but in practice they are subordinated to the military commands of the countries in which they are stationed. Brigades: Hittin (attached to the Syrian Army), Ein Jaloud (was with the Egyptian army), Qadisiya (Iraqi army).

Militia – The various Palestinian organizations have militia units. Theoretically they are under the command of the PLO Executive Committee Chairman (Arafat), but in practice, they belong to different organizations.

Palestine National Fund – responsible for PLO budget and its implementation. Receives Arab subsidies from Arab governments. However, some Arab states prefer to finance various organizations directly, enabling them to exercise a certain measure of control over them.

Head: Walid Al-Qamhawi.

Center for Palestinian Planning – functions – political and military research and advisory status, responsible for coordination between various organizations, and for links in the West Bank and Gaza, and for education of Palestinian youth in Lebanon.

PLO Structure

Palestine National Council
Palestine Central Council
Executive Committee

Independent

Organizations

Palestinian Red Crescent

Center for Palestinian Planning

Center for Palestinian studies

Central Council for Occupied Homeland

Department of Occupied Homeland

Department of National (Arab) and International Relations

Department of Social Affairs

Department of Higher Education

Central Council for Education and Culture

Department of Information and Culture

Voice of Palestine Broadcasts

Palestine Liberation Army (PLA)

United Command: Supreme Military Council

Palestine National Fund (Financial Department)

Political Department

Military Department

Department for Administrative Affairs, Secretary of Executive Committee

PLO offices in Arab and other countries

Popular Organizations Department

Palestine General Unions of students, workers, women, writers, lawyers, doctors, youth, journalists

PFLP Mergers and Splits

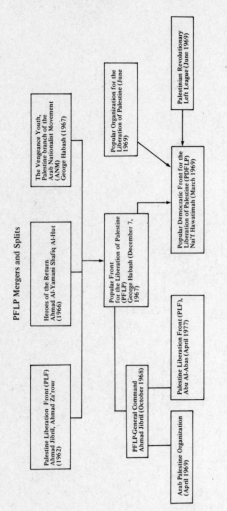

In parenthesis: Date of foundation, merger or split

Center for Palestinian Studies — issues publications on the Palestinian problem and Arab-Israeli conflict. Has a documentation center, archives and library.

Popular Organizations — organizations of Palestinian students, women workers, lawyers, teachers, etc. Activated by the PLO and used by it, mainly for publicity and fund-raising.

PLO Offices — The PLO maintains offices in a great number of countries. Some are officially recognized, others are unofficial, acting as Information Centers in the Arab League offices in the host country. The PLO has an interest in them as their mere existence implies recognition as representing Palestinians. The offices' activities include ties with local governemnts, resident Palestinians and friendly organizations. Also supplies informations and attempts to create a avorable public opinion for the PLO.

PALESTINIAN ORGANIZATIONS

Most of them were established in the 1960's and since then underwent many transformations and splits as a result of ideological and personal differences, or because particular Arab states wish to have their "own" organizations or to control existing ones. Some organizations completely disappeared, some continue as small groups having only a few members and existing only on paper.

Some organizations appeared for a limited period only (or from time to time), serving as a cover for other organizations, with the aim of conducting terrorist or other activities for which the parent organizations preferred not to be responsible.

"The Palestine National Liberation Movement" — Fath — Largest organization, began activities in 1965, dominates the PLO and its members and holds the most important positions in it. Nationalist, pragmatic, without ideological commitments, tries to maintain good relations with all Arab states — radical and conservative, and to receive aid from all of them. Has three regular brigades (Yarmuq, Karami, Qastel) and non-regular military forces.

Leader: Yasir Arafat. No. of members: 8,000

"Vanguards of the Popular Liberation War" — Al-Sa'iqa — Established by Syria's Ba'th regime in 1968 and acts in accordance with its instructions, following the Syrian line. Pan-Arab, wants a Palestinian state as a part of a united Arab world under Syria's leadership. Its leader, Zuhayr Muhsin (assassinated on July 25, 1979 in Cannes, France), denied the very existence of a separate Palestinian people. Al-Sa'iqa is the second to Fath in size and in organization in the PLO.

"Popular Front for the Liberation of Palestine" (PFLP) — The principal and the most powerful organization in the "Rejection Front", established late in 1966; leftist, Marxist, but closer to the "new left" and anarchist organizations than to communist parties. In accordance with its ideology which calls for world wide revolutions, it established close ties with a number of other terroris organizations, as the Japanese "Red Army", the German Bader-Meinhoff group the Irish Republican Army, etc. The ties expressed themselves in training mem bers of such organizations in PFLP bases in Lebanon, Iraq and in the People' Democratic Republic of Yemen, in supplies of arms and equipment. The PFL also used members of such organizations to conduct for it terror activities.

Since 1974 there appeared differing positions within the PFLP concernin the continuation of "foreign operations" such as hijackings of planes or attack on Israeli and Jewish institutions in Europe. The PFLP General Secretary Georg Habash objected to these activities and ordered a stop to them. He said that th movement's aim of bringing the Palestinian problem before world public opinio had been achieved and that the continuation of the struggle should be concen trated in Israel. The PFLP rejects any political settlement of the Arab-Israel conflict.

Leader: George Habash.

Top leadership includes Ahmad Yamani, Tayasir Qub'a.

No. of members, excluding militia — 800.

PFLP — Wadi' Haddad Group — The PFLP 1974 decision to stop terro activities outside the Middle East was sharply opposed by Dr. Wadi' Haddad whc headed PFLP foreign operations. After the PFLP decision in mid-1975 to dis solve his staff, he decided to continue with these activities independently anc conducted a number of terrorist acts, including the kidnapping of OPEC minister in Vienna on October 1975, an attempt to hit an "El Al" plane in Nairob (January 1976), the hijacking of an "Air France" plane to Entebbe (June 1976) the attack on "El Al" passengers in Istanbul (August 1976), and the hijacking o a "Lufthansa" plane to Mogadishu (October 1977). Dr. Haddad was reported tc be ill and dying on April 1978 as a result of his being poisoned by the Iraq Intelligence. Since then the Haddad group has seemed to return to the PFLP.

"Popular Democratic Front for the Liberation of Palestine" (PDFLP) – Split from the PFLP in early 1969. Marxist, has close ties with the USSR. Fol lowed the political line of Arafat but since civil war in Lebanon tends to more radicalization. Its relative pragmatism often made it the first to adopt positions that were later accepted by other organizations. The PDFLP was the first tc adopt the policy of stages (that was later adopted by the PLO) — and accepted a Palestinian National Authority in the West Bank and Gaza Strip as a part of a political settlement and as a step to a Palestinian state in all of Palestine. It was the first to use the slogan of a "secular democratic state" and to establish ties with Israeli leftist groups such as "Matzpen". While the PDFLP is, in principle ready to enter the political process, it appears to be against this, since it would mean a strengthening of US positions and of Arab conservatives. In this way it maneuvers between Arafat and the "Rejection Front", its position being some where in the middle.

The PDFLP objected in principle to terror activities abroad, concentrating them instead in the Israel-Lebanon border and in Israel. Among these acts were the murder of over twenty schoolchildren in Ma'alot (May 15, 1974), and of civilians in Beit Shean (November 19, 1974).

Leader: Na'if Hawatimah.

Top leadership includes Yasir Abd Rabu', Salah Rafat.

No. of members — 600.

"PFLP-General Command" — Split from the PFLP in 1968, less ideological, has a higher military and technical level, was Syrian-controlled for a long time.

With the outbreak of the civil war in Lebanon, the PFLP-GC took the side of the leftists against the Christians. The arrival of Syrian forces in Lebanon and their anti-left and anti-PLO position created sharp differences of opinion within the Front which, because of its traditional ties with Syria, tried, on the one hand, to avoid fighting Syrian forces, but on the other hand was committed to fight with the left and the PLO against the Christians. The PFLP-GC leftists and pro-Iraqis, headed by Mahmoud Zeidan (Abu Al-Abas) demanded opposition to Syrian forces and a continuation of the alliance with other "Rejection Front" organizations, while Ahmad Jibril refused to fight the Syrians.

On April 1977, the Front split into two separate organizations:

PFLP-GC pro-Syrian.

Leader: Ahmad Jibril.

Top members include Talal Naji.

No. of members — 200.

Palestine Liberation Front (PLF) — pro-Iraqi, supported by Iraq and having close ties with Libya.

Leader: Mahmoud Zeidan (Abu Al-Abbas).

No. of members — 100.

Terror activities of the PFLP-GC included the attack on a school bus of children from Avivim, a Jewish settlement on the Lebanese border, the explosion of an airborne "Swissair" plane, and the attacks on Kiryat Shmone (April 1974) and Shamir (June 1974).

Arab Liberation Front (ALF) — Established by Iraqi Ba'th regime on April 1969 as a counter-weight to Syrian-controlled Al-Sa'iqa. Most of its members are non-Palestinians (Iraqi, Lebanese, Jordanian).

Leader: Abd Al-Rahim Ahmad. Former leader: Abd Al-Wahhab Al-Kayyali.

No. of members — 300 (depended on Iraq will).

Claimed responsibility for the attack on Misgav Am, a Kibbutz on the Lebanese border (April 7, 1980)

The Front of Palestinian Popular Struggle — Small organization, established in 1967 in the West Bank. In July 1971 merged with Fath. The merger was however, not complete. Joined the "Rejection Front", was supported primarily by Iraq, also by Libya.

Leader: Samir Ghoshe.

Top members included Bahjat Abu G'harbayya.

No. of members — 80

Palestine National Front (PNF) — Established in the West Bank in 1973 a a political coalition in which the Communist Party played a major role. PNF members participated in the April 1976 West Bank municipal elections and suc ceeded in getting seats in some municipal councils. PNF leaders banished by Israel were given leading positions in the PLO, to demonstrate PLO ties with the West Bank population. For example, the PLO Executive Committee elected in March 1977 included three PNF leaders that were expelled by Israel (Abd Al Muhsin Abu-Maizer, PLO spokesman, Abd Al-Jawad Salah, and Walid Al-Qam hawi).

Fath Baghdad based dissidents, headed by Abu Nidhal — Sabri Al-Bana (Abu Nidhal) was head of Fath Baghdad office. In 1974, he declared himself independent and was backed by Iraq. Acted against Syria and Fath. Not a part of the PLO.

● **TERRORIST COVER ORGANIZATIONS**

Black September. Named after the September 1970 civil war in Jordan. A cover for Al Fath. Conducted a great number of terror activities for which Fath did not wish to be responsible.

Black June. Named after the entry of Syrian troops into Lebanon in June 1976. Activated by Iraq and Abu Nidha'l group. Attacked Syrian and othe Arab targets, such as attempts to hit the Semiramis and Intercontinental hotels in Damascus and Amman, the Syrian Embassies in Italy and Pakistan (September— November 1976).

Eagles of the Palestinian Revolution. Appeared on the scene from time to time as a cover for Al-Sa'iqa. Among their activities — the attack on the Egyptian Embassy in Ankara in July 1979.

Appendix two

DOCUMENTS

1. THE PALESTINIAN NATIONAL COVENANT

The full text of the Palestinian National Covenant as adopted by the Palestinian National Assembly (PNA) in 1968 and that of the original Covenant of 1964 have been arranged for easy comparisons. The articles are given as numbered in the new version. The sequence of the 1964 articles has been re-arranged, disregarding their former numerical order, so as to place corresponding articles next to each other.

The texts are from *Middle East Record*, Volume four, 1968, edited by Daniel Dishon, (Jerusalem, Israel Universities Press for the Shiloah Center, Tel-Aviv University, 1973), pp. 432–436.

The 1968 Covenant	*The 1964 Covenant*
This Covenant will be called The Palestinian National Covenant (*al-mithaq al-watani al-filastini*).	The Palestinian National Covenant (*al-mithaq al-qawmi al-filastini*)
Article 1: Palestine is the homeland of the Palestinian Arab people and an integral part of the great Arab homeland, and the people of Palestine is a part of the Arab nation.	Palestine is an Arab homeland bound by strong ties to the rest of the Arab countries, which together form the great Arab homeland.
Article 2: Palestine with its boundaries that existed at the time of the British mandate is an integral regional unit.	[No change]
Article 3: The Palestinian Arab people possesses the legal right to its homeland, and when the liberation of its homeland is completed it will exercise self-determination solely according to its own will and choice.	The Palestinian Arab people possesses the legal right to its homeland and it is an inseparable part of the Arab nation and shares its expectations and sufferings and its struggle for liberty, sovereignty, progress and unity.
Article 4: The Palestinian personality is an innate, persistent characteristic that does not disappear, and it is transferred from fathers to sons. The Zionist occupation, and the dispersal of the Palestinian Arab people as a result of the disasters which came over it, do not deprive it of its Palestinian personality and affiliation and do not nullify them.	The Palestinian personality is an innate, persistent characteristic that does not disappear, and it is transferred from father to sons.
Article 5: The Palestinians are the Arab citizens who were living permanently in Palestine until 1947, whether they were expelled from there or remained. Whoever is born to a Palestinian Arab father after this date, within Palestine or outside it, is a Palestinian.	The Palestinians are the Arab citizens who were living permanently in Palestine until 1947, whether they were expelled from there or remained. Whoever is born to a Palestinian father after this date, within Palestine or outside it, is a Palestinian.
Article 6: Jews who were living permanently in Palestine until the beginning of the Zionist invasion will be considered Palestinians.	Jews who are of Palestinian origin will be considered Palestinians if they will undertake to live loyally and peacefully in Palestine.
Article 7: The Palestinian affiliation and	The upbringing of the [present] Palestinian

the material, spiritual and historical tie with Palestine are permanent realities. The upbringing of the Palestinian individual in an Arab and revolutionary fashion, the undertaking of all means of forging consciousness and training the Palestinian, in order to acquaint him profoundly with his homeland, spiritually and materially, and preparing him for the conflict and the armed struggle, as well as for the sacrifice of his property and his life to restore his homeland, until the liberation – all this is a national duty.

generation in an Arab national fashion, the undertaking of all means of forging consciousness and training [the Palestinian generation]; in order to acquaint it profoundly with its homeland, [and to create] a deep spiritual acquaintance with it which will link [this generation] to it strongly and forever – all this is a national duty.

Article 8: The phase in which the people of Palestine is living is that of national (*watani*) struggle for the liberation of Palestine. Therefore, the contradictions among the Palestinian national forces are of secondary order which must be suspended in the interest of the fundamental contradiction between Zionism and colonialism on the one side and the Palestinian Arab people on the other. On this basis, the Palestinian masses, whether in the homeland or in places of exile (*mahajir*) organizations and individuals, comprise one national front which acts to restore Palestine and liberate it through armed struggle.

The ideological schools, whether they be political, social or economical will not divert the Palestinians from their primary task of liberating their homeland. All Palestinians present one national front and they will work for the liberation of their homeland with all their feelings and all their mental and material abilities.

Article 9: Armed struggle is the only way to liberate Palestine and is therefore a strategy and not tactics. The Palestinian Arab people affirms its absolute resolution and abiding determination to pursue the armed struggle and to march forward towards the armed popular revolution, to liberate its homeland and return to it [to maintain] its right to a natural life in it, and to exercise its right of self-determination in it and sovereignty over it.

[No corresponding article]

Article 10: Fida'iyyun action forms the nucleus of the popular Palestinian war of liberation. This demands its promotion, extension and protection, and the mobilization of all the masses and scientific capacities of the Palestinians, their organization and involvement in the armed Palestinian revolution and cohesion in the national (*watani*) struggle among the various groups of the people of Palestine, and between them and the Arab masses, to guarantee the continuation of the revolution, its advancement and victory.

[No corresponding article]

Article 11: The Palestinians will have three mottoes: national (*wataniyya*) unity; national (*qawmiyya*) mobilization and liberation.

The Palestinians will have three mottoes: national (*wataniyya*) unity; national (*qawmiyya*) mobilization and liberation. After the liberation of the homeland is accomplished the Palestinian people will choose for its way of life any political, economical and social systems it wishes.

Article 12: The Palestinian Arab people believes in Arab unity. In order to fulfill its role in realizing this, it must preserve, in this phase of its national (*watani*) struggle, its Palestinian personality and the constituents thereof, increase consciousness of its existence and resist any plan that tends to disintegrate or weaken it.

The Palestinian people believes in Arab unity. In order to fulfill its role in realizing this, it must preserve in this phase of its struggle, its Palestinian personality and the constituents thereof, increase consciousness of its existence and resist any plan that tends to disintegrate or weaken it.

Article 13: Arab unity and the liberation of Palestine are two complementary aims. Each one paves the way for realization of the other. Arab unity leads to the liberation of Palestine, and the liberation of Palestine leads to Arab unity. Working for both goes hand in hand.

[No change]

Article 14: The destiny of the Arab nation, indeed the very Arab existence, depends upon the destiny of the Palestine issue. The endeavour and effort of the Arab nation to liberate Palestine follows from this connection. The people of Palestine assumes its vanguard role in realizing this sacred national (*qawmi*) aim.

[No change]

Article 15: The liberation of Palestine, from an Arab viewpoint, is a national (*qawmi*) duty to repulse the Zionist, Imperialist invasion from the great Arab homeland and to purge the Zionist presence from Palestine. Its full responsibility falls upon the Arab nation, peoples and governments, with the Palestinian Arab people at their head. For this purpose, the Arab nation must mobilize all its military, human, material and spiritual capacities to participate actively with the people of Palestine in the liberation of Palestine. They must especially in the present stage of armed Palestinian revolution, grant and offer the people of Palestine all possible help and every material and human support, and afford it every sure means and opportunity enabling it to continue to assume its vanguard role in pursuing its armed revolution until the liberation of its homeland.

The liberation of Palestine, from an Arab viewpoint, is a national (*qawmi*) duty. Its full responsibilities fall upon the Arab nation, peoples and governments, with the Palestinian Arab people at their head.

For this purpose, the Arab nation must mobilize all its military, material and spiritual capacities for the sake of the liberation of Palestine. They must grant and offer the people of Palestine all possible help and every material and human support, and afford it every sure means and opportunity enabling it to continue to assume its role.

Article 16: The liberation of Palestine, from a spiritual viewpoint, will prepare an atmosphere of tranquility and peace for the Holy Land in the shade of which all the Holy Places will be safeguarded, and freedom of worship and visitation to all will be guaranteed, without distinction or discrimination of race, colour, language or religion. For this reason, the people of Palestine looks to the support of all the spiritual forces in the world.

[No change]

Article 17: The liberation of Palestine from a human viewpoint, will restore to the Palestinian man his dignity, glory and freedom. For this, the Palestinian Arab people looks to the support of those in the world who believe in the dignity and freedom of man.

[No corresponding article]

Article 18: The liberation of Palestine, from an international viewpoint is a defensive act necessitated by the requirements of self-defence. For this reason the Arab people of Palestine, desiring to befriend all peoples, looks to the support of the states which love freedom, justice and peace in restoring the legal situation to Palestine, establishing security and peace in its territory, and enabling its people to exercise national (*wataniyya*) sovereignty and national (*qawmiyya*) freedom.

The liberation of Palestine, from an international viewpoint, is a defensive act necessitated by the requirements of self-defence as laid down in the UN Charter. For this reason the people of Palestine, desiring to befriend all peoples, looks to the support of the states which love freedom, justice and peace in restoring the legal situation to Palestine, establishing security and peace in its territory and enabling its people to exercise national (*wataniyya*) sovereignty and national (*qawmiyya*) freedom.

[No change]

Article 19: The partitioning of Palestine in 1947 and the establishment of Israel is fundamentally null and void, whatever time has elapsed, because it was contrary to the wish of the people of Palestine and its natural right to its homeland, and contradicts the principles embodied in the Charter of the UN, the first of which is the right of self-determination.

Article 20: The Balfour Declaration, the Mandate document, and what has been based upon them are considered null and void. The claim of a historical or spiritual tie between Jews and Palestine does not tally with historical realities nor with the constituents of statehood in their true sense. Judaism, in its character as a religion of revelation, is not a nationality with an independent existence. Likewise, the Jews are not one people with an independent personality. They are rather citizens of the states to which they belong.

[No change]

Article 21: The Palestinian Arab people, in expressing itself through the armed Palestinian revolution, rejects every solution that is a substitute for a complete liberation of Palestine, and rejects all plans that aim at the settlement of the Palestine issue or its internationalization.

[No corresponding article]

Article 22: Zionism is a political movement organically related to world Imperialism and hostile to all movements of liberation and progress in the world. It is a racist and fanatical movement in its formation; aggressive, expansionist and colonialist in its aims; and fascist and Nazi in its means. Israel is the tool of the Zionist movement and a human and geographical base for world Imperialism. It is a concentration and jumping-off point for Imperialism in the heart of the Arab homeland, to strike at the hopes of the Arab nation for liberation, unity and progress.

Zionism is an Imperialist movement in its development; aggressive [and] expansionist in its aims; racist and fanatical in its formation; and fascist in its means. Israel, which is the front line of this destructive movement and a stanchion of Imperialism, is an endless source of trouble and annoyance for the ME and the international community. Therefore, the Palestinian people deserves the help of the international community and its support.

Article 23: The demands of security and peace and the requirements of truth and justice oblige all states that preserve friendly relations among peoples and maintain the loyalty of citizens to their homelands to consider Zionism an illegitimate movement and to prohibit its existence and activity.

[No change]

Article 24: The Palestinian Arab people believes in the principles of justice, freedom, sovereignty, self-determination, human dignity and the right of peoples to exercise them.

The Palestinian Arab people believes in the principles of justice, freedom, sovereignty, self-determination, human dignity and the right of peoples to exercise them, and it will support all the international efforts that aim to establish peace on the basis of law and free international co-operation.

Article 25: To realize the aims of this covenant and its principles the Palestine Liberation Organization will undertake its full role in liberating Palestine.

To realize the aims of this covenant and its principles the Palestine Liberation Organization will undertake its full role in the liberating of Palestine in accordance with the political constitution of this organization.

Article 26: The Palestine Liberation Organization, which represents the forces of the Palestinian revolution, is responsible for the movement of the Palestinian Arab people in its struggle to restore its homeland, liberate it, return to it and exercise the right of self-determination in it. This responsibility extends to all military, political and financial matters, and all else that the Palestine issue requires in the Arab and international spheres.

The Palestine Liberation Organization is responsible for the movement of the Palestinian people in its struggle to restore its homeland. This responsibility extends to all matters of liberation and to organizational, political and financial matters, and all else that the Palestine issue requires in the Arab and international spheres.

Article 27: The Palestine Liberation Organi-

The Palestine Liberation Organization will

zation will co-operate with all Arab states, each according to its capacities, and will maintain neutrality in their mutual relations in the light of and on the basis of the requirements of the battle of liberation and will not interfere in the internal affairs of any Arab state.

Article 28: The Palestinian Arab people insists upon the originality and independence of its national (*wataniyya*) revolution and rejects every manner of interference, guardianship and subordination.

Article 29: The Palestinian Arab people possesses the prior and original right in liberating and restoring its homeland and will define its position with reference to all states and powers on the basis of their positions with reference to the issue [of Palestine] and the extent of their support for [the Palestinian Arab people] in its revolution to realize its aims.

Article 30: The fighters and bearers of arms in the battle of liberation are the nucleus of the popular army, which will be the protecting arm of the gains of the Palestinian Arab people.

Article 31: This organization shall have a flag, oath and anthem, all of which will be determined in accordance with a special system.

Article 32: To this covenant is attached a law known as the fundamental law of the Palestine Liberation Organization, in which is determined the manner of the organization's formation, its committees, institutions, the special functions of every one of them and all the requisite duties associated with them in accordance with this covenant.

[No corresponding article]

[No corresponding article]

---

co-operate with all Arab states, each according to its capacities and will not interfere in the internal affairs of any Arab state.

[No corresponding article]

[No correpsonding article]

[No corresponding article]

[No change]

[No change]

The Palestinian people believes in peaceful co-existence on the basis of legitimate existence as there cannot be any co-existence with hostility and no peace with occupation and imperialism.

This organization has no regional sovereignty over the West Bank in the Hashimite Kingdom of Jordan nor over the Gaza Strip nor al-Hamma region. Its activity will be in the popular national (*qawmi*), organizational, political, and financial fields.

Article 33: This covenant cannot be amended except by a two-thirds majority of all the members of the National Assembly of the Palestine Liberation Organization in a special session called for this purpose.

[No change]

2. PLO-LEBANESE SECRET AGREEMENT, CAIRO, NOVEMBER 3, 1969
Al-Nahar, (Beirut), April 20, 1970.

On Monday, 3 November 1969, a Lebanese delegation headed by army Commander Gen. Emile al-Bustani and a Palestine Liberation Organization (PLO) delegation headed by PLO Chairman Yasir Arafat met in Cairo. The meeting was attended for the UAR by Foreign Minister Mahmud Riyad and War Minister Muhammad Fawzi.

On the basis of the principles of fraternity and common destiny, relations between Lebanon and the Palestinian revolution must always be characterized by confidence, frankness, and positive cooperation in the interests of Lebanon and the Palestinian revolution within the framework of Lebanon's sovereignty and safety.

The two delegations agreed on the following principles and measures:

Palestinian existence — It was agreed to reorganize Palestinian existence in Lebanon on the following bases:

1. The right of work, residence, and free movement of Palestinians residing in Lebanon.

2. Formation of local committees of Palestinians in the camps to look after the interests of Palestinian residents in these camps through cooperation with the local authorities and within the framework of Lebanon's sovereignty.

3. Establishment of Palestine Armed Struggle Command (PASC) posts within the camps to cooperate with the local committee to insure good relations. These posts will be responsible for organizing and specifying the existence of arms in the camps within the framework of Lebanon's security and the Palestinian revolution's interest.

4. Palestinians residing in Lebanon shall be allowed to participate in the revolution through the PASC within the principles of Lebanon's sovereignty and safety.

Fedayeen action — It was agreed to facilitate fedayeen action by:

1. Facilitating movement by specifying passage and reconnaissance points along the border.

2. Insuring passage to the Al-Urqub region.

3. PASC maintenance of the discipline of all members of the organizations so they will not interfere in Lebanese affairs.

4. Establishment of a joint disciplinary system between the PASC and the Lebanese Army.

5. Cessation of propaganda campaigns by the two sides.

6. A census of armed struggle elements in Lebanon through the organizations' leaders.

7. Appointment of PASC representatives to the Lebanese Army staff to help solve all urgent matters.

8. Study of suitable concentration points along the border which will be agreed on with the Lebanese Army staff.

9. Regulation of the entry, exit and movement of PASC elements.

10. Liquidation of (Jayrun) base.

11. Posts for medical treatment, evacuation and supply for fedayeen action specified by the Lebanese Army.

12. Release of detainees and confiscated arms.

13. Exercise of full powers and responsibilities in all Lebanese regions and under all circumstances by Lebanese civilian and military authorities.

14. The two delegations emphasize that Palestinian armed struggle is in the interest of Lebanon as well as of the Palestinian revolution and all Arabs.

15. This agreement shall remain top secret and shall be accessible only to the leaders.

The agreement was signed by Al-Bustani and Arafat.

3. "DEMOCRATIC PALESTINIAN STATE"

A. Proceedings of a Symposium of Representatives of Palestinian Organizations
Al Anwar, (Beirut), March 8 and 15, 1970 (Excerpts)

A representative of the Democratic Front (PDFLP):

" . . . the victory of the national Palestinian liberation movement and its success in liberating Palestine . . . cannot be carried out except within the framework of a federation of Arab countries: it can only be carried out after the elimination of the entity presently existing on Palestinian soil, since, as long as the Israeli entity exists, a progressive technological entity representing a cross-section of European culture forcibly planted in this area, it will be impossible to attain any democratic solution to the Palestinian question and to the matter of the Arab revolution in general.

"Co-existence with this entity is impossible . . . the uprooting of imperialistic influence in the Middle East means the uprooting of the Israeli entity. This is a matter on which no compromises can be reached . . . a Democratic state in Palestine cannot be established save through the Palestinian and Arab liberation movement . . . ."

Representative of the Arab Liberation Front (ALF):

"There exists no special, separate solution to the Palestine problem. The solution is to be found within the framework of the Arab Revolution . . .

"There is agreement between the factors of the resistance movement that the political translation of the idea of a Palestinian state means the elimination of the Zionist entity . . . not to establish a fifteenth [Arab] state which would deepen division [but] an alternative to the Zionist entity . . . democratic by necessity . . . In the unified Arab state, all minorities – ethnic or other – will have equal rights . . . .

"When the slogan of the Democratic Palestinian state was brought up, it was implied that it was intended to pacify progressive public opinion and the world leftist movements. However, the idea cannot be realized by unrealistic slogans . . ."

Shafiq Al Hut [PLO]:

". . . it is useless to talk of the slogan of a Democratic Palestinian state . . .

With regard to the humane attitude towards the Jews . . . such an attitude must be expressed . . . by telling the Jews that . . . you must return to your countries of origin to seek a different way of attaining a solution to the problem called the 'persecuted Jew' in the world. As Marx said, you have no alternative but to assimilate in your society . . .

Even if we would be interested, as a result of the situation, in a Democratic Palestinian, non-Arab, state, this would mean – let us speak openly – that we abolish our Arab identity. I say that in this matter we cannot negotiate . . . This land and those who dwell in it belong to a certain [Arab] environment, to a certain area to which we are connected by the ties of one nation and legacy, and one hope – unity, freedom and socialism.

. . . Eventually it will be an Arab state . . . Eventually the Democratic state will be submerged in human and cultural terms into the Arab sphere.

If the slogan of a Democratic State is only designed to reply to the contention that we aim to throw the Jews into the sea, then it is a successful slogan and an effective political and propaganda tool, but if we wish to see it as the final strategical aim . . . then I am convinced that it demands continued consideration . . . ."

Representative of Sa'iqa:

"It is not right to take away its Arab character from Palestine, as long as it exists within the heart of the Arab homeland. No force can deny the Arab character of Palestine . . ."

Shafiq Al-Hut:

"I do not believe that there exists a people by the name of the Jewish people ... Does an Islamic people, an Orthodox, Protestant or Buddhist people exist ... There is no Jewish people .... Do religious ties create people in the world ..."

Representative of Democratic Front:

"Regarding the question of the Jewish people – any group living together under certain circumstances creates, in time, something like a unit. That happened in America. Immigrants from all over the world were grouped together and over hundreds of years became a people."

Shafiq Al-Hut:

"At the expense of the Indians?"

Democratic Front:

"Obviously, and in order that we may not become like the Indians ... The process should be stopped by the victory of the Palestinian revolution."

Shafiq Al-Hut:

"When we speak of democracy, it must be clear that we do not mean the liberal democracy according to the one man–one vote system. Our intention is a popular democracy ...

... the idea [of a Democratic state] ... cannot be described without the following fundamentals:

– The hoped-for State in Palestine is from the historical point of view a part of the Arab East ...

– The state can only be created on the ruins of the Zionist entity and the destruction of the State of Israel;

– This aim will be attained by armed struggle directed at destroying this entity and all its establishment ...

It is according to this concept which is based on the above-mentioned fundamentals that we think that the true historical solution to the problem of the national liberation of Palestine will be founded.

B. "Al-Ahram" Article

Clovis Maqsud, "Democratic State of Palestine – initial notes on the plan debated by the Palestine National Council", *Al-Ahram*, (Cairo), September 14, 1969, (Excerpts).

The article is based on the 6th PNC session (Cairo, September 1–6, 1969) debates and resolutions.

The state of Palestine was the subject of a lengthy debate at the recent meetings of the Palestine National Council ...

.... the majority in the Palestinian resistance as well as the earnest and genuine leaders consider discussion of the democratic state of Palestine an opportunity to assert the main conviction of the Palestinian revolution. These convictions are:

1. Removal of the Zionist existence in Palestine does not necessarily mean removal of Jews from Palestine.

2. Admission of the right of the Jews to Palestinian citizenship and rejection of their right to a national existence in Palestine.

3. Being a Jew does not give one additional privileges and rights, as Zionism and the state of Israel want to insure. Being a Jew also does not prevent one from enjoying the right of equality and "belonging," as antisemitism and racism suggest.

4. It must be stressed that the Jews as a group have no historical, religious, or political

right to Palestine, but the democratic state of Palestine will guarantee the rights of the Jews as individual citizens of the state.

5. The Palestinian resistance cannot accept the existence of a Jewish "people." But naturally it will recognize the existence of Jews as part of the people of Palestine.

6. Zionism continues its efforts to make Israel synonymous with what it terms the Jewish nation. This means Israel should become a gathering place for all world Jewry. The Palestinian resistance cannot under any circumstances agree that Jews have a special right to Palestine. Jews do not have any special link to Palestine other than religion, similar to Christianity's link to Palestine. Since the religious link does not give Christians or Moslems any political rights or the right to exist as a distinct group, similarly this spiritual-religious link does not give the Jews any political right or the right to exist as a distinct group in Palestine. This means the basic right of political and national existence in Palestine belongs to the Palestinians alone. Thus the right of self-determination cannot be abandoned. The liberation movement expresses this right.

7. The Palestinian resistance is gaining complete legality, not through its opposition to the occupation, but through its opposition to the Zionist usurpation and the political entity emerging from it. Therefore, the Palestinian resistance is definitely confronting the Zionist entity as a whole, because it perpetuates the right of a Jewish "group" or the Jewish "people" to existence as a political ethnic [*qawmi*] entity at the expense of the Palestinian people's national and political right. Moreover, should the existence of a Jewish "people" be acknowledged, the land on which Israel intends [as published] to establish its state would become a secondary question. *The Palestinian resistance's opposition to Israel is actually opposition to the latter's right to existence and not the extent of this existence.*

While the Palestine resistance to Israel's existence is regarded as a fundamental change, this revolutionary step, arising from the humanitarian concept referred to above, will achieve the following objectives:

1. Escalation of clashes between the Palestine people and Israel will deter world Zionism from making Israel a local point for world Jews stripped of their citizenship. Zionist Jews will realize that they are immigrating to an entity with diminishing chances of survival and increasing chances of extinction, thanks to the resistance.

2. Escalation of the Palestine armed struggle, while abiding by humanitarian democratic concepts, will in turn promote doubt and opposition. Anti-Zionist Jews are already expressing this opposition . . .

By rejecting the principle of making religion a springboard for ethnic [*qawmi*] existence, the Palestine resistance emphasizes the modern trend toward nationalism . . . .

The democratic state of Palestine, as manifested in the Palestine resistance's fundamental conviction, is a secular and multisociety state.

The Palestinian resistance is not immediately expected to give more details about how it visualizes the structure of the state and society. A great many of these details will be defined by the battle and the circumstances in which liberation is achieved. The resistance cannot and must not give hints of details about the constitutional-administrative aspect during liberation. It is not part of the resistance's civilian-philosophical-ideological commitment to give such details before liberation . . . .

A final point on this subject is that the "democratic state of Palestine," which is presented as a substitute for the Zionist existence in our nation, must be linked to that general national entity the Arab nation. In other words, the democratic Palestine formula will be the Palestinian extension of the unified democratic Arab entity. This means that the Palestinian resistance must be the leading expression of the general Arab will for liberation, because Palestine is part of a homeland and not a homeland in itself.

Consequently, the Arab nation must also assume partial responsibility for finding formulae for solving postliberation problems. It must consider from now on the possibility of returning to the various Arab countries those Jews who originated there and who may wish to return, since their deportation — under reactionary regimes — was collusion with an imperialist plan. Thus, discussion of the establishment of the "democratic state of Palestine" was accompanied by a call to the Arab countries to return any Arab Jew wishing to return to his country of origin .... Therefore, it is important that the Arab countries should now proclaim their political commitments in principle by giving Arab Jews the right to return to the Arab countries they left.

It is obvious from all this that we completely reject the plan of a dual Palestinian state based on sociological structure, such as the proposed Arab-Jewish state. We reject it because the word "Arab" has a national meaning, while the word "Jew" has a religious one. Any confusion between the two could lead to recognition of a national existence, although on a more restricted scale than in Zionism's absolute meaning. Therefore, the Palestinian state will stress one citizenship — Palestinian citizenship. This citizenship will be given to Jews who decide to link their future to the state. But the Palestinian state will not acknowledge any additional rights to Jews which give usurpation any recognition, no matter how small.

Most Jews who emigrated after 1917 did so against their will. They were forced out by imperialism. Therefore, as a group they do not enjoy any rights which the Arabs must recognize. But Jews as individuals — regardless of the harm and injustice they did to the Palestinians — have the right to belong to the Palestinian Arab state, enjoy their rights, and perform the duties everyone will have. Although some of us may not like this open approach, it will be considered part of our contribution in laying civilized and humanitarian foundations for human relations. This will not be the first time the Arabs have contributed in this field.

4. PROPOSAL BY KING HUSAYN FOR "A UNITED ARAB KINGDOM", MARCH 15, 1972

Amman Radio Home Service, March 15, 1972.

I am pleased to meet you and to speak to you about the affairs of the current stage and their connection with the affairs and experiences of the past and the aspirations and hopes of the future. The establishment of the State of Jordan in 1921 was the most important stage of the Arab revolution following the exposure of the conspiracy against this revolution during the First World War. After the issue of the Balfour Declaration in 1917, the establishment of the state became even more significant because it spared the territory east of the Jordan river from that declaration and consequently from the Zionist plans at that time.

When the Arab armies entered Palestine in 1948, the Jordanian army was the smallest in terms of men and equipment. Yet, this army was able to save from Palestine that area which extends from Janin in the north to Hebron in the south and from the Jordan river in the east to a point not more than 15 km from the coast in the west. It was also able to save the entire Holy City of Jerusalem and other areas outside the city walls — those areas north, south and east of the walls which later became known as Arab Jerusalem. That area which later became known as the West Bank was all that was left for the Arabs from Palestine, in addition to that narrow strip which later became known as the Gaza Strip.

After a short period of temporary administration in the West Bank, a group of leaders, notables and elders representing Palestinian Arabs who had emigrated from the occupied territories, considered joining the East Bank a patriotic and nationalist demand and a guarantee against Israeli dangers. They held two great historic meetings. The first was in Jericho on 1 December 1948 and the second in Nablus on 28 December 1948. These meetings were attended by the representatives of all the people — leaders, thinkers, youth, the aged, workers and farmers — and their organisations.

Those present adopted resolutions calling on the late King Abdullah Bin al-Husein to take immediate steps to unify and merge the two banks in a single state under his leadership. The old king responded to the nation's call and ordered that constitutional and practical measures be taken to achieve that important patriotic and nationalist demand. The measures included holding elections to select the legitimate representatives of the West Bank people in the Chamber of Deputies.

On 24 April 1950, the new Jordanian National Assembly — with its two chambers, deputies and senators — representing the two banks held an historic meeting which marked the first real step in modern Arab history towards Arab unity, which the revolution has advocated since its inception. The meeting announced the unity and merger of the two banks in a single independent Arab state, a parliamentary monarchy known as the Hashemite Kingdom of Jordan.

The ship of unity sailed in seas which were not all calm and easy. There were many currents secretly manipulated by foreign hands and quarters. They tried to cause storms around the ship to push it gradually towards the rocks. But the vigilance of the people in the two banks of the country, their faith in the unity of their soil and in their sons and their understanding of the real danger to them which lurks across the border were a great guarantee for the safety of the trip and saved the ship from the evils harboured against it.

The primary fact the unity of the two banks represented day after day has been that the people in both banks are one and not two peoples. This fact was manifested for the first time in the reunion of the sons of the East Bank, with their emigrant brothers, the sons of the Palestine areas occupied in 1948. It was manifested when the former shared with the latter food and shelter and the sweetness and bitterness of life. This fact became more salient and took deeper roots with every step the state took.

The unity of blood and destiny reached its greatest significance in 1967 when the sons of the two banks stood together on the West Bank as they have been doing for 20 years and jointly sacrificed their blood on its pure soil. But the struggle was too great for them and its conditions and complexities were too much for their valour. The catastrophe occurred and what happened did happen.

In the sea of suffering the June catastrophe left behind, the objectives of the Jordanian State in the post war era have been summarised as (1) valiant steadfastness in the face of the unabating and unending aggressions against the East Bank and (2) confident resolve to liberate the land, the people and the brothers in the West Bank. All the efforts were directed towards these two objectives in an atmosphere of reassurance about the Arab States' support for Jordan in its ordeal and of unlimited confidence that the unity of all Arab destiny has become a concrete fact to the entire Arab nation and unshaken by regional interests no matter how great and cannot be harmed by plans and intentions, no matter what these advocate or how they are disguised.

A New Catastrophe

But suddenly Jordan found itself face to face with a new catastrophe whose inevitable result, if it had been destined to come true, would have been the loss of the East Bank and the establishment of the situation needed to liquidate the Palestine issue once and for all on the ruins of the East Bank. The driving forces of the catastrophe had enlisted numerous elements to serve their aims. Numerous other elements and quarters fell into the trap of these forces. Some of the former and the latter of these elements had assumed Palestinian identity as bearers of the holy cause. They played their role under the guise and cover of that name. Many of the paradoxes and conflicting currents in the world found their way among these elements. Many international contradictions and various world disputes penetrated them.

Naturally Jordan had to stand up and deal with the imminent catastrophe. This it did by taking a stand in which that unique mixture of its sons, the emigrants and the supporters, participated equally. The dissension was crushed on the solid rock of national unity. The dissension ceased to exist thanks to the enlightenment of the new man who had been born on that distant day in 1950 and grew up on the challenges which the ordeals have been posing for the past 20 years.

Throughout all this, since the June 1967 war and perhaps even before then, the Jordanian leaders have been thinking and planning for the future of the state. The leaders have based this thinking on their faith in Jordan's Arab mission, which stems from the mission of the great Arab revolution and on their faith in the man of the two banks of the river and in his ability to carry out his role in serving and achieving the aims of this mission. The Palestine issue was viewed from all the aspects of the entire Arab-Zionist conflict. Palestine was the first objective of the Zionist plans. The people in Palestine were the first prey and victim of these plans. The next were the people of the two dear banks.

Even if the expansionist ambitions had a limit, it would be in the interest of Zionism to keep the Arab world weak with its ranks scattered to enable Zionism to keep its gains forever. Since the opposing camp stands as one force and bloc as a whole, all the Arabs should stand united with closed ranks in the opposite camp. Moreover, unity in itself is insufficient unless it includes a true concept of the requirements of sound civilisation and modern progress.

Jordan understood the magnitude of the catastrophe which had befallen the Palestinian people. When the Zionist plot dispersed them, the sons of this people could not find in any country, Arab or non-Arab, the honourable and dignified life found by those who came to Jordan for shelter in 1948 and afterwards. Under the unity of the two banks in Jordan, the real Palestinian regrouping, the vast majority of the people, came to live on the two banks of the immortal river. The Palestinian found the sound framework within which he could work and move and found the real springboard for the desire of liberation and for the great hopes.

The Palestinian people existed for hundreds of years before 1948. The Palestinian people continued to exist after 1948. But the forces and currents behind the conditions which had started to prevail in the Arab world began overriding and ignoring these facts in view of the nation's confused situation and dismemberment from which it has been suffering for years. The pressure and eruption of these fabricated conditions intensified through the conferences, campaigns and plans we have been hearing of and witnessing. It was as if it was desired that the Palestinian should cut off his domestic and national links and place himself in a small bottle which could be easily smashed at any time. It was as if a new plan was being designed against that people, or rather was a move in the long chain of plots against the Palestinian people and the entire Arab nation. This suspicious move is not confined to the Palestinian minority outside the two banks but is aimed at the majority here. It desires to push the people in the West Bank into a separation from everything with which they are connected and from everything around them. If certain powers who are encouraging and strengthening these trends do not conceal their desire to rid themselves of the responsibilities for the Palestinian issue and people, the glitter of this situation, no matter how attractive to some, should not blind us to the danger that the Palestinian people may end up in a position in which they will once again be an easy and isolated prey to Israel and its insatiable ambitions. That is why this move is trying to portray the Jordanian regime as coveting booty and gain. That is why it is trying to penetrate the national unity to weaken it and cast doubt on it.

The Arab World

The first inevitable result of all the conditions prevailing in the Arab world – the dispersed ranks, scattered efforts, non-existent co-ordination, rivalry in establishing axes and camps, abandonment of the essence of the issue and its prerequisites, paying lip service to the issue once and exploiting it several times, the abandonment of real work for liberation and the devotion of efforts to domination and achievement of power – has been the continued Israeli occupation of the West Bank of Jordan and other dear Arab territories. The second inevitable result has been a further intensification of the Palestinian people's suffering. It has also been pushing the Palestinians into more confusion, bewilderment and ruin which is on the point of overtaking the Arabs everywhere. The talk about the municipal elections in the West Bank is but one of the signs of this suffering just as it is also one of the means to exploit and use this suffering.

Despite all this, Jordan has never for one day stopped advocating the unity of ranks and the pooling and coordination of efforts. Jordan has never hesitated to extend a true capable hand to all the brothers out of its belief in the unity of the cause and fate. Jordan has never spared any effort in working for the goal of liberation.

Though Arab conditions have obstructed Jordan and impeded its steps, contemplation of the future of the state has continued along its course. This is because none of the attitudes or events could shake our faith in the inevitable triumph of the right in the end and the dissipation of the catastrophe of the dear land and the beloved kinsmen.

Though basically that faith depended on the faith in the right itself and its inevitable triumph, it derived its strength from faith in the country and the people on both banks of the river and in the nation throughout the greater homeland.

For this reason it has been decided to move the country into a new phase which basically centres on liberation and which in essence responds to the aspirations and expectations of man in our country and incorporates his faith in the unity of his nation and his affinity for it. Furthermore, it is based on absolute adherence to the legitimate rights of the Palestinian people and aims at leading the Palestinian people to the point which will enable them to regain and safeguard these rights.

This was the pledge we took — to give the people the right of self-determination. This is our reply to all those who chose to cast doubts on this pledge and to render it void of all meaning. This pledge today finds its way to the ears of every citizen in this country, every member of this nation and every person in this world. Today this pledge is growing in size, exceeding the limits of its words to face all the possibilities of dispersement and scattering and to incorporate all the patriotic and national goals and manifest them in all clarity.

We wish to declare here that planning for the new phase has come as a blessed result of a long series of uninterrupted discussions and continued consultations which we have had with people's representatives, personalities, leaders and thinkers of both banks. All have expressed the unanimous opinion that the primary formula of the phase embodies the most modern concepts of the modern state and the best models of objective democracy. Furthermore, the formula has come to help build the new society which the new man is building to be the new force which will drive us along the road of victory, progress, unity, freedom and a better life.

We are happy to declare that the bases of the proposed formula for the new phase are as follows:

(1) The Hashemite Kingdom of Jordan will become a united Arab kingdom and will bear this name.

(2) The United Arab Kingdom will consist of two regions: (a) The Palestine region which will consist of the West Bank and any other Palestinian territories which are liberated and whose inhabitants desire to join it. (b) The Jordan region which will consist of the East Bank.

(3) Amman will be the central capital of the kingdom as well as capital of the Jordan region.

(4) Jerusalem will be the capital of the Palestine region.

(5) The Head of State will be the king, who will assume the central executive authority with the help of a central cabinet. The central legislative authority will be vested in the king and an assembly to be known as the National Assembly. Members of this assembly will be elected by direct secret ballot. Both regions will be equally represented in this assembly.

(6) The central judicial authority will be vested in a central supreme court.

(7) The kingdom will have unified armed forces whose supreme commander is the king.

(8) The responsibilities of the central executive authority will be confined to affairs connected with the kingdom as an international entity to guarantee the kingdom's security, stability and prosperity.

(9) The executive authority in each region will be assumed by a governor-general from among its sons and a regional cabinet also from among its sons.

(10) Legislative authority in each region will be assumed by a council to be called the People's council. It will be elected by a direct secret ballot. This council will elect the region's governor-general.

(11) The judicial authority in the region will be in the hands of the region's courts and nobody will have power over them.

(12) The executive authority in each region will assume responsibility for all the affairs of the region except such affairs as the Constitution defines as coming under the jurisdiction of the central executive authority.

Naturally, the implementation of this formula and its bases must be according to the constitutional principles in force. It will be referred to the (Jordanian) National Assembly to adopt the necessary measures to prepare a new constitution.

The new phase which we look forward to will guarantee the reorganisation of the Jordanian-Palestinian house in a manner which will provide it with more intrinsic power and ability to work to attain its ambitions and aspirations. Proceeding from this fact, this formula will bind the two banks with ties of stronger fibre and with closer bonds and will strengthen their brotherhood and march as a result of enhancing man's responsibility in each bank on bases more suitable for serving their national aspirations without prejudice to any of the rights gained by any citizen, whether he be of Palestinian origin living in the Jordanian region or of Jordanian origin living in the Palestinian region.

This formula gathers and does not disperse, strengthens and does not weaken, unites and does not divide. It does not contain anything to change anything gained by any person during a unity of 20 years.

Every attempt to cast doubt on any of this or discredit it is treason against the unity of the kingdom, the cause, the people and the homeland. The experience, vigilance and ability gained by our people make them capable of facing the forthcoming responsibilities with greater confidence and more determination. If ability is a debt for a person to use for himself and others and if vigilance is a weapon to be used for his and others' welfare, then the time has come for that person to stand up and face his responsibilities, perform them sincerely and faithfully and practise them bravely and with dignity. For this reason this formula is the title for a new bright, shining and confident page in the history of this country in which each citizen has a part and responsibility. It is partly based on sound allegiance to his faithful country and sincere devotion to his nation.

The armed forces, which from the very beginning marched under the banner of the great Arab revolution and which included and will always include in its ranks the best sons of the people in both ranks, will always be prepared to welcome more sons of both banks. They will always be at peak efficiency, ability and organisation, and will remain open to anyone anxious to serve the homeland and the cause with absolute loyalty to homeland and the cause and to the aims.

This Arab country is the country of the cause, just as it is from the Arabs and for all the Arabs. The record of its sacrifices for the nation and the cause is long and well known. This record was written by its brave armed forces and free and loyal people with their blood and honourable sacrifices. In as much as the attitudes toward this country change to attitudes of fraternity, assistance and support, this country will continue on the path of sacrifice with strength and hope until it and its nation regain their rights and achieve their objectives.

This Arab country belongs to all, Jordanians and Palestinians alike. When we say Palestinians we mean every Palestinian throughout the world, provided he is Palestinian by loyalty and affinity. When we call on every citizen to rise to play his part and carry out his responsibilities in the new stage, we call on every Palestinian brother outside Jordan to respond to the call of duty – unaffected by appearances and attempts to outdo others and free from weaknesses and deviations – to proceed with his relatives and brothers in a march whose basis is this formula and to be united in rank and clear in aim in order that all may participate in attaining the aim of liberation and establishing the cherished edifice and strong structure.

If God helps you, none can defeat you. For God is mighty and strong. Peace be with you.

5. U.N. SECURITY COUNCIL RESOLUTION 242 (1967), NOVEMBER 22, 1967
U.N. Monthly Chronicle, Vol. IV, No. II, December 1967, p. 19.

The Security Council

 Expressing its continuing concern with the grave situation in the Middle East.

 Emphasizing the inadmissability of the acquisition of territory by war and the need to work for a just and lasting peace in which every State in the area can live in security,

 Emphasizing further that all Member States in their acceptance of the Charter of the United Nations have undertaken a commitment to act in accordance with Article 2 of the Charter,

 1. *Affirms* that the fulfilment of Charter principles requires the establishment of a just and lasting peace in the Middle East which should include the application of both the following principles:

  (i) Withdrawal of Israeli armed forces from territories occupied in the recent conflict;

  (ii) Termination of all claims or states of belligerency and respect for and acknowledgment of the sovereignty, territorial integrity and political independence of every State in the area and their right to live in peace within secure and recognized boundaries free from threats or acts of force;

 2. *Affirms further* the necessity

  (a) For guaranteeing freedom of navigation through international waterways in the area;

  (b) For achieving a just settlement of the refugee problem;

  (c) For guaranteeing the territorial inviolability and political independence of every State in the area, through measures including the establishment of demilitarized zones;

 3. *Requests* the Secretary-General to designate a Special Representative to proceed to the Middle East to establish and maintain contacts with the States concerned in order to promote agreement and assist efforts to achieve a peaceful and accepted settlement in accordance with the provisions and principles in this resolution;

 4. *Requests* the Secretary-General to report to the Security Council on the progress of the efforts of the Special Representative as soon as possible.

6. U.N. SECURITY COUNCIL RESOLUTION 338 (1973), OCTOBER 22, 1973
U.N. Monthly Chronicle, Vol. X, No. 10, November 1973, p. 30.

THE SECURITY COUNCIL

1. *Calls upon* all parties to the present fighting to cease all firing and terminate all military activity immediately, no later than 12 hours after the moment of the adoption of this decision, in the positions they now occupy;

2. *Calls upon* the parties concerned to start immediately after the cease-fire the implementation of Security Council resolution 242 (1967) in all of its parts;

3. *Decides* that, immediately and concurrently with the cease-fire, negotiations start between the parties concerned under appropriate auspices aimed at establishing a just and durable peace in the Middle East.

7. ALGIERS ARAB SUMMIT CONFERENCE SECRET RESOLUTIONS, NOVEMBER 26–28, 1973
Al-Nahar, (Beirut), December 4, 1973, (Excerpt)

The sixth Arab summit conference meeting in Algiers discussed the latest developments in the Arab and international situations and the circumstances of the confrontation with the enemy.

The conference heard the statements of the Arab kings and presidents and adopted the following resolutions:

First: The temporary objective of the Arab nation

The conference resolves that the objectives of the current stage of the joint Arab struggle are:

1. The complete liberation of all the Arab territories occupied in the June 1967 aggression and the nonrelinquishment of any part of these territories or the infringement upon the national sovereignty over them.

2. The liberation of the Arab city of Jerusalem and the rejection of any status that many infringe upon the complete Arab sovereignty over the holy city.

3. The commitment to the restoration of the national rights of the Palestinian people in the manner decided by the Palestine Liberation Organization (PLO) in its capacity as the sole representative of the Palestinian people. (The Hashimite Kingdom of Jordan expressed reservations on this clause.)

4. The question of Palestine is the cause of all the Arabs. It is impermissible for any Arab side to give up this commitment as affirmed by the resolutions of the previous Arab summit conferences.

Second: In the military field

In view of the need to continue the battle against the enemy until achieving our nation's objectives of liberating the occupied territories and regaining the national rights of the Palestinian people, the conference decides the following:

1. The solidarity of all the Arab states with Egypt, Syria and the Palestinian people in the common struggle to achieve the just Arab objectives.

2. Giving all means of military and financial support to the Egyptian and Syrian battlefronts to strengthen their military ability to wage the battle of liberation and to counter the enormous aid and the limitless assistance which the enemy is receiving.

3. Backing the Palestinian resistance with all possible means to guarantee its effective role in the battle.

8. DRAFT PROGRAMMES OF FATH, SA'IQA, PDFLP AND PFLP
Al-Nahar, (Beirut), March 10, 1974, (Excerpts).

Over the last few weeks, all groups of the Palestinian resistance movement held meetings and seminars and conducted discussions and dialogs on one subject, namely, the short-term political action program of the Palestinian Liberation Organization (PLO), . . .

Throughout the history of the Palestinian resistance movement, the various organizations and commands have never held discussions in such a frank and democratic manner as they did during recent weeks in order to arrive at a short-term program for the PLO. During that period, the Fatah movement Al-Sa'iqah Organization and the Democratic Front (Democratic Popular Front for the Liberation of Palestine (DPFLP) prepared a draft for a short-term political program. The Popular Front (for the Liberation of Palestine – PFLP) also prepared a draft . . . .

I. Text of the draft program of Fath, Al-Sa'iqa and the PDFLP

This program constitutes the guidelines of the national action at this stage for the PLO, the resistance movement and the overall Palestinian national movement, through the definition of the aims which the Palestinian national struggle, in all its forms is seeking to achieve in order to attain the general strategic aims of the Palestinian revolution, the foremost being the liberation of Palestine, the elimination of the Zionist entity and the establishment of the democratic Palestinian state over all the Palestinian soil where everybody will have equal rights and duties.

The fulfillment of any short-term program must certainly constitute a step on the road to the general strategic aim and not be a substitute for that aim. The draft of the short-term program for the revolution was formulated in view of the general strategic aim, on the basis of the potentials for struggle available to the Palestinian people and the Arab nation under the current cirucmstances . . .

This program is based on the following fundamental principles:

1. Unity of the Palestinian people wherever they may be inside and outside the homeland. The Palestinian revolution and the Palestinian national movement should endeavor to consolidate this fact by their struggle in order to preserve the national identity of our people inside the territory occupied since 1948 and the independent national Palestinian identity of all sections of our people in the fraternal Arab countries and in foreign countries; protect the Palestinian people from the plots which aim at forcing them to migrate, settling them [outside Palestine], and making them dissolve [within other societies] ; consolidate their unity with the revolution and the homeland, and cement their feeling of the common destiny of the one Palestinian people.

2. The Palestinian people fight for the establishment of justice and peace in the land of Palestine and the guaranteeing of the right to freedom and honorable life to all citizens in the democratic Palestinian state.

3. Palestine is part of our Arab homeland and the Palestinian struggle is a part of the Arab national liberation movement and its just and legitimate aspiration to build a comprehensive Arab unity.

4. The Palestinian question is an Arab question and the liberation of Palestine is an overriding national and pan-Arab responsibility.

5. The Palestinian national movement is part of the world liberation and progressive movement and is organically linked with it by the common struggle to liquidate Zionism and imperialism so that peace and justice may prevail throughout the world.

The General Strategic Aim

It is the liberation of Palestine from Zionist colonialism, the establishment of a democratic Palestinian state in the whole of the Palestinian territory, the return of all the Palestinian nationals to their homeland, and their exercise of their right to self-determination and complete national sovereignty.

The democratic Palestinian state shall uphold the aims of the Arab struggle for unity, freedom and progress.

The Short-Term Aims

A. To uphold the UN resolutions in all Arab and international fields as the minimum limit of legitimate Palestinian rights in this stage, and to ask the Arab states to abide by this, to keep the state of war with the Zionist entity alive and to support the Palestinian revolution to enable it to continue its armed popular struggle until the attainment of its aims.

B. To ask the Arab states to continue and escalate the economic and political measures against the United States and other countries supporting the Zionist enemy until the complete Israeli withdrawal from all occupied Arab territories and the establishment of the national legitimate rights of the Palestinian people.

C. To approach friendly and supporting forces in the world with a view to securing their stand on the side of our people and their solidarity with them until the attainment of these aims.

D. To continue struggling together with the national masses and forces in Jordan to liquidate the agent Hashimite regime and renew Jordanian-Palestinian unity on national democratic bases.

E. To consolidate ties of unity with the masses of our people who have been under the yoke of the Zionist colonial occupation since 1948, to bolster their national struggle and steadfastness in the face of the occupation in order to safeguard their national identity and to link their struggle internally with the struggle of our people everywhere for the realization of their aims.

F. To continue the struggle of the masses of our people who have been forced out of their homeland to preserve their unity and wrest their right to return and to determine their destiny in their homeland.

G. To devleop the fighting capabilities of the revolution, develop its weapons, training, and organization, and work to secure the unity of the forces of the Palestinian revolution on democratic bases and to escalate the armed struggle against the enemy.

The Immediate and Direct Aims of the Palestinian Arab Struggle

A. To put an end to the occupation and force the enemy to unconditionally withdraw from the West Bank and the Gaza sector without making any political concessions to him in return. This demand represents only a part of the minimal program of the Palestinian people's demands and legitimate rights at this stage.

B. To refuse the return of the Hashimite authority over any Palestinian territory from which occupation has receded.

C. To wrest back under the PLO leadership the Palestinian people's legitimate and just right to self-determination, national independence and complete sovereignty in the Palestinian land whose liberation has been completed.

Fields and Means of Political Action:

In the Palestinian Field:

A. To seek to rally all the Palestinian forces, factions and masses around this program through constant dialog among all the groups and on all levels.

B. To have the Executive Committee issue a comprehensive political statement concentrating on the following points:

1. Commitment to the general strategic objective.

2. Commitment to continue the armed struggle and struggle by various other methods.

3. Struggle to defeat occupation, to prevent the return of the Hashimite authority over Palesitnian territory and to insist on our people's right to self-determination and national sovereignty over their land.

4. Demand that the Arab countries support all forms of Palestinian struggle and maintain the conflict with the Zionist entity until our people's objectives are fully realized.

5. Appeal to the friendly states to support the Palestinian struggle, to maintain their break of diplomatic and economic relations with it, and to emphasize this stand by withdrawing recognition [of Israel].

6. The continued refusal of Security Council Resolution no. 242 which does not meet the Palestinian people's minimum demands and legitimate rights, which denies the existence of the Palestinian people and their political rights, and which considers the problem of our people as a problem of refugees while it is actually the problem of a people who have been expelled from their land.

In the Arab Field

6. To hold immediate contacts on the highest level with the Arab countries, particularly Egypt and Syria, in order to commit them to this short-term program, to stand with the PLO in order to achieve it, to lay down a unified Palestinian-Arab stand and to seek to create a unified Egyptian-Syrian-Palestinian stand on this basis.

II. Text of the PFLP program.

Introduction

The October 1973 war has sorted out a number of facts which should be taken into consideration. The most important of these facts are:

1. The stressing of the conviction of the Palestinian and Arab masses that:

A. The continuation of the fighting will ensure the fulfillment of the liberation of all the Palestinian national soil.

B. Palestinian national unity, Arab solidarity and the state of advancement at the various levels are most firmly accomplished through armed clashes with the enemy.

C. The escalation and continuation of the fighting will force the forces — which affect international policy in view of their interests in our region — to review their stands toward our causes and will also force them to make a proportionate adjustment in these stands.

2. The international community is now throwing its weight to find a political settlement of the struggle between us and our enemies. There are:

A. The United States — a principal power at the world level and which affects the course of events in this part of the world which is, exerting efforts to eliminate the revolutionary pit in this region in order to protect its interests, especially its agents and allies — especially Israel. This makes it work strenuously to abort the developing revolutionary state and to find a settlement of the Arab-Israeli struggle on the basis of Resolution no. 242 with amendments in favor of Israel.

B. The Soviet Union also a principal power at the world level and which also affects the course of events — which is exerting efforts (but from prerequisites which are different from those of the United States) to find a settlement of the Arab-Israeli struggle on the basis of Resolution no. 242 and of the need to implement it completely which will ensure the evacuation of Israel from all the Arab and Palestinian territories which it occupied by force in 1967.

3. As to the official Arab level, the October war has formed the beginning of a new

stage which strengthened the imposition of a settlement because it provides a better position for some regimes to proceed along the course of settlement and to confront the movement of the masses which reject the course of bargaining.

4. As to Israel, it cannot ignore the new international situation nor the American drive toward finding a settlement. Within this framework, it will try to achieve – politically and economically – the most it can of its expansionist ambitions.

5. As to the Palestinian level, the pressure on the PLO to become a party to the settlement will increase. Several sides will try to push the resistance movement to the table of negotiations and into the quagmire of capitulation. This will abort the revolutionary state which the Palestinian resistance represents at the level of the whole Arab area and cause it to lose its revolutionary meaning.

Despite all the above, there is a possibility for foiling this settlement. There is the stand of the Arab revolutionary forces, the Arab movement of national liberation, which rejects the capitulationist solutions. And there is, especially, the Palestinian masses, their revolutionary commands and the PLO – the sole legitimate representative of the Palestinian people – which refuses in any form whatsoever to relinquish its historic right to any inch of its national soil and which is determined to continue along the road of struggle in all its forms, in order to achieve all the aims for whose sake it has been established in accordance with the Palestinian National Charter.

In light of these new and significant conditions and in light of the Palestinian revolution's responsibilities, the PLO groups and forces inside and outside the occupied territories have approved their short-term political program which is based on four principal strategic points:

1. To continue the mobilization and organization of all our people's potentialities inside and outside the homeland in a long-term popular war for the sake of comprehensive liberation and the establishment of a democratic state and society within the framework of the Arab nation's aims for national [qawmi] liberation and comprehensive unity.

2. To fuse our people's struggle with the fraternal Jordanian people's struggle in a Palestinian-Jordanian Liberation Front that will, in addition to its duties in the Palestinian arena, struggle for the establishment of a domestic [watani] rule in Jordan.

3. To link the Palestinian struggle with the general Arab struggle in a front comprising all the domestic [watani] and progressive forces that are against imperialism, Zionism and neoimperialism.

4. To unite with the world struggle movement against imperialism, Zionism and reaction for the sake of domestic [watani] liberation.

Short-Term Tasks

The PLO in light of the above mentioned, in adherence to the Palestinian National [watani] Charter, and in confirmation of the contents of the political program approved by the National [watani] Council at its 11th session, defines its short-term tasks as follows:

1. On the Palestinian level.

A. To work to consolidate Palestinian national [watani] unity among and between the various resistance movement groups and masses in order to confront and confound the conspiracies aimed at dividing the Palestinian national [watani] movement.

B. To protect the gains achieved by the Palestinian Arab people during their years of struggle. Moreover, to protect the Palestinian Arab people's right to carary arms for continuing their struggle until the liberation of the entire Palestinian national [watani] soil is achieved.

C. To mobilize and organize the Palestinian Arab masses; to strengthen the ties of national [watani] unity and unity of struggle of our masses in the land occupied in

1948, in the West Bank and the Gaza Strip and outside the occupied homeland; to build the unified Palestinian national [watani] front based on the Palestinian National [watani] Charter and the PLO political program; and to fight any call for division in our people's ranks.

D. To contain and fight all reactionary and agents' calls demanding the return of the Hashimite regime and fighting any settlement attempt of that reactionary regime at the expense of our rights.

E. To initiate serious and studied work to establish the Palestinian-Jordanian National [wataniyah] Front and to continue the struggle against the agent Hashimite regime in order to topple it and establish democratic national [watani] rule that will facilitate the continuation of the struggle to liberate Palestine.

F. To resolutely and seriously struggle to bring about the failure of the Geneva conference – convened on the basis of UN Resolution no. 242 – or any other conference based on the same resolution. To frustrate all the capitulationist settlements aimed at our people's issue and at diminishing the issue by submitting proposals for the establishment of a Palestinian authority or state in a part of Palestine, and to resist these proposals with armed struggle and the massive political struggle that is associated with it.

G. Resolve to keep the PLO, the sole legitimate representative of the Palestine people, outside the framework of any settlement leading to negotiations with or recognition of the Zionist enemy; and to fight any Palestinian side that goes to Geneva or elsewhere to participate in the negotiations.

H. To impose sovereignty of the Palestinian and people over all Palestinian territory so that from it our people may continue their fighting, armed strife and mass political struggle for the liberation of the other parts.

It must be stressed that any Palestinian authority established in any Palestinian territory as a result of a political settlement based on UN Security Council Resolutions 242 and 338 cannot but be reactionary and capitulationist and the PLO should not recognize it as the authority representing the national Palestinian struggle.

2. In the Arab Field

A. To consider the Arab front participating [in the Palestinian revolution] as an instrument of struggle to instigate and mobilize the Arab masses to rise in the face of the imperialist plots which aim at the liquidation of the Palestinian question and to ask the Arab front to play an effective and active role for thwarting these plots.

B. To ask the nationalist Arab fronts which reject the UN Security Council Resolution no. 242 to translate their stand into active and effective action to foil the settlement and to form themselves into a front which would prepare itself to deal with the imperialist-Israeli-reactionary aggression. The nucleus of this front should consist of Syria, Iraq and the resistance movement and the nationalist countries which reject the capitulationist solutions. The front shall work to persuade the Arab Republic of Egypt not to march forward along the road of concessions and to prevent the agent in Jordan from discussing and implementing any bilateral agreement with the enemy.

C. To continue solidarity and cooperation with the national liberation movements and the Arab revolution groups and to continue the struggle with them to liquidate all the existing forms of imperialism in the Arab homeland whether they are political influence, military bases, investment, cultural activities on institutions, and to fight the reactionary forces which propagate and promote imperialist existence. And to support the Arab national and progressive strugglers against all oppressions which they are facing.

3. In the International Field

A. To continue to stress that the Palestinian national Arab struggle is firmly and decisively on the side of the unity of the world revolution forces.

B. To consider that the Arab national struggle contribution toward settling the differences within the world revolution movement can be primarily achieved by the Arab struggle's successful and effective settlement of the problems and challenges facing this struggle.

C. To realize that the aims and methods of the Arab struggle which are based on the general rules of the revolution and which are the result of the experiences of the world national liberation movements are matters that concern the Arab national and progressive forces alone, though this should not mean disregarding and ignoring the remarks and advice of friends.

D. To strengthen alliances with the forces of liberation and progress in the world, intensify the dialog with friends in all the socialist countries and to work to win their support for our political stand.

The Conclusion

Our own action to perform and achieve these tasks is the only genuine way out of the political crisis which we are facing. Our own action shall remain the basis for any decision, though we are not in a position at present to prevent the Arab official circles from adopting a decision accepting the settlement and its consequences. But it is certainly within our power to obstruct the way for such a decision and under no circumstances should we contemplate paving the way for such a decision.

9. PLO PHASED POLITICAL PROGRAM (RESOLUTIONS OF THE 12TH PALESTINE NATIONAL COUNCIL, CAIRO, JUNE 1–9, 1974)
Voice of Palestine, Cairo, June 8, 1974. Quoted from BBC Monitoring Serivce, ME/4622/A/2, June 11, 1974.

Proceeding from the Palestinian National Covenant and the PLO's Political Program which was approved during the 11th session held from January 3–12, 1973, believing in the impossibility of the establishment of a durable and just peace in the area without the restoration to our Palestinian people of all their national rights, foremost of which is their right to return to and determine their fate on all their national soil, and in the light of the study of the political circumstances which arose during the period between the Council's previous and current sessions, the Council decides the following:

1. The assertion of the PLO position regarding Resolution 242 is that it obliterates the patriotic (wataniyah) and national (qawmiyah) rights of our people and deals with our people's cause as a refugee problem. Therefore, dealing with this resolution on this basis is rejected at any level of Arab and international dealings including the Geneva Conference.

2. The PLO will struggle by every means, the foremost of which is armed struggle, to liberate Palestinian land and to establsh the people's national, independent and fighting authority on every part of Palestinian land to be liberated. This requires making more changes in the balance of power in favor of our people and their struggle.

3. The PLO will struggle against any plan for the establishment of a Palestinian entity the price of which is recognition [of Israel], conciliation [with it], secure borders, renunciation of the national right, and our people's deprivation of their right to return and their right to determine their fate on their national soil.

4. Any liberation step that is achieved constitutes a step for continuing [the efforts] to achieve the PLO strategy for the establishment of the Palestinian democratic state that is stipulated in the resolutions of the previous National Councils.

5. The PLO will struggle with the Jordanian national forces for the establishment of a Jordanian-Palestinian national front whose aim is the establishment of a national democratic government in Jordan: a government that will cohere with the Palestinian entity to be established as a result of the struggle.

6. The PLO will strive to establish a unity of struggle between the two peoples and among all the Arab liberation movement forces that agree on this program.

7. In the light of this program the PLO will struggle to strengthen national unity and to elevate it to a level that will enable it to carry out its duties and its patriotic and national tasks.

8. The Palestinian national authority, after its establishment, will struggle for the unity of the confrontation states for the sake of completing the liberation of all Palestinian soil and as a step on the path of comprehensive Arab unity.

9. The PLO will struggle to strengthen its solidarity with the socialist countries and the world forces of liberation and progress to foil all the Zionist, reactionary and imperialist schemes.

10. In the light of this program, the Revolutionary Command will work out the tactics that serve and lead to the achievement of these aims.

A recommendation has been added to the political program. The recommendation stipulates that the Executive Committee implement this program:

Should a fateful situation connected with the future of the Palestinian people arise, the Council will be called to hold a special session to decide on it.

An Iraqi News Agency (INA) dispatch datelined Cairo, June 8, 1974 (BBC Monitoring

Service, June 11, 1974, ME/4622/A/5, June 11, 1974), extended the last paragraph saying:

The Palestine National Council has decided to commit the PLO to call the Council for an extraordinary meeting should a matter of destiny concerning the Palestinian people's future arise. This decision has been added to the ten points submitted by the Executive Committee at the request of the Palestinian forces which reject a settlement. This means the Executive Committee will be unable to participate in the Geneva Conference or to negotiate without going back to the Council.

10. "PLO REPRESENTS PALESTINIANS EXCEPT THOSE RESIDING IN JORDAN" (SADAT-HUSAYN STATEMENT, JULY 18, 1974)

Cairo Voice of the Arabs in Arabic, July 18, 1974. Cited in FBIS, ME, July 19, 1974, pp. D1–D2, (Excerpts).

At the invitation of President Muhammad Anwar Al-Sadat of the Arab Republic of Egypt, King Hussayn bin Talal of the Jordan Hashimite Kingdom, paid a visit to the Arab Republic of Egypt from 16 to 18 July 1974. President Al-Sadat and his guest held talks on Arab and international affairs of interest to the two countries . . .

The two sides expressed satisfaction at the progress attained by the Arab nation and the growing international support it has gained in its struggle to achieve its just demand for the withdrawal of the Israeli forces from all the occupied Arab territories including Arab Jerusalem and the realization of the legitimate national rights of the Palestinian people . . .

The two sides agreed on the necessity of undertaking continued and regular coordination between the Arab Republic of Egypt, the Syrian Arab Republic, the Hashemite Kingdom of Jordan and the PLO . . .

The two sides declared that the PLO is the legitimate representative of the Palestinians, except for those Palestinians residing in the Hashimite Kingdom of Jordan. The two sides concur on the need to have the PLO take part independently in the Geneva conference at the appropriate stage, in support of the right of the Palestinian people to self-determination. The two sides also agreed on the need to reach a disengagement agreement on the Jordanian front as a first step toward a just peaceful solution . . . .

11. REPORT ON RABAT ARAB SUMMIT SECRET SESSIONS, OCTOBER 26–29, 1974
Musa Sabri, "The full story of seven secret sessions which have defied all storms",
Akhbar Al Yawm, (Cairo), November 2, 1974, pp. 3–4, (Excerpts).

After King Hassan's speech, the public session of the Arab summit conference turned into a closed session for the discussion of procedural matters. This session lasted for only a few minutes.

The Arab kings, presidents and foreign ministers began their first closed session the following morning at King Hassan's palace. What actually happened during the meeting of the Arab kings and presidents?

King Husayn spoke during this session. He read a statement which covered 30 large sheets of paper. He reviewed the history of the Hashimite dynasty's work for the Arab cause and its right to the land. He referred to the [December 1, 1948] Jericho conference and repeated his reservations about the resolutions of the sixth Arab summit in Algiers concerning the PLO's representation of the Palestinian people. He concluded by saying that he was prepared to accept all resolutions adopted by the Rabat conference but that he would not feel responsible for anything after that.

The focal point of the king's statement was that Kissinger had told him that there can be no solution with the Resistance. This represented an adamant Israeli stand. King Husayn also spoke of his efforts in the international field in search of a solution.

King Husayn also spoke of an offer made to him which is still under discussion, but he refrained from giving any details. Deep silence then engulfed the meeting hall. For this meant that all the efforts exerted during the bilateral and tripartite contacts held the night before to persuade the king to change his attitude have failed.

Syrian President Hafiz al-Asad also spoke. He warned of an American plot. He said that King Husayn would be the first victim of this plot because all contacts made [by the Arabs] with the King will be of no avail.

President al-Asad objected to all talk about the past. He said in the past Syria had no independent entity and the same was true of Lebanon. But things have since changed. Today we are facing the question of Palestine, the question of a people who want their land back.

In his speech Yasir Arafat expressed opposition to every word uttered by King Husayn. He called on the conference to shoulder its responsibilities. He said that there are past resolutions stating that the PLO is the sole representative of the Palestinian people. We have not come here to discuss these resolutions again. We have come to find out what steps have been taken to implement these resolutions. Arafat then reminded the kings and president of all the tragedies of the Palestinian people and of the September 1970 events.

Sudanese President Numayri also spoke. He reviewed the Arab gains after 6 October [1973] and said that these gains must be expanded with the changes in the international situation. He said that the situation between the resistance and Jordan must be settled with complete frankness.

Algerian President Boumediene spoke. He commented on King Husayn's talk of the past. He said: We in Algeria have asked the schools to cut down on the use of the verb "was," which denotes the past. We demand the use of the future tense always. In the past, nobody ever listened to us when we spoke of the Palestinian question. But today the international community has recognized the Palestinian people. The name of Palestine must rise and its flag must be hoisted, even if only on a 5-square centimeter piece of land.

Tunisian President Bourguiba spoke very frankly. He said the matter must be settled and a choice must be made between the king and the PLO. He said he personally favors the PLO.

At this point the situation became violent — indeed increased in fierceness — and all talk about compromises was forgotten.

President Al-Sadat had postponed making his speech, so Arafat spoke again. But this time he spoke as a statesman. He spoke of the future horizons and the colossal struggle awaiting the Arab nation. He said that Palestine cannot live in the future without cooperation with Jordan, Egypt, Syria and all the Arab states. He added that the experience of independence in Lebanon and Syria has imposed a new type of cooperation between them such as the unification of currency and so forth. Arafat was realistic when he said that he does not deny that the Resistance had committed some mistakes but that severe conditions which the Palestinian people face demand that we excuse them.

At this juncture the atmosphere began to ease up. But we must not forget in this respect King Hassan's role during the bilateral talks, particularly his contacts with King Husayn.

President Al-Sadat then spoke. He postponed his speech because he preferred to listen to the views of his colleagues first. He said: Cairo welcomed the establishment of a Palestinian government two or more years ago. At the time, some people thought that this was a maneuver on the part of Egypt. But our idea had its reasons and causes: First, the Palestinian struggle must take its true form, and second, the Israeli establishment insists on denying the existence of anything called Palestine.

President Al-Sadat added: We are still in a state of battle. The result of any battle depends in the first place on economic, political and military steadfastness. If we were to depart from this course for one single day, Israel would try to change the course of events and assume the initiative once more. With all hope and in the spirit of the October war, I expect that we here will meet on the following basis, which I have previously enumerated: There can be no squandering of an inch of the land, there can be no bargaining on or squandering of the rights of the Palestinian people and the Palestinian people shall determine their own fate.

I am saying this again, the President said, because Israel says that it will only talk with King Husayn and will not talk with the Palestinians. I am afraid that we might fall into Israel's trap. The important thing is that every inch we can retrieve by any means we must grasp so that the name of Palestine will become prominent. We must seek for and preserve all progress we can make with our movement. We must take all we can. Arafat has spoken realistically. He has shown understanding of the international changes and has admitted the use of working in stages.

President Al-Sadat said: All pending questions can be solved. There is no problem without a solution. We must submit more than one solution for every problem. In my speech when Nixon was in Cairo, I stressed that the Palestine problem is the core and that there can be no peace without its solution. I asked him to see that the United States exerts efforts to insure further withdrawals from all the occupied Arab territories.

Al-Sadat concluded his speech by defining the road. He said: Arab solidarity is the only road open. The only contradiction at present is between Jordan and the PLO. This cotradiction must be resolved at this conference, as there is no room for delay. The important thing is to tell Israel: Get out of our land, and we will deal with the rest, for it is not Israel's concern. Israel insists on exploiting the Jordanian—PLO differences. The Palestinian people must be sovereign in their land. We must act. We must concentrate on depriving Israel of this abnormal excuse.

President Ja-far Numaryi had proposed the formation of a working committee of the Presidents to bring King Husayn and Yasir Arafat together and have them conduct a dialog in front of them and to intervene when necessary to conciliate between them. The committee was formed of Morocco, Egypt, Syria, Saudi Arabia, Jordan and the PLO. King Faysal declined, saying that the frontline states are capable of finding a solution. He then blessed the work of the committee.

The committee was formed on Monday evening. Then an emissary from the Resistance came to the Hilton Hotel to say that King Husayn has announced his readiness to abide in advance by any decision the heads of states take. This announcement came as a surprise, and many of the delegates did not even believe it. For why, then, did the king insist for three years on not recognizing the Palestinian entity and why did he make reservations against the resolution of the Algerian conference? Why was there a violent start to the foreign minister's conference which had prepared the working paper for the heads of states?

In fact, the Arab foreign ministers' meetings were noisy. Jordan's representative Zayd ar-Rifa'i adopted an extremely rigid stand and intimated that Resistance was about to undermine a solution which Jordan was about to achieve. No such rigidness was evident during the Jordanians' meetings with President Al-Sadat in Alexandria. Indeed, the Jordanian stand was then marked with flexibility. What has happened? What is behind this extreme rigidness in the Jordanian stand? Is it a tactic agreed upon between Jordan and Kissinger?

There was also a misunderstanding between Egypt and Syria at the Arab foreign minister's meetings. The Syrian foreign minister, Abd al-Halim Khaddam had submitted a working paper advocating against "running after unilateral solutions." The Egyptians saw it as an intimation that Egypt was "running" after a unilateral solution by seeking a partial withdrawal in Sinai without Syria securing a similar partial withdrawal in the Golan. The Syrian working paper also asked the Arab states to provide $13 billion worth of military and economic support.

The first point was then removed from the Syrian working paper in a spirit of understanding, on the grounds that phased political struggle does not constitute and will never constitute "running" and that Egyptian-Syrian work is the basis of struggle.

As to the second point, it was agreed to replace it by a word of thanks to the Arab states for their present and past support, without asking for any new support. This matter was left for the Arab states to decide in the light of their responsibilities under Arab solidarity. This is the way Al-Sadat operates. Egypt does not ask for anything other than solidarity.

The summit conference resulted in the fixing of annual aid to the frontline states and the PLO. Iraq participated in this aid for the first time. This participation was announced by Saddam Husayn during the final and seventh closed session of the conference.

President Al-Sadat called on Saddam Husayn on Wednesday morning, after the conclusion of the work of the conference, to return Saddam Husayn's visit to him. Al-Sadat told him he was glad to see Iraq attending because its absence would have created a gap, a big gap. The president and Saddam Husayn discussed the deepening of cooperation between Egypt and Iraq.

Asked by a PLO member about what was actually offered to him by Israel, King Husayn said openly: Israel has offered to give Jordan two passageways to the West Bank, while continuing to occupy some fortified points. It also offered a civilian Arab administration of the West Bank with a military presence provided that peace is concluded with Israel. King Husayn said that he has rejected the offer and does not advise its acceptance.

This statement was recorded in the minutes of the meeting so that it would not be possible to say in the future that taking a decision on who is to govern the West Bank after its deliberation has impeded its liberation and that Israel's withdrawal from the West Bank had been agreed upon [between the king and Israel].

The formulation of the five-man committee resolutions were unanimously approved in a short time.

Iraq said it agrees to these resolutions provided that the PLO would not participate in the Geneva conference. Iraq said it approves the reaching of a peace through the efforts of the USSR and the United States, but without direct talks with Israel at one table attended by the United States and Israel.

The resolutions were written in such a form as to prevent any future contradictory interpretations. The PLO was described as the sole legitimate representative of the Palestinian territory. The word "legitimate" was added so that the "legitimacy" of the PLO presence in the West Bank would not be questioned. It was also stated that "support would be given to the PLO in the exercise of its national and pan-Arab responsibilities," instead of just "the PLO will exercise its national and pan-Arab responsibilities." The above form was put to commit the Arab states to sharing the responsibility.

I understand from the PLO leaders that a new chapter of cooperation will begin with King Husayn. I only hope that nothing unexpected will be made by those around the king to spoil this cooperation. The Palestinian information media will henceforth follow a line which reflects the real conditions in the near and distant future.

I also understand from them that King Husayn has pledged to implement everything that is agreed upon between the frontline states and the PLO and that the king will very readily give any political gain for the liberation of any part of the land to the Palestinian government to help it assume its legitimate authority.

I also understand from these leaders that they will form a Palestinian government after securing from the United Nations positive resolutions pertaining to the question of Palestine which would become the basis of their political struggle.

I also understand from all the parties that all matters pertaining to the Geneva conference and any other phased steps will be coordinated by the four-member committee of cooperation consisting of Egypt, Syria, Jordan and the PLO. This committee was entrusted by the summit conference to draw up the form of relations that will exist among the various parties concerned in implementation of the summit resolutions.

12. RABAT ARAB SUMMIT PUBLISHED RESOLUTIONS
Al-Ahram, (Cairo), October 31, 1974, (Excerpt).

The Arab kings and presidents have decided to offer economic and military support to the frontline states. The Arab kings and presidents have agreed on the figures for this support during a closed session they held here yesterday morning.

The Arab kings and presidents have defined the basis of the joint Arab action in the coming stage as follows:

1. To strengthen the intrinsic military, economic and political power of the Arab states and to continue the building of the military power of the frontline states and provide all the requisites for it;

2. To establish effective Arab political, military and economic coordination leading to comprehensive Arab integration in the various fields;

3. To reject all attempts for partial settlements on the basis that the issue is a pan-Arab unified one;

4. To have all the Arab states commit themselves to the liberation of all the occupied Arab territories and the retrieval of the national rights of th Palestinian people;

5. To adopt the necessary Arab measures within the framework of political action to check the political, military and economic support which Israel receives from any source in the world;

6. To assert the Palestinian people's right to return to their homeland and determine their own fate; to stress that any Palestinian territory liberated through struggle in any form shall revert to its legitimate Palestinian ownership under the leadership of the PLO; to assert the Palestinian people's right to establish their own independent national authority in all liberated territories; and to insure the support of the frontline states for such an authority, when established, in all fields and on all levels.

13. U.N. GENERAL ASSEMBLY DEBATE ON THE "QUESTION OF PALESTINE", NOVEMBER 1974

U.N. Monthly Chronicle, Vol. XI, No. 11, December 1974. pp. 80-136

Speeches of Arafat (pp. 80-82) and representatives of Israel (pp. 82-84), the USSR (pp. 95-96) and the USA (pp. 136-137).

Note of *UN Monthly Chronicle*, [p. 80] :

During November, the General Assembly held a debate on the "Question of Palestine" in which 82 Member States participated. Due to limitations of space, it has been necessary to compress these statements. The summaries, which are given in the order in which the statements were made, are based on the provisional records of the General Assembly and, in many instances, on interpretations from the languages in which they were delivered.

Palestine Liberation Organization
Yasser Arafat,
Chairman, Executive Committee:
The General Assembly is re-examining the question of Palestine. The Assembly's decision to consider the question, and to invite a representative of the Palestine Liberation Organization (PLO) to address it, is as much a victory for the United Nations as it is for the Palestinian cause. The United Nations of today is not the United Nations of the past. The representatives of the 138 Member States more clearly reflect the will of the international community.

Great efforts are required if the world's goals of peace, freedom, justice, equality and development are to be realized and victory is to be achieved in the struggle to overcome colonialism, imperialism, neo-colonialism and racism in all its forms, including Zionism. The question of Palestine must be viewed within the perspective of the emerging struggle as the old world order crumbles. The same opportunity afforded PLO to address the General Assembly must be given to all liberation movements fighting racism and imperialism.

The question of Palestine is not merely a refugee problem; the Middle East question does not concern a border dispute between the Arab states and the Zionist entity. Those distortions are the basis for the hostile positions taken by the United States and others who imagine that the Palestinian people claim rights not rightfully theirs, who fight without logic or valid motive simply to disturb the peace and to terrorize wantonly. The United States supplies the enemy with planes and bombs. All that is done is at the expense of the Palestinian people, as well as the American people. The PLO appeals to the American people, in friendship, to endorse right and justice, to support the heroic Palestinian people, bearing in mind the heroic achievements of Washington, Lincoln and Wilson.

The roots of the Palestine question reach back to the end of the 19th century, the period of colonialism and settlement. Zionism was born in that era. It aimed at the conquest of Palestine by Eurpoean immigrants. That situation persists with the usurpation of Palestine and with its people hounded from their homeland. Zionism is imperialist, colonialist, racist and united with anti-Semetism in its retrograde tenets. The Zionists promised Britain an imperialist base on Palestinian soil. They succeeded in having Britain issue the Balfour Declaration. In the guise of a League of Nations Mandate, British imperialism was imposed on the Palestinian people and the Zionist invaders consolidated their gains in the homeland. As a result of the collusion between the mandatory Power and the Zionist movement, the General Assembly approved a recommenadtion to partition the Palestinian land. In an atmosphere poisoned with questionable actions and strong pressure, the Assembly partitioned what it had no right to divide and a people were dispersed and uprooted. The colonialist and racist entity managed to be accepted as a United Nations Member.

That entity became an arsenal of weapons; it ignored Security Council decisions; and despite the experience of October 1973, which demonstrated the bankruptcy of its policy of occupation and expansion, it is preparing for the fifth war of aggression. There is the grave likelihood that this war would bring nuclear destruction.

It pains the Palestinian people greatly to witness propagation of the myth that the homeland was a desert until it was made to bloom by the toil of foreign settlers. For thousands of years, the Arab people farmed, built, spread culture, and set an example of freedom of worship, and were faithful guardians of the holy places of all religions. Religious brotherhood was the hallmark of the Arab people's Holy City before it succumbed to catastrophe. The Arab people condemned the massacres of Jews under Nazi rule. At that time the Zionist leadership seemed more interested in exploiting them to realize the goal of immigration into Palestine. If the immigration of Jews had had as its objective the goal of living side by side with the Arab people of Palestine, the doors would have been opened to the extent of capacity for absorption. No one can demand acquiescence in usurpation and dispersion.

The Palestinian revolution is not aimed at the Jews but at racist Zionism and aggression. The goal of the struggle is for Jew, Christian and Moslem to live in equality. The PLO urges peoples and Governments to stand firm against Zionist attempts at encouraging world Jewry to emigrate from their countries and to usurp the Palestinian land. Why should the Arab Palestinian people pay the price of discrimination and be responsible for the problems of Jewish emigration? Why do not the supporters of Jewish emigration open their own countries?

The difference between the revolutionary and the terrorist lies in the reason for which each fights. Whoever stands by a just cause and fights for liberation from invaders and colonialists cannot be called terrorist. Those who wage war to occupy, colonize and oppress other people are the terrorists. The record of the Israeli rulers is replete with acts of terror in Sinai, the Golan Heights and with the total destruction of the city of Kuneitra. They have been condemned in numerous Assembly resolutions for violating human rights, aggression, and the annexation of Jerusalem which they have made lose its Moslem and Christian character. The Israeli rulers should keep in mind the General Assembly resolution which called for the one-year suspension of membership of South Africa—the inevitable fate of every racist country.

The Palestinian people had to resort to armed struggle when they lost faith in the international community, which ignored their rights, and when it became clear that not one inch of Palestine could be recuperated through exclusively political means. Through armed struggle and political leadership, a national liberation movement comprising all the Palestinian factions materialized into the Palestine Liberation Organization. That organization had earned its legitimacy by sacrifice and dedicated leadership. The Palestinian masses chose PLO to lead the struggle according to their directives. The legitimacy of PLO was strengthened by the support of the entire Arab nation and consecrated during the last Arab Summit Conference, which reiterated the right of the PLO, as the sole representative of the Palestinian people, to establish an independent national State on all liberated Palestinian territory.

The PLO dreams and hopes for one democratic State where Christian, Jew and Moslem live in justice, equality, fraternity and progress. The Jews of Europe and the United States have led the struggle for the separation of church and State and have fought religious discrimination. How can they refuse that humane paradigm for the Holy Land? The Palestine of tomorrow would include all Jews living there who choose to remain to live in peace and without discrimination. The Jews should turn away from the illusory promises made by Zionist ideology and Israeli leadership.

The Chairman of the PLO and leader of the Palestinian revolution appeals to the General Assembly to accompany the Palestinian people in its struggle to attain its right to self-determination—a right consecrated in the Charter and confirmed in Assembly resolutions. The Assembly is asked to aid the Palestinian people to return to their homeland from an involuntary exile. The Chairman of the PLO has come bearing an olive branch and a freedom-fighter's gun. He asks that the Assembly not let the olive branch fall.

(Meeting 2283/13 November)

Israel
Yosef Tekoah,
Permanent Representative:
On 14 October the General Assembly turned its back on the United Nations Charter, on law and humanity, and virtually capitulated to a murder organization which aims at destruction of a State Member of the United Nations. Today this rostrum was defiled by the chieftan of that murder organization, who proclaimed that the shedding of Jewish blood would end only when the murderers' demands have been accepted and their objectives achieved.

The United Nations has lavished great attention on the Arab inhabitants of Palestine Is it because the problems of others have been solved? Has the Kurdish people, subjected to a continuing war of annihilation by Iraqi Government, ever had its plight discussed and its rights upheld by the United Nations? Has the organization tried to avert the massacre of half a million non-Moslem Africans in South Sudan? Have the fundamental human and political rights of the hundreds of millions living under totalitarian regimes been ensured by the United Nations?

Are the Arabs of Palestine suffering starvation as are, according to United Nations statistics, almost 500 million people in Asia, Africa and Latin America? Has the United Nations left the Palestinian refugees the only one who as it has tens of millions of refugees all over the world, including Jewish refugees in Israel from Arab lands? Are the Palestinian refugees without assistance, cannot be reintegrated as others have been?

The real reason for the special consideration accorded to questions concerning the Arabs of Palestine has been the continuous exploitation of those questions as a weapon of Arab belligerency against Israel. As King Hussein said of the Arab leaders: "They have used the Palestinian people for selfish political purposes." That is also the real motivation of this debate.

No nation has enjoyed greater fulfilment of its political rights or been endowed with territory, sovereignty and independence more abundantly than the Arabs. As a result of centuries of acquisition of territory by war, the Arab nation is represented in the United Nations by 20 sovereign States. Among them is the Palestinian Arab State of Jordan. Geographically and ethnically, Jordan is Palestine. The population of Jordan is composed of two elements—the sedentary population and the nomads. Both are Palestinian.

It is false to allege that the Palestinian people has been deprived of a State of its own, or that it has been uprooted from its national homeland. Most Palestinians continue to live in Palestine, in a Palestinian State. The vast majority of Palestinian Arabs are citizens of that Palestinian State. On 9 December 1970, the late Dr. Kadri Toukan, a prominent West Bank leader and former Foreign Minister of Jordan said: "Jordan is Palestine and Palestine is Jordan."

The initiators of the discussion of the so-called question of Palestine are concerned primarily not with the realization of the rights of the Palestinians, but with annulment of the rights of the Jewish people. The PLO did not emerge from within the Palestinian community. It is not a representative of the Palestinian community. It is a creation of the Arab Governments. It was established at the first summit meeting of the Heads of Arab States in Cairo in 1964 as an instrument for waging terror warfare against Israel. Its Covenant stipulates: "The establishment of Israel is fundamentally null and void."

In a press conference held at United Nations Headquarters, after the General Assembly vote on 14 October, the PLO representative said: "Our short-term goal, which has been approved by our congress, is to establish in any and every part liberated in Palestine a national authority provided that in no way should that compromise our right to the whole of Palestine."

Arafat's design is to deprive the Jewish people of its independence, to liquidate the Jewish State and to establish on its ruins another Arab State in which Jews would live again as a minority as they do today, persecuted and tortured in Syria, and as they did in the past in countries such as Iraq, Yemen or Algeria, suffering all the pain and sorrow of oppression.

The speakers who opened the debate have confirmed its real purpose—to establish a PLO springboard from which the murder organization can continue its efforts to destroy the Jewish State. This is what the PLO's olive branch is. The choice before the Assembly is clear: On the one hand there is the Charter of the United Nations; on the other there is the PLO, whose sinister objectives, defined in its Covenant, and savage outrages are a desecration of the Charter.

On the one hand, there is Israel's readiness and desire to reach a peaceful settlement with the Palestnian Arab State of Jordan in which the Palestinian national identity would find full expression. On the other hand, there is PLO's denial of Israel's right to independence and of the Jewish people's right to self-determination.

The question is: Should there be peace between Israel and its eastern neighbor or should there be an attempt made to establish a PLO base to the east of Israel from which the terrorist campaign against the Jewish State's existence could be pursued?

The murderers of athletes in the Olympic Games of Munich, the butchers of children in Ma'alot, the assassins of diplomats in Khartoum do not belong to the international community. Israel shall see to it that they have no place in international diplomatic efforts. Israel will pursue the PLO murderers until justice is meted out to them. It will continue to take action against their organization and their bases until a definitive end is put to their atrocities. The blood of Jewish children will not be shed with impunity. Israel will not permit the establishment of PLO authority in any part of Palestine. The PLO will not be forced on the Palestinian Arabs; it will not be tolerated by the Jews of Israel.

Israel will continue to strive for peace with the Arab States. However, if the peacemaking process becomes paralyzed as a result of the Rabat and General Assembly resolutions, Israel will find a way, by the exercise of its sovereignty, to ensure its political and security interests while doing justice to the Arab population living in the administered areas.

No General Assembly resolution can establish the authority of an organization which has no authority, which does not represent anyone except the few thousand agents of death it employs, which has no foothold in any part of the territories it seeks to dominate. The PLO will remain what it is and where it is—outside the law and outside Palestine.

(Meeting 2283/13 November)

USSR
Yakov Malik,
Permanent Representative:

Thanks primarily to the efforts of the socialist and other peace-loving countries, considerable positive changes have occured tending towards the reduction of international tension. In those conditions, particular concern is aroused by the dangerous situation in the Middle East. The main reason is rooted in the fact that Israel, with the support of external forces, continues to pursue an aggressive and expansionist policy vis-a-vis the Arab States and stubbornly refuses to withdraw from the Arab lands it has seized; it is grossly flouting the legitimate national rights of the Arab peoples and is provocatively ignoring United Nations decisions.

The USSR has been consistently in favour of establishing a just and lasting peace in the Middle East which takes into account the interests of all the States and peoples in that area. To do that, it is essential to ensure the withdrawl of Israeli forces from all Arab lands seized in 1967 and to ensure the legitimate national rights of the Arab people of Palestine. There should be no delay to bring about a radical political settlement. The USSR is in favour of the immediate resumption of the Geneva peace conference which provides the most appropriate forum for ensuring that the Middle East problem is considered in its full complexity and that its decisions would satisfy the parties involved, including the representatives of the Arab peoples of Palestine.

The United Nations took an historic step towards recognizing the legitimate rights of the Arab people of Palestine when the Assembly decided to invite the PLO to participate in the discussion of the Palestine question. The vote on that resolution showed that the international community is mindful of the urgent need to settle the question as an integral part of an over-all Middle East settlement. The Palestine question is primarily a political one which affects the fate of an entire people defending its legitimate national rights. It cannot simply be reduced to one of refugees. The aggressor and those who protect are still trying to reduce it to that single aspect. Only by guaranteeing the rights of the Palestine people, including the right to self-determination and to their own statehood, can a realistic approach be found to bring about a just Middle East settlement.

The Israeli aggressor has not only expelled an entire people from its traditional lands but uses force and threats even against those States, such as Lebanon, which have welcomed the Palestinians into their territory. The aggressiveness and the illegitimacy of the actions of Israel and Zionist circles towards the Arab people of Palestine and its legitimate rights have been clearly demonstrated in recent days. The Zionist circles have carried out demonstrations unprecedented in their character and cynicism against both the Palestinians and the United Nations aimed at preventing the Assembly from discussing the question of Palestine with the participation of all the parties concerned. They have covered themselves with infamy before the entire world by burning the flag of the United Nations.

The ruling circles in Israel have planned and instigated that entire campaign of hostility and hatred by their warlike statements and refusal to hold negotiations with the representatives of the Arab people of Palestine, threatening a new bloody war. Israeli statesmen, who so often say such a great deal about the right of their State and their people to an independent and secure existence, deliberately forget or directly deny that the same right to an independent and secure existence should be acknowledged as belonging to every people, including the Arab people of Palestine.

In an attempt to mislead world public opinion regarding the genuine purposes of the Palestinian struggle, Zionist propaganda and the representatives of Israel in the United Nations are depicting the Palestinian movement as merely terrorist activities by small and inconsiderable groups of Palestinians. The whole world has become convinced, particularly after the statement of Yasser Arafat, that the Palestinian people are fighting for a just cause, for their legitimate rights, against cruel and unscrupulous usurpers.

Year by year the authority of the PLO, the guiding force in the struggle of the Palestinian people, has been growing. The Palestinian movement, a resistance movement, is becoming more mature and has turned into a weighty and genuine factor in the political situation in the Middle East. No solution to the problem of how the Arab people of Palestine can regain their legitimate rights can be achieved without the full participation of the Palestine representatives at all stages of the talks relating to the Palestinian problem. It is essential that the representatives of the Palestinian people, in the form of a delegation from the PLO, should take an independent part in the efforts made to bring about a peace settlement in the Middle East on an equal footing with other participants in the Geneva peace conference. The duty of the United Nations is to condemn those who try to prevent that and who threaten not to allow the Palestinians not to return to their homeland.

The USSR firmly supports the struggle of the Arab peoples, including those of Pale-stine, against the imperialist policies of aggression, for a just and durable peace, and for a solution to the key problems relating to the Middle East settlement; it is in favour of guaran-teeing the free development of the Arab peoples and their social and economic progress. The USSR has consistently striven to establish a genuine Middle East peace in accordance with the interests of all people in that area without exception; it will spare no efforts to achieve that end.

(Meeting 2287/15 November)

United States
John Scali,
Permanent Representative:
Those who seek a genuine resolution of the Middle East problem must keep ever in mind the continuing plight of people who have left their homes because of that conflict and have been unable to return. Continuing efforts by the international community to alleviate the hardships of those people are essential, but those efforts alone are not a solution. The goal of the Organization must be to seek ways to promote movement to a just and lasting solu-tion to the Arab-Israeli dispute while avoiding any measure which might make such move-ment more difficult.

The sole alternative to the sterile pursuit of change through violence is negotiation. The great achievement of the past year has been that the parties to the conflict have at last accepted that alternative and they have for the first time begun to make it work. A land-mark in that effort, and in Arab-Israeli relations, is set forth in Security Council resolution 338 (1973), in which the Council for the first time called for immediate negotiations "be-tween the parties concerned under appropriate auspices aimed at establishing a just and dur-able peace."

The consequences of a possible breakdown in that negotiating process cannot be overemphasized. The primary objective of the United States has been to maintain the momentum of the negotiating process. When the parties agreed to attend the Geneva confer-ence, they agreed that the role of the other participants would be discussed there. It is ne-cessary that all parties to the negotiations engage in give and take with the objective of achieving a permanent peace settlement that all parties can accept. That is the governing principle of resolution 338 (1973). If any of the parties rejects that governing principle or questions the right to exist of any of the parties to the negotiation, the best hopes for nego-tiation and peace are lost. Certainly it must be understood by all that Israel has a right to exist as a sovereign, independent State within secure and recognized boundaries.

During the debate there have been speakers who sought to equate terror with revolu-tion, who professed to see no difference between the slaughter of innocents and a struggle for national liberation. Some wished to compare the American Revolution and many other wars of liberation of the past 200 years with indiscriminate terrorism. If there were in-stances during the American Revolution where innocent people suffered, there was no in-stance where the revolutionary leadership boasted of or condoned such crimes. There were no victims, on either side, of a deliberate policy of terror.

The United States hopes all Member nations will reaffirm their support for a nego-tiated Middle East settlement, and their support fro Council resultions 242 (1967) and 338 (1973). To seek to alter them not only risks dangerous delays but could destroy prospects for peace in the foreseeable future.

The way to move towards a situation more responsive to Palestinian interests is not through new resolutions or dramatic parliamentary manoeuvres, but by weaving the Palestinian interests into the give and take of the negotiating process. The most important contribution the Assembly can make towards resolving the issue in the Middle East is to help establish an international climate in which the parties will be encouraged to maintain the momentum towards peace. The legitimate interests of the Palestinian people can be promoted in that negotiating process, and those negotiations will lead to a just and lasting peace for all the peoples in the Middle East.

(Meeting 2294/21 November)

14. U.N. GENERAL ASSEMBLY RESOLUTION 3236 (XXIX) ON PALESTINIANS' RIGHTS, NOVEMBER 22, 1974

The resolution was adopted by a roll-call vote of 89 in favour to 8 against, with 37 abstentions.

U.N. Monthly Chronicle, Vol. XI, No. 11, December 1974, pp. 36–37.

The General Assembly,

Having considered the question of Plaestine,

Having heard the statement of the Palestine Liberation Organization, the representative of the Palestinian people,

Having also heard other statements made during the debate,

Deeply concerned that no just solution to the problem of Palestine has yet been achieved and recognizing that the problem of Palestine continues to endanger international peace and security,

Recognizing that the Palestinian people is entitled to self-determination in accordance with the Charter of the United Nations,

Expressing its grave concern that the Palestinian people has been prevented from enjoying its inalienable rights, in particular its right to self-determination,

Guided by the purposes and principles of the Charter,

Recalling its relevant resolutions which affirm the rights of the Palestinian people to self-determination,

1. Reaffirms the inalienable rights of the Palestinian people in Palestine, including:

(a) The right to self-determination without external interference;

(b) The right to national independence and sovereignty;

2. Reaffirms also the inalienable right of the Palestinians to return to their homes and property from which they have been displaced and uprooted, and calls for their return;

3. Emphasizes that full respect for and the realization of these inalienable rights of the Palestinian people are indespensable for the solution of the question of Palestine;

4. Recognizes that the Palestinian people is a principal party in the establishment of a just and durable peace in the Middle East;

5. Further recognizes the right of the Palestinian people to regain its rights by all means in accordance with the purposes and principles of the Charter of the United Nations;

6. Appeals to all States and international organizations to extend their support to the Palestinian people in its struggle to restore its rights, in accordance with the Charter;

7. Requests the Secretary-General to establish contacts with the Palestine Liberation Organization on all matters concerning the question of Palestine;

8. Requests the Secretary-General to report to the General Assembly at its thirtieth session on the implementation of the present resolution;

9. Decides to include the item "Question of Palestine" in the provisional agenda of its thirtieth session.

15. U.N. GENERAL ASSEMBLY RESOLUTION 3237 (XXIX), OBSERVER STATUS FOR PLO, NOVEMBER 22, 1974

The resolution was adopted by a recorded vote of 95 in favour to 17 against, with 19 abstentions.

U.N. Monthly Chronicle, Vol. XI, No. 11, December 1974, p. 37.

The General Assembly,

Having considered the question of Palestine . . .

1. Invites the Palestine Liberation Organization to participate in the sessions and the work of the General Assembly in the capacity of observer;

2. Invites the Palestine Liberation Organization to participate in the sessions and the work of all international conferences convened under the auspices of the General Assembly in the capacity of observer;

3. Considers that the Palestine Liberation Organization is entitled to participate as an observer in the sessions and the work of all international conferences convened under the auspices of other organs of the United Nations;

4. Requests the Secretary-General to take the necessary steps for the implementation of the present resolution.

16. U.S. POLICY WITH RESPECT TO THE PLO, SECRET MEMORANDUM APPENDED TO THE SINAI INTERIM AGREEMENT, SEPTEMBER 1975

The memorandum was signed by U.S.A. Secretary of State Henry Kissinger and Israeli Foreign Minister, Yigal Allon. It was not officially published, but leaked out in *New York Times*, September 18, 1975.

1. The Geneva peace Conference will be reconvened at a time coordinated between the United States and Israel.

2. The United States will continue to adhere to its present policy with respect to the Palestine Liberation Organization, whereby it will not recognize or negotiate with the Palestine Liberation Organization so long as the Palestine Liberation Organization does not recognize Israel's right to exist and does not accept Security Council Resolutions 242 and 338. The United States Government will consult fully and seek to concert its position and strategy at the Geneva peace conference on this issue with the Government of Israel. Similarly, the United States will consult fully and seek to concert its position and strategy with Israel with regard to the participation of any other additional states. It is understood that the participation at a subsequent phase of the conference of any possible additional state, group or organization will require the agreement of all of the initial participants.

3. The United States will make every effort to insure at the conference that all the substantive negotiations will be on a bilateral basis.

4. The United States will oppose and, if necessary, vote against any initiative in the Security Council to alter adversely the terms of reference of the Geneva peace conference or to change Resolutions 242 and 338 in ways which are incompatible with their original purpose.

5. The United States will seek to insure that the role of the co-sponsors will be consistent with what was agreed in the memorandum of understanding between the United States Government and the Government of Israel of December 20, 1972.

6. The United States and Israel will concert action to assume that the conference will be conducted in a manner consonant with the objectives of this document and with the declared purpose of the conference, namely the advancement of a negotiated peace between Israel and its neighbors.

A statement made by the State Department Legal Counsel on October 6, 1975, said that the memorandum was "not legally binding" (*Washington Post*, January 6, 1976).

Secretary of State, Dr. Kissinger said it was not an "international commitment," but the USA was not "morally or politically" free to act as if it did not exist. It was an "important statement of diplomatic policy [that] will engage the good faith of the US. as long as the circumstances that gave rise to [it] continue." (Secretary Kissinger discusses Egypt-Israel Agreement. Statement before the Senate Committee on Foreign Relations made on October 7, 1975", *Department of State Bulletin*, vol. 73, no. 1896, October 27, 1975, p. 613).

17. SAUNDERS STATEMENT ON PALESTINIAN ISSUE, NOVEMBER 12, 1975

Statement by Harold M. Saunders, Deputy Assistant Secretary of State for Near Eastern and South Asian Affairs, made before the Special Sub-committee on Investigations of the House of Representatives Committee on International Relations on November 12, 1975, (*Department of State Bulletin*, December 1, 1975, pp. 797–800).

A just and durable peace in the Middle East is a central objective of the United States. Both President Ford and Secretary Kissinger have stated firmly on numerous occasions that the United States is determined to make every feasible effort to maintain the momentum of practical progress toward a peaceful settlement of the Arab-Israeli conflict.

We have also repeatedly stated that the legitimate interests of the Palestinian Arabs must be taken into account in the negotiation of an Arab-Israeli peace. In many ways, the Palestinian dimension of the Arab-Israeli conflict is the heart of that conflict. Final resolution of the problems arising from the partition of Palestine, the establishment of the State of Israel, and Arab opposition to these events will not be possible until agreement is reached defining a just and permanent status for the Arab peoples who consider themselves Palestinians.

The total number of Palestinian Arabs is estimated at a little more than 3 million. Of these, about 450,000 live in the area of Israel's pre-1967 borders; about 1 million are in the Israeli-occupied West Bank, East Jerusalem and Gaza; something less than a million are in Syria and Lebanon; and somewhat more than 200,000 or so are elsewhere, primarily in the gulf states.

Those in Israel are Israeli nationals. The great majority of those in the West Bank, East Jerusalem, and Jordan are Jordanian nationals. Palestinian refugees, who live outside of pre-1967 Israel and number 1.6 million, are eligible for food and/or services from the U.N. Relief and Works Agency (UNRWA); more than 650,000 of these live in camps.

The problem of the Palestinians was initially dealt with essentially as one involving displaced persons. The United States and other nations responded to the immediate humanitarian task of caring for a large number of refugees and trying to provide them with some hope in life.

In later years, there has been considerable attention given to the programs of UNRWA that help not only to sustain those people's lives but to lift the young people out of the refugee camps and to train them and give them an opportunity to lead productive lives. Many have taken advantage of this opportunity, and an unusually large number of them have completed secondary and university education. One finds Palestinians occupying leading positions throughout the Arab world as professionals and skilled workers in all fields.

The United States has provided some $620 million in assistance – about 62 percent of the total international support ($1 billion) for the Palestinian refugees over the past quarter of a century.

Today, however, we recognize that, in addition to meeting the human needs and responding to legitimate personal claims of the refugees, there is another interest that must be taken into account. It is a fact that many of the 3 million or so people who call themselves Palestinians today increasingly regard themselves as having their own identity as a people and desire a voice in determining their political status. As with any people in this situation, they have differences among themselves, but the Palestinians collectively are a political factor which must be dealt with if there is to be a peace between Israel and its neighbors.

The statement is often made in the Arab world that there will not be peace until the "rights of the Palestinians" are fulfilled; but there is no agreed definition of what is meant, and a variety of viewpoints have been expressed on what the legitimate objectives of the Palestinians are:

— Some Palestinian elements hold to the objective of a binational secular state in the area of the former mandate of Palestine. Realization of this objective would mean the end of the present State of Israel — a member of the United Nations — and its submergence in some larger entity. Some would be willing to accept merely as a first step toward this goal the establishment of a Palestinian state comprising the West Bank and Gaza, based on acceptance of Israel's right to exist as an independent state within roughly its pre-1967 borders.

— Some Palestinians and other Arabs envisage as a possible solution a unification of the West Bank and Gaza with Jordan. A variation of this which has been suggested would be the reconstitution of the country as a federated state, with the West Bank becoming an autonomous Palestinian province.

— Still others, including many Israelis, feel that with the West Bank returned to Jordan, and with the resulting existence of two communities — Palestinian and Jordanian — within Jordan, opportunities would be created thereby for the Palestinians to find self-expression.

— In the case of a solution which would rejoin the West Bank to Jordan or a solution involving a West Bank-Gaza state, there would still arise the property claims of those Palestinians who before 1948 resided in areas that became the State of Israel. These claims have been acknowledged as a serious problem by the international community ever since the adoption of Resolution 194 on this subject in 1948, a resolution which the United Nations has repeatedly reaffirmed and which the United States has supported. A solution will be further complicated by the property claims against Arab states of the many Jews from those states who moved to Israel in its early years after achieving statehood.

— In addition to property claims, some believe they should have the option of returning to their original homes under any settlement.

— Other Arab leaders, while pressing the importance of Palestinian involvement in a settlement, have taken the position that the definition of Palestinian interests is something for the Palestinian people themselves to sort out, and the view has been expressed by responsible Arab leaders that realization of Palestinian rights need not be inconsistent with the existence of Israel.

No one, therefore, seems in a position today to say exactly what Palestinian objectives are. Even the Palestine Liberation Organization (PLO), which is recognized by the Arab League and the U.N. General Assembly as the representative of the Palestinian people, has been ambivalent. Officially and publicly, its objective is described as a binational secular state, but there are some indications that coexistence between separate Palestinian and Israeli states might be considered.

When there is greater precision about those objectives, there can be clearer understanding about how to relate them to negotiations. There is the aspect of the future of the West Bank and Gaza — how those areas are to be defined and how they are to be governed. There is the aspect of the relationship between Palestinians in the West Bank and Gaza to those Palestinians who are not living in those areas, in the context of a settlement.

What is needed as a first step is a diplomatic process which will help bring forth a reasonable definition of Palestinian interests — a position from which negotiations on a solution of the Palestinian aspects of the problem might begin. The issue is not whether Palestinian interests should be expressed in a final settlement, but how. There will be no peace unless an answer is found.

Another requirement is the development of a framework for negotiations – a statement of the objectives and the terms of reference. The framework for the negotiations that have taken place thus far and the agreements they have produced involving Israel, Syria, and Egypt has been provided by UN Security Council Resolutions 242 and 338. In accepting that framework, all of the parties to the negotiations have accepted that the objective of the negotiations is peace between them based on mutual recognition, territorial integrity, political independence, the right to live in peace within secure and recognized borders, and the resolution of the specific issues which comprise the Arab-Israeli conflict.

The major problem that must be resolved in establishing a framework for bringing issues of concern to the Palestinians into negotiation, therefore, is to find a common basis for the negotiation that Palestinians and Israelis can both accept. This could be achieved by common acceptance of the above-mentioned Security Council resolutions, although they do not deal with the political aspect of the Palestinian problem.

A particularly difficult aspect of the problem is the question of who negotiates for the Palestinians. It has been our belief that Jordan would be a logical negotiator for the Palestinian-related issues. The Rabat summit, however, recognized the Palestine Liberation Organization as the "sole legitimate representative of the Palestinian people."

The PLO was formed in 1964, when 400 delegates from Palestinian communities throughout the Arab world met in Jerusalem to create an organization to represent and speak for the Palestinian people. Its leadership was originally middle-class and relatively conservative, but by 1969 control had passed into the hands of the Palestinian fedayeen, or commando, movement, which had existed since the mid-1950's but had come into prominence only after the 1967 war. The PLO became an umbrella organization for six separate fedayeen groups: Fatah; the Syrian-backed Saiqa; the Popular Democratic Front for the Liberation of Palestine; the General Command, a subgroup of the PFLP; and the Iraqi-backed Arab Liberation Front. Affiliated with the PLO are a number of "popular organizations" – labor and professional unions, students groups, women's groups, and so on. Fatah, the largest fedayeen group, also has a welfare apparatus to care for widows and orphans of deceased Fatah members.

However, the PLO does not accept the UN Security Council resolutions, does not recognize the existence of Israel, and has not stated its readiness to negotiate peace with Israel; Israel does not recognize the PLO or the idea of a separate Palestinian entity. Thus we do not at this point have the framework for a negotiation involving the PLO. We cannot envision or urge a negotiation between two parties as long as one professes to hold the objective of eliminating the other – rather than the objective of negotiating peace with it.

There is one other aspect to this problem. Elements of the PLO have used terrorism to gain attention for their cause. Some Americans as well as many Israelis and others have been killed by Palestinian terrorists. The international community cannot condone such practices, and it seems to us that there must be some assurance if Palestinians are drawn into th negotiating process that these practices will be curbed.

This is the problem which we now face. If the progress toward peace which has now begun is to continue, a solution to this question must be found. We have not devised an "American" solution, nor would it be appropriate for us to do so. This is the responsibility of the parties and the purpose of the negotiating process. But we have not closed our minds to any reasonable solution which can contribute to progress toward our overriding objective in the Middle East – an Arab-Israeli peace. The step-by-step approach to negotiations which we have pursued has been based partly on the understanding that issues in the Arab-Israeli conflict take time to mature. It is obvious that thinking on the Palestinian aspects of the problem must evolve on all sides. As it does, what is not possible today may become possible.

Our consultations on how to move the peace negotiations forward will recognize the need to deal with this subject. As Secretary Kissinger has said:

We are prepared to work with *all* the parties toward a solution of *all* the issues yet remaining – including the issue of the future of the Palestinians.

We will do so because the issues of concern to the Palestinians are important in themselves and because the Arab governments participating in the negotiations have made clear that progress in the overall negotiations will depend in part on progress on issues of concern to the Palestinians. We are prepared to consider any reasonable proposal from any quarter, and we will expect other parties to the negotiation to be equally open-minded.

Secretary Kissinger said on November 15, 1975 that the statement was "a somewhat academic exercise explaining in a purely theoretical manner several aspects of the Palestinian problem as Mr. Saunders saw them," but a State Department spokesman said that Saunders "had spoken for the administration." Theere were reports saying that Kissinger took part in its preparation and "personally approved the carefully written paper word for word." (*New York Times*, December 31, 1975)

18. BROOKINGS REPORT, DECEMBER 1975
Toward Peace in the Middle East.
Report of a Study Group. The Brookings Institution (Washington, D.C., December 1975), pp. 10–11.

The Palestinians for the most part believe that they have a right to self-determination. For a peace settlement to be viable, indeed for it even to be negotiated and concluded, this right will have to be recognized in principle and, as part of the settlement, given satisfaction in practice.

Whoever represents the Palestinians must recognize the equal right to self-determination of Israel and Jordan. In particular, the Palestinians must recognize the sovereignty and integrity of Israel within agreed frontiers and must accept whatever security arrangements, mutual guarantees, demilitarized zones, or UN presence are embodies in the peace settlement.

Such a settlement also cannot be achieved unless Israel accepts the principle of Palestinian self-determination and some generally acceptable means is found of putting that principle into practice.

Possibilities for doing so might include (1) an independent Palestine state accepting the obligations and commitments of the peace agreements or (2) a Palestine entity voluntarily federated with Jordan but exercising the extensive political autonomy King Hussein has offered. Either of these arrangements might be supplemented by close economic cooperation with Israel and Jordan, possibly evolving into a wider regional common market.

Moreover, a peace settlement should include provision for the resettlement of those Palestinian refugees desiring to return to whatever new Palestinian entity is created, for reasonable compensation for property losses for Arab refugees from Israel and for Jews formerly resident in Arab states, and for sufficient economic assistance to the state or entity in which Palestinian self-determination is realized, from its neighbors and from the international community, to enable it to survive and to develop.

Accomplishment of these essential aspects of a settlement is complicated by disagreement and uncertainty as to who can negotiate authoritatively on behalf of the Palestinians.

While the Arab states at the Rabat meeting in 1974 accepted the Palestine Liberation Organization as representing the Palestinians, and many other states have also done so, its claim is not unchallenged. Many Jordanians continue to believe Jordan has a better right to this representation. It is not clear to what extent the PLO can negotiate on behalf of the Palestinians on the West Bank, in Gaza, or in Jordan, to whom it does not have ready access. The PLO has not publicly recognized Israel's right to exist. Israel has not recognized the PLO or agreed to accept the establishment of a Palestine state.

Nevertheless, it can certainly be said that a solution to the Palestinian dimension of the conflict will require the participation of credible Palestinian representatives who are prepared to accept the existence of Israel.

19. 13TH PNC SESSION, CAIRO, MARCH 12–20, 1977

MENA, Cairo, March 20, 1977. Quoted from FBIS, ME, March 21, 1977. pp. A7–A12.

A. Political Declaration (excerpts)

Proceeding from the Palestine National Charter and the previous National Council's resolutions; out of care for the decisions and political gains achieved by the PLO on the Arab and international levels during the period following the 12th session of the PNC; after studying and debating the latest developments in the Palestine issue; and stressing support for the Palestinian national struggle in Arab and international forums, the PNC affirms the following:

1. The PNC affirms that the Palestine issue is the essence and root of the Arab-Zionist conflict. Security Council Resolution 242 ignores the Palestine people and their firm rights, and therefore the PNC confirms its rejection of this resolution and rejects dealings on the Arab and international levels on the basis of this resolution.

2. The PNC affirms the PLO's stand in its determination to continue the armed struggle and its concomitant forms of political and mass struggle to achieve our inalienable national rights.

3. The PNC affirms that the struggle in the occupied territory in all its military, political and popular forms constitutes the central link of its program of struggle. On this basis, the PLO will strive to escalate the armed struggle in the occupied land, to escalate all forms of concomitant struggle, and to give all kinds of moral support to the masses of our people in the occupied land so as to escalate this struggle and strengthen their steadfastness to defeat and liquidate the occupation.

4. The PNC affirms the PLO's stand which rejects all kinds of American capitulationist settlements and all liquidationist projects. The council affirms the PLO's determination to abort any settlement achieved at the expense of our people's firm national rights. The PNC calls upon the Arab nation to shoulder its pan-Arab responsibilities and to pool all its energies to confront these imperialist and Zionist plans.

5. The PNC stresses the importance and necessity of national unity, political and military, among all contingents of the Palestine revolution within the framework of the PLO, because this is one of the basic conditions for victory. That is why it is necessary to coordinate national unity of all levels and in all spheres on the basis of commitment to all these resolutions and to draw up programs that will insure the implementation of this.

6. The PNC affirms the right of the Palestinian revolution to be present on the soil of fraternal Lebanon within the framework of the Cairo Agreement and its appendexes concluded between the PLO and the Lebanese authorities. The council also affirms adherence to implementation of the Cairo Agreement in letter and spirit, including preservation of revolution's position and the security of the camps. The PNC rejects any unilateral interpretation of this agreement. Meanwhile, it affirms its concern over Lebanon's sovereignty and security.

7. The PNC greets the heroic fraternal Lebanese people and affirms the PLO's concern over Lebanon's territorial integrity, the unity of its people, and its security, independence, sovereignty and Arabism. The PNC affirms its pride in the support rendered by this heroic fraternal people to the PLO, which is struggling for our people's regaining their national rights to their homeland as well as their right to return to this homeland. The PNC strongly affirms the need for deepening and consolidating cohesion between all Lebanese nationalist forces and the Palestinian revolution.

8. The council affirms the need to strengthen the Arab front participating in the Palestinian revolution and to deepen cohesion with all forces participating in it in all Arab

countries, as well as to escalate the joint Arab struggle and to further strengthen the Palestinian revolution in order to cope with the imperialist and Zionist designs.

9. The PNC has decided to consolidate Arab struggle and solidarity on the basis of struggle against imperialism and Zionism, to work for the liberation of all the occupied Arab areas, and to continue to support the Palestinian revolution in order to regain the eternal national rights of the Palestinian Arab people without any conciliation [sulh] or recognition [of Israel].

10. The PNC affirms the PLO's right to exercise its struggle responsibilities on the pan-Arab level and through any Arab land for the sake of liberating the occupied areas.

11. The PNC has decided to continue the struggle to regain the national rights of our people, particularly their rights of return, self-determination and establishing their independent national state of their national soil.

12. The PNC affirms the significance of cooperation and solidarity with socialist, non-alined, Islamic and African countries, and with all the national liberation movements in the world.

13. The PNC hails the stands and struggle of all democratic countries and forces against Zionism, in its capacity as one form of racism, as well as against its aggressive practices.

14. The PNC affirms the significance of establishing relations and coordinating with the progressive and democratic Jewish forces inside and outside the occupied homeland, since those forces are struggling against Zionism as a doctrine and practice. The PNC calls upon all states and forces who love freedom, justice and peace in the world to cut off all forms of assistance to and cooperation with the racist Zionist regime and to stop contacting it and its tools.

15. Taking into consideration the important accomplishments achieved in the Arab and international arenas since the conclusion of the PNC's 12th session, the PNC, which has reviewed the political report submitted by the PLO, has decided the following:

    A. The council confirms its care for the PLO's rights to participate in an independent manner and on an equal footing in all conferences and international forums concerned with the Palestine issue and the Arab-Zionist conflict, with a view to achieving our inalienable national rights as approved by the UN General Assembly in 1974, specifically in Resolution 3236.

    B. The council declares that any settlement or agreement affecting the rights of our Palestinian people in the absence of this people will be completely null and void. Long live the Palestine revolution, long live Palestinian unity among the revolution's contingents, glory and immortality for our innocent martyrs! This revolution will continue until victory!

PNC official spokesman Mahmud Al-Labadi said that the Arab Front for the Liberation of Palestine, headed by 'Abd al-Wahhab al-Kayyali, and the PFLP-GC, headed by Ahmad Jibril – two organizations which are well known for their position within the rejectionist front – voted for the Political Declaration approved by the council. However, 13 members who attended on behalf of the Popular Front [presumably the PFLP] voted against the Political Declaration and the PNC resolution.

Al-Labadi added that the representatives of the Popular Front expressed reservations concerning two points in the Political Declaration and requested that these two points be amended. But the council refused and the Political Declaration was put to a vote as a whole. The vast majority approved its issuance. Thus, 194 out of 207 members present at the session voted for the issuance. Al-Labadi said the representatives of the Popular Front will also express reservations concerning their representation in the PLO Executive Committee.

B. Final Statement (Summary)

The PNC has affirmed the Palestinian people's determination to exercise their natural, legitimate right to continue the struggle with all means against the Zionist racist entity to defend themselves, attain the liberation of Palestine and achieve a just peace in the area. This came in the final statement issued today by the 13th session of the PNC, which ended its 9-day meetings at the Arab League premises in Cairo today. The council called on the international community to tackle the Palestine issue – the core of the Arab-Zionist conflict – on the basis of UN General Assembly Resolution 3236, which provides for the return of all Palestinians to their homes and property and their rights to self-determination, national sovereignty and the establishment of an independent national state on their national soil.

The council also affirmed its adherence to the PLO'S strategic objective, the liberation of the Palestine from the racist Zionist occupation so that it can become a homeland to the people of Palestine in which a democratic state of Palestine can be established where its citizens can live without any discrimination by color or race.

In its statement, the PNC said that when the PLO speaks of the Palestine of tomorrow, it includes in its aspirations – as it announced at the UN rostrum – "all Jews who live with us in peace and without discrimination" and who cast aside Zionist racist affiliation.

In its final statement today, the PNC underlined the distinction between Zionism and racism and the right of every Jew to a dignified life in his homeland [watanahu]. The statement said that the PLO and the Arab states will seek means to apply this right with the Jews of the Arab homeland who wish to return to their homelands.

Taking into consideration the daily practices of the Zionist entity which epitomize the meaning of occupation, the PNC explained that attaining a just peace in the area will still mean days of struggle and that there is no scope for anything except struggle aimed at the liberation of the Arab land. The council said that the means of achieving this objective is through reconstructing and strengthening the bonds of national unity in the Palestinian arena, escalating the armed struggle and the resistance of the Palestinian people against occupation, mobilizing Arab potentials through a unified Arab position to steer these potentials in this struggle, and affirming the bonds with the Arab frontline states and the Arab depth ['umq] states in general.

Concluding its statement, the PNC said that the means for achieving this objective in the international arena is further political struggle in cooperation with the Third World states, the states of the Islamic world and the socialist states to isolate the Zionist racist entity.

20. JOINT US-USSR STATEMENT ON THE MIDDLE EAST, OCTOBER 1, 1977

US State Department release. (Soviet text: TASS in English and *Pravda,* October 2, 1977).

Having exchanged views regarding the unsafe situation which remains in the Middle East, United States Secretary of State Cyrus Vance and member of the Politburo of the Central Committee of the Communist Party of the Soviet Union, Minister for Foreign Affairs of the USSR A. A. Gromyko, have the following statement to make on behalf of their countries which are cochairmen of the Geneva Peace Conference on the Middle East:

1. Both governments are convinced that vital interests of the peoples of this area as well as the interests of strengthening peace and international security in general urgently dictate the necessity of achieving as soon as possible a just and lasting settlement of the Arab-Israeli conflict. This settlement should be comprehensive, incorporating all parties concerned and all questions.

The United States and the Soviet Union believe that, within the framework of a comprehensive settlement of the Middle East problem, all specific questions of the settlement should be resolved, including such key issues as withdrawal of Israeli armed forces from territories occupied in the 1967 conflict; the resolution of the Palestinian question including insuring the legitimate rights of the Palestinian people; termination of the state of war and establishment of normal peaceful relations on the basis of mutual recognition of the principles of sovereignty, territorial integrity and political independence.

The two governments believe that, in addition to such measures for insuring the security of the borders within Israel and the neighboring Arab states as the establishment of demilitarized zones and the agreed stationing in them of UN troops or observers, international guarantees of such borders as well as of the observance of the terms of the settlement can also be established, should the contracting parties so desire. The United States and the Soviet Union are ready to participate in these guarantees subject to their constitutional processes.

2. The United States and the Soviet Union believe that the only right and effective way for achieving a fundamental solution to all aspects of the Middle East problem in its entirety is negotiating within the framework of the Geneva Peace Conference, specially convened for these purposes, with participation in its work of the representatives of all the parties involved in the conflict including those of the Palestinian people, and legal and contractual formalization of the decisions reached at the conference.

In their capacity as cochairmen of the Geneva Conference, the US and the USSR affirm their intention through joint efforts and in their contacts with the parties concerned to facilitate in every way the resumption of the work of the conference not later than December 1977. The cochairmen note that there still exist several questions of a procedural and organizational nature which remain to be agreed upon by the participants to the conference.

3. Guided by the goal of achieving a just political settlement in the Middle East and of eliminating the explosive situation in this area of the world, the US and the USSR appeal to all the parties in the conflict to understand the necessity for careful consideration of each other's legitimate rights and interests and to demonstrate mutual readiness to act accordingly.

21. CAMP DAVID AGREEMENT, SEPTEMBER 17, 1978

"A Framework for Peace in the Middle East Agreed at Camp David" signed by President A. Sadat for the Government of the Arab Republic of Egypt and Prime Minister M. Begin for the Government of Israel. Witnessed by President J. Carter of the United States of America.

US Department of State Publication 8954, Near East and South Asian Series 88, September 1978, pp. 7–8, (Excerpt).

A. West Bank and Gaza

1. Egypt, Israel Jordan and the representatives of the Palestinian people should participate in negotiations on the resolution of the Palestinian problem in all its aspects. To achieve that objective, negotiations relating to the West Bank and Gaza should proceed in three stages:

(a) Egypt and Israel agree that, in order to ensure a peaceful and orderly transfer of authority, and taking into account the security concerns of all the parties, there should be transitional arrangements for the West Bank and Gaza for a period not exceeding five years. In order to provide full autonomy to the inhabitants, under these arrangements the Israeli military government and its civilian administration will be withdrawn as soon as a self-governing authority has been freely elected by the inhabitants of these areas to replace the existing military government. To negotiate the details of a transitional arrangement, the Government of Jordan will be invited to join the negotiations on the basis of this framework. These new arrangements should give due consideration both to the principle of self-government by the inhabitants of these territories and to the legitimate security concerns of the parties involved.

(b) Egypt, Israel, and Jordan will agree on the modalities for establishing the elected self-governing authority in the West Bank and Gaza. The delegations of Egypt and Jordan may include Palestinians from the West Bank and Gaza or other Palestinians as mutually agreed. The parties will negotiate an agreement which will define the powers and responsibilities of the self-governing authority to be exercised in the West Bank and Gaza. A withdrawal of Israeli armed forces will take place and there will be a redeployment of the remaining Israeli forces into specified security locations. The agreement will also include arrangements for assuring internal and external security and public order. A strong local police force will be established, which may include Jordanian citizens. In addition, Israeli and Jordanian forces will participate in joint patrols and in the manning of control posts to assure the security of the borders.

(c) When the self-governing authority (administrative council) in the West Bank and Gaza is established and inaugurated, the transitional period of five years will begin. As soon as possible, but not later than the third year after the beginning of the transitional jperiod, negotiations will take place to determine the final status of the West Bank and Gaza and its relationship with its neighbors, and to conclude a peace treaty between Israel and Jordan by the end of the transitional period. These negotiations will be conducted among Egypt, Israel, Jordan, and the elected representatives of the inhabitants of the West Bank and Gaza. Two separate but related committees will be convened, one committee, consisting of representatives of the four parties which will negotiate and agree on the final status of the West Bank and Gaza, and its relationship with its neighbors, and the second committee, consisting of representatives of Israel and representatives of Jordan to be joined by the elected representatives of the inhabitants of the West Bank and Gaza, to negotiate the peace treaty between Israel and Jordan, taking into account the agreement reached on the final status of the West Bank and Gaza. The negotiations shall be based on all the provisions and principles of UN Security Council Resolution 242. The negotiations will resolve, among other matters, the location of the boundaries and the nature of the security arrangements. The solution from the negotiations must also recognize the legitimate rights of the Palestinian people and their just requirements. In this way, the Palestinians will participate in the determination of their own future through:

1) The negotiations among Egypt, Israel, Jordan and the representatives of the inhabitants of the West Bank and Gaza to agree on the final status of the West Bank and Gaza and other outstanding issues by the end of the transitional period.

2) Submitting their agreement to a vote by the elected representatives of the inhabitants of the West Bank and Gaza.

3) Providing for the elected representatives of the inhabitants of the West Bank and Gaza to decide how they shall govern themselves consistent with the provisions of their agreement.

4) Participating as stated above in the work of the committee negotiating the peace treaty between Israel and Jordan.

2. All necessary measures will be taken and provisions made to assure the security of Israel and its neighbors during the transitional period and beyond. To assist in providing such security, a strong local police force will be constituted by the self-governing authority. It will be composed of inhabitants of the West Bank and Gaza. The police will maintain continuing liaison on internal security matters with the designated Israeli, Jordanian, and Egyptian officers.

3. During the transitional period, representatives of Egypt, Israel, Jordan and the self-governing authority will constitute a continuing committee to decide by agreement on the modalities of admission of persons displaced from the West Bank and Gaza in 1967, together with necessary measures to prevent disruption and disorder. Other matters of common concern may also be dealt with by this committee.

4. Egypt and Israel will work with each other and with other interested parties to establish agreed procedures for a prompt, just and permanent implementation of the resolution of the refugee problem.

22. SOVIET TRAINING FOR PLO

Robert Moss, "Moscow Backs Terror, Inc.", *Daily Telegraph*, (London), July 16, 1979, p. 5 (Excerpt).

In the storm of controversy inspired by the red-carpet reception that the Austrian chancellor, Bruno Kreisky, recently accorded PLO leader Yasir Arafat, one vital fact passed largely neglected.

This is that it is a tragic error for any Western government to confer any degree of legitimacy on the PLO, not only because of its methods – the deliberate assault on innocent men, women and children in many different countries – but because its operations are directly supported and, in some cases, controlled by the Soviet Union.

I have called attention in this column in the past to the services that the PLO has rendered to the Soviet KGB; for example, by providing a link, or "cut-out," between Moscow and Ayatollah Khomeyni's entourage before the overthrow of the Shah; by helping to set up a new revolutionary secret police in Teheran; and by arming and advising extreme left-wing groups in Turkey.

I can now make public some important new evidence of the degree of Soviet involvement in PLO activities. The Russians are currently training hundreds of Palestinians – in addition to recruits from the radical Arab states and carefully-picked non-Arabs of the "Carlos" type – in establishments near Moscow and along the Black Sea.

There are similar training camps (at which the East Germans figure prominently as instructors) near Varna in Bulgaria and in Czechoslovakia.

The military academy at Simferopol in the Crimea is a primary reception centre for PLO men selected for sabotage and terrorist training in the Soviet Union. Courses specially tailored for the Palestinians (according to sources inside the PLO) include river crossings and all types of sabotage.

These courses are attended by mixed groups of 50–60 PLO trainees, drawn from different guerrilla organisations according to a quota system.

At a typical course at Simferopol, there were recruits from Fatah, As-Sa'iqah (a Syrian-based group whose foreign operations are under the direct supervision of Syrian military intelligence), the Palestine Liberation Front (PLF) and George Habash's Popular Front for the Liberation of Palestine (PFLP).

The differences between these rival terror groups were apparently submerged, on this occasion, for the sake of collective self-advancement.

However, two other Palestinian groups that were invited to send trainees to the course declined the invitation: the Iraqi-based Arab Liberation Front (nominally headed by Abu Shamil but in reality a wholly owned subsidiary of Iraq's G-2) because it was jealous of the preponderance of Fatah members; the overtly Marxist Democratic Front for the Liberation of Palestine (DFLP), headed by Nayif Hawatimah, on the grounds that, as communists, their members already had ample facilities available to them in the Soviet Union that were not open to other Palestinians.

Significantly, efforts to indoctrinate PLO trainees in the virtues of the Soviet system begin even before their departure – equipped with doctored Jordanian, Iranian or Lebanese passports – from the camps in Lebanon and Syria.

Officers from the "Political Department" of Fatah like Abu Khalid Husayn, formerly based at the Shatila camp, provide crash courses in the achievements of the Bolshevik revolution and the Soveit model of society.

On arrival in Moscow, Palestinian recruits are received by Al-Amid ash-Sa'ir and Hikmat Abu Zayd, the director and deputy director (respectively) of the PLO office in Russia.

Palestinian trainees of above-average aptitudes are sometimes transferred for special courses in KGB or GRU (Soviet military intelligence) schools, which also receive a steady intake of intelligence officers from Libya, Syria, Iraq and South Yemen.

In the Soviet view, the PLO is a tremendously useful asset. It can supply (a) shock troops, like the members of Idi Amin's bodyguard in Uganda; (b) subversive agents, like the networks in the gulf sheikdoms and Saudi Arabia that can now hold a knife to the throats of pro-Western monarchs and (c) all-purpose terrorists – without automatically implicating the Russians in PLO operations.

The PLO can serve as the middleman in supplying arms to the "national liberation movements" that the Soviet Union is pledged to support under article 28 of its revised (1977) constitution – a document that openly defines support for terrorism as a permanent element in Soviet policy, under the euphemistic phrasing, and should therefore bring down on the Russians' heads the opprobrium deserved by a "terrorist state."

In the view of some Western analysts, it was thanks to the PLO that Joshua Nkomo' ZAPU terrorists were able to shoot down two Rhodesian civilian airliners with Soviet-made Strela (SAM-7) missiles.

The inventory of Soviet-made arms in the hands of the PLO is long and impressive including many types of anti-tank and anti-aircraft missiles, artillery, and the same kind of submachine gun (the Czech-made Skorpion) that Italian ballistics experts have now concluded was the murder weapon in the Aldo Moro case.

The PLO under Soviet guidance has not been parsimonious about making its extensive armoury available to sympathetic groups in other parts of the world. Gen. Ergun Gokdeniz in a recent interview with a Turkish Army magazine, confirmed my reports in this column about the PLO's role in arming Turkish rebels, and commented that, thanks to the Russians the PLO "have been trained for wars of liberation to be fought with Marxist-Leninist methods."

23. EUROPEAN COMMUNITY, VENICE DECLARATION, JUNE 13, 1980
Official English text, AP, June 13, 1980.

1. The heads of state and government and the ministers of foreign affairs held a comprehensive exchange of views on all aspects of the present situation in the Middle East, including the state of negotiations resulting from the agreements signed between Egypt and Israel in March 1979. They agreed that growing tensions affecting this region constitute a serious danger and render a comprehensive solution to the Israeli-Arab conflict more necessary and pressing than ever.

2. The nine member states of the European Community consider that the traditional ties and common interests which link Europe to the Middle East oblige them to play a special role and now require them to work in a more concrete way towards peace.

3. In this regard, the nine countries of the community base themselves on (UN) Security Council resolutions 242 and 338 and the positions which they have expressed on several occasions, notable in their declarations of 29 June 1977, 19 September 1978, 26 March and 18 June 1979, as well as in the speech made on their behalf on 25 September 1979 by the Irish minister of foreign affairs at the 34th UN General Assembly.

4. On the bases thus set out, the time has come to promote the recognition and implementation of the two principles universally accepted by the international community: the right to existence and to security of all the states in the region, including Israel, and justice for all the peoples, which implies the recognition of the legitimate rights of the Palestinian people.

5. All of the countries in the area are entitled to live in peace within secure, recognized and guaranteed borders. The necessary guaranties for a peace settlement should be provided by the UN by a decision of the Security Council and, if necessary, on the basis of other mutually agreed procedures. The nine declare that they are prepared to participate within the framework of a comprehensive settlement in a system of concrete and binding international guarantees, including (guarantees) on the ground.

6. A just solution must finally be found to the Palestinian problem, which is not simply one of refugees. The Palestinian people, which is conscious of existing as such, must be placed in a position, by an appropriate process defined within the framework of the comprehensive peace settlement, to exercise fully its right to self-determination.

7. The achievement of these objectives requires the involvement and support of all the parties concerned in the peace settlement which the nine are endeavouring to promote in keeping with the principles formulated in the declaration referred to above. These principles apply to all the parties concerned, and thus to the Palestinian people, and to the PLO, which will have to be associated with the negotiations.

8. The nine recognize the special importance of the role played by the question of Jerusalem for all the parties concerned. The nine stress that they will not accept any unilateral initiative designed to change the status of Jerusalem and that any agreement on the city's status should guarantee freedom of access for everyone to the holy places.

9. The nine stress the need for Israel to put an end to the territorial occupation which it has maintained since the conflict of 1967, as it has done for part of Sinai. They are deeply convinced that the Israeli settlements constitute a serious obstacle to the peace process in the Middle East. The nine consider that these settlements, as well as modifications in population and property in the occupied Arab territories, are illegal under international law.

10. Concerned as they are to put an end to violence, the nine consider that only the renunciation of force or the threatened use of force by all the parties can create a climate of confidence in the area, and constitute a basic element for a comprehensive settlement of the conflict in the Middle East.

11. The nine have decided to make the necessary contacts with all the parties concerned. The objective of these contacts would be to ascertain the position of the various parties with respect to the principles set out in this declaration and in the light of the results of this consultation process to determine the form which such an initiative on their part could take.

Bibliography

Books and Pamphlets

Ben-Dor, Gabriel, ed., *The Palestinians and the Middle East Conflict,* Tel Aviv, Turtledove Publishing, 1978.

Bell, J. Bowyer, *The Myth of the Guerrilla: Revolutionary Theory and Malpractice*, New York, Knopf, 1971.

Cooley, John K., *Green March, Black September, The Story of the Palestinian Arabs,* London, Frank Cass, 1973.

Curtiss, Michael, ed., *The Palestinians, People, History, Politics,* New Brunswick, New Jersey, Transaction Books, 1975.

Dobson, Christopher, *Black September; its short, violent history*, New York, Macmillan, 1974.

Eran, Oded, *The Soviet Union and the Palestine Guerrilla Organizations,* Tel Aviv, Shiloah Center for Middle Eastern and African Studies, Tel Aviv University, 1971 (Occasional papers).

Golan, Galia, *The Soviet Union and the PLO,* London, The International Institute for Strategic Studies, Adelphi Papers no. 131, 1977.

Harkabi, Yehoshafat, *Fedayeen Action and Arab Strategy,* London, The Institute for Strategic Studies, Adelphi Papers no. 53, 1968.

———, *Arab Attitudes to Israel,* London, Valentine, Mitchell, 1972.

———, *Palestinians and Israel,* New York, J. Wiley, 1974.

———, *Arab Strategies and Israel's Response,* New York, Free Press, 1977.

Hirst, David, *The Gun and the Olive Branch,* London, Faber and Faber, 1977.

Howley, Dennis C., *The United Nations and the Palestinians,* New York, Exposition Press, 1975.

Hussain, Mehmood, *The Palestine Liberation Organisation: A Study in Ideology, Strategy and Tactics,* New Delhi, University Publishers, 1975.

Institute for the Study of Conflict, *Since Jordan; the Palestinian Fedayeen,* London, Conflict Studies no. 38, 1973.

Jansen, Michael, *The United States and the Palestinian People,* Beirut, Institute for Palestinian Studies, 1968.

Joiner, Charles Adrian, *The Fedayeen and Arab World Politics,* Morristown, New Jersey, General Learning Press, 1974.

Jones, W. M., *Predicting Insurgent and Government Decision,* Santa Monica, California, Rand Corporation, 1970, (RM–6358–PR).

Kadi, Leila, *Basic Political Documents of the Armed Palestinian Resistance Movement,* Beirut, PLO Research Centre, 1969.

Kazziha, Walid W., *Revolutionary Transformation in the Arab World; Habash and his comrades from nationalism to Marxism,* London, C. Knight, 1975.

———, *Palestine in the Arab Dilemma,* London, Croom Helm, 1979.

Khalid, Laila (pseud.), *My people shall live; the autobiography of a revolu-*

tionary, edited by George Hajjar, London, Modder and Stoughton, 1973.

Kiernan, Thomas, *Arafat: the man and the myth*, New York, W. W Norton, 1976.

Laffin, John, *Fedayeen; the Arab-Israeli dilemma*, London, Cassel, 1973.

Maoz, Moshe, *Soviet and Chinese Relations with the Palestinian Guerrilla Organizations*, Jerusalem, Hebrew University, The Leonard Davis Institute for International Relations, 1974.

———, ed., *Palestinian Arab Politics*, Jerusalem, Academic Press, 1975 (Truman Institute Studies, Middle East Services).

Maron, Ran, *The Development of US Policy on the Palestine Issue, October 1973–November 1976*, Tel Aviv, The Shiloah Center for Middle Eastern and African Studies, Tel Aviv University, 1978 (Occasional papers).

Norton, Augustus R., *Moscow and the Palestinians; a new tool of Soviet policy in the Middle East*, Coral Gables, Florida, University of Miami, Center for Advanced International Studies, 1974.

O'Ballance, Edgar, *Arab Guerrilla Power, 1967–1972*, London, Faber and Faber, 1974.

O'Neill, Bard Emmett, *Revolutionary Warfare in the Middle East; the Israelis vs. the Fedayeen*, Boulder, Colorado, Paladin Press, 1974.

———, *Armed Struggle in Palestine*, Boulder, Colorado, Westview Press 1979.

Pearlman, Maurice, *Mufti of Juersalem: the story of Haj Amin el Husseini*, London, V. Gollancz, 1947.

Peretz, Don, Evan M. Wilson and Richard J. Ward, *A Palestine Entity?*, Washington, DC, The Middle East Institute, 1970.

Porath, Yehoshua, *The Emergence of the Palestinian Arab National Movement, 1918–1929*, London, F. Cass, 1974.

———, *The Palestinian Arab National Movement, from riots to rebellion*. Volume 2: 1929–1939, London, F. Cass, 1977.

Price, David Lynn, *Jordan and Palestinians: the PLO's prospects*, London, Institute for the Study of Conflict, Conflict Study no. 66, 1975.

Price-Jones, David, *The Face of Defeat: Palestinian Refugees and Guerrillas*, London, Weidenfeld and Nicolson, 1972.

Quandt, William B., Fuad Jabber, Ann Mosely Lesch, *The Politics of Palestinian Nationalism*, Berkeley, University of California Press, 1973.

———, *Palestinian Nationalism: its political and military dimensions*, Santa Monica, California, Rand Corp. 1971 (R–782–ISA).

Al-Rayyin, Riyad Najib and Dunia Nahas, *Guerrillas for Palestine*, London, C. Melin, 1976.

Schiff, Zeev and Raphael Rothstein, *Fedayeen: guerrillas against Israel*, New York, D. McKay Co., 1972.

———, *Fedayeen: the story of the Palestinian guerrillas*, London, Valentine, Mitchel, 1972.

Sharabi, Hisham, *Palestine guerrillas: their credibility and effectiveness*, Beirut, Institute for Palestine Studies, 1970.

Al-Shuqayri, Ahmed, *Liberation — not negotiation,* Beirut, PLO Research Centre, 1966.

Snow, Peter and David Phillips, *The Arab Hijack War,* New York, Ballantine, 1970.

Sobel, Lester, ed., *Palestine Impasse: Arab Guerrillas and International Terror,* New York, Facts on File, 1977.

Tsai Ching-lang. *Chinese Communists' Support to Palestinian Guerrilla Organizations,* Taipei, Taiwan, World Anti-Communist League, 1973.

Tuma, Elias H. and Haim Darin-Drabkin, *The Economic Case for Palestine,* London, Croom Helm, 1978.

US Congress, House Committee on International Relations, *The Palestinian Issue in Middle East Peace Efforts: hearings* . . . , 94th Conf., 1st session, September 30, October 1, 8 and November 12, 1975, Washington, DC, GPO, 1976.

Ward, Richard J., Don Peretz, Evan M. Wilson, *The Palestinian State: a rational approach,* New York, Fort Washington, Keunikat Press, 1977.

Yaari, Ehud, *Strike Terror; the story of Fatah,* New York, Sabra Books, 1970.

Yodfat, Aryeh, *Between Revolutionary Slogans and Pragmatism: The PRC and the Middle East,* Bruxelles, Centre d'Etude du Sud-Est Asiatique et de l'Extreme Orient, 1979.

Articles

Abbreviations:
JPS — Journal of Palestine Studies, Beirut
MEJ — Middle East Journal, Washington, DC
NME — New Middle East, London
WT — The World Today, London

Abdul Mohsen, Assem, "Palestinians agree on strategy but not on tactics," *The Middle East,* (London), May 1977, pp. 23–28.

Armanasi, Ghath, "The rights of Palestinians: the international definition," *JPS,* vol. 3, no. 3 (Spring 1974), pp. 88–96.

Ben-Meir, Alon, "The Arab Palestinians," *Current History,* (New York), vol. 74, January 1978, pp. 24–28, 41–42.

Brown, Neville, "After the showdown: Jordan is on the move," *NME,* no. 48, September 1972, pp. 20–24.

———, "Jordanian Civil War," *Military Review,* (US Army), vol. 51, September 1971, pp. 38–48.

———, "Palestinian nationalism and the Jordanian state," *WT,* vol 26, no. 9, (September 1970), pp. 370–378.

Cooley, John K., "Iran, the Palestinians and the Gulf," *Foreign Affairs,* vol. 57, no. 5, (Summer 1979), pp. 1017–1034.

"Europe plays now-you-see-it-now-you-don't with the PLO," *The Economist,* (London), August 25, 1979, pp. 33–35.

Franjieh, S., "How revolutionary is the Plaestinian resistance: a Marxist interpretation;" *JPS,* vol. 1, no. 2, (Winter 1972), pp. 52–60.

Gaspard, J., "Palestine: who's who among the guerrillas, *NME,* no. 18, March 1970, pp. 12–16.

Gazit, M., "Forgotten aspects of the Palestinian diaspora," *NME,* no. 10, July 1969, pp. 11–13.

Gutmann, David, "The Palestinian Myth," *Commentary,* vol. 60, no. 4, (October 1975), pp. 43–47.

Hagopian, Edward and A. B. Zahlan, "Palestine's Arab population: the demography of the Palestinians," *JPS,* vol. 3, no. 4, (Summer 1974), pp. 32–73.

Hamami, Said, "A Personal View from co-existence to reconciliation," *The Middle East,* November 1977, pp. 34–39.

Hamid, Rashid, "What is the PLO?," *JPS,* vol. 4, no. 4, (Summer 1975), pp. 90–109.

Harkabi, Yehoshafat, "The position of the Palestinians in the Israeli-Arab conflict and their National Covenant (1968); an Israeli commentary," *Journal of International Law and Politics,* (New York University), vol. 3, no. 1, (Spring 1970), pp. 209–244.

———, "The meaning of 'a democratic Palestinian state'," *Wiener Library Bulletin,* (London), vol. 24, no. 2, (1970), pp. 1–6.

———, "Scope and limit of a fadyeen consensus," *ibid.,* no. 4, (1970–1971), pp. 1–8.

————, "The debate at the 12th Palestinian National Council," *Middle East Review,* no. 1, Fall 1974, pp. 8–13.

Hottinger, A., "Black September," *Swiss Review of World Affairs* (Zurich), vol. 22, no. 7, (August 1972), p. 5.

Howard, N. F., "Jordan: The commando state," *Current History,* vol. 58, January 1970, pp. 16–20.

Hudson, Michael, "The Palestinian Arab resistance movement: its significance in the Middle East crisis," *MEJ,* vol. 23, Summer 1969, pp. 291–307.

————, "Fedayeen are forcing Lebanon's hand," *Mideast,* vol. 10, no. 1, (February–May 1970), pp. 7–14.

————, "Developments and setbacks in the Palestinian resistance movement, 1967–1971," *JPS,* vol. 1, no. 3, (Spring 1972), pp. 64–84.

————, "The Palestinian factor in the Lebanese Civil War," *MEJ,* vol. 32, Summer 1978, pp. 261–278.

Jiryis, Sabri, "A political settlement in the Middle East: the Palestinian dimension," *JPS,* vol. 7, no. 1, (Autumn 1977), pp. 3–25.

Kamleh, J., "The Palestine Liberation Army: ten years of challenge," *Arab Palestinian Resistance,* (Damascus), vol. 2, March 1975, pp. 17–42.

Khalidi, Walid, "Thinking the unthinkable: a sovereign Palestinian state," *Foreign Affairs,* vol. 56, no. 4, (July 1978), pp. 695–713.

Khan, Rais A., "Lebanon at the crossroads," *WT,* vol. 25, no. 12, (December 1969), pp. 530–536.

Kyle, Keith, "The Palestinian Arab State: collision course or solution," *WT,* vol. 33, no. 9, (September 1977), pp. 343–352.

Landes, David S., "Palestine before the Zionists," *Commentary,* vol. 61, no. 2, (February 1976), pp. 47–56.

Lehn, Walter, "The Palestinians: refugees to guerrillas," *Middle East Forum,* vol. 48, no. 1, (1972), pp. 27–44.

Lewis, Bernard, "The Palestinians and the PLO: a historical approach," *Commentary,* (New York), vol. 59, no 1, January 1975, pp. 320–348.

————, "The return of Islam," *ibid.,* vol. 61, no. 1, (January 1976), pp. 39–49;

————, "Settling the Arab-Israeli conflict," *ibid.,* vol. 63, No. 6, (June 1977), pp. 50–56.

Little, Shelby, "Fedayeen: Palestinian commandos," *Military Review,* vol. 50, November 1970, pp. 49–55.

Little, Tom, "The nature of the Palestine resistance movement," *Royal Central Asian Journal,* (London), vol. 57, June 1970, pp. 157–169.

Macintyre, Ronald R., "The Palestine Liberation Organization: tactics, strategies and options towards the Geneva conference," *JPS,* vol. 4, no. 4, (Summer 1975), pp. 65–89.

Mansfield, Peter, "PLO: a time for decisions," *Middle East International,* October 1977, pp. 4–6.

————, "Will the PLO miss the tide," *ibid.,* November 1977, pp. 6–7.

Medzini, R., "China and the Palestinians: a developing relationship," *NME,* no. 32, May 1971, pp. 34–40.

Mertz, Robert Anton, "Why George Habash Turned Marxist," *Mideast,* vol. 10, no. 4, (August 1970), pp. 31–36.

Meron, Theodor, "Some legal aspects of Arab terrorists' claims to privileged combatancy," In: Shlomo Shoham, ed., *Of Law and Man: Essays in Honor of Haim C. Cohen,* (New York and Tel Aviv, Sabra, 1971), pp. 225–268.

Moore, John Norton, "The Arab-Israeli conflict and the obligation to pursue peaceful settlement of international disputes," *Kansas Law Review,* vol. 19, no. 3, (Spring 1971), pp. 403–440.

Moughrabi, Fuad, "The Palestine Resistance movement: evolution of a strategy," *XVIII Annual Convention of the International Studies Association,* (Toronto, 1976), pp. 1–16.

Musleh Muhammad Y., "Moderates and rejectionists within the Palestine Liberation Organization," *MEJ,* vol. 30, Spring 1976, pp. 127–140.

Nakhleh, Emile E., "The anatomy of violence: theoretical reflections on Palestinain resistance," *MEJ,* vol. 25, Spring 1971, pp. 180–200.

Nevo, Yosef, "How many Palestinians?," *New Outlook,* vol. 12, no. 4, (May 1969), pp. 28–31.

Nissan, Mordechai, "PLO 'moderates'," *The Jerusalem Quarterly,* vol. 1, Fall 1976, pp. 70–82.

O'Ballance, Edgar, "Some Arab Guerrilla problems," *Military Review,* vol. 25, October 1972, pp. 27–34.

Peretz, Don, "Palestinian social stratification: the political implication," In: *The Tenth Annual Meeting of the Middle East Studies Association,* (Los Angeles, 1976), pp. 1–36.

Porath, Y., "Palestinian historiography," *The Jerusalem Quarterly,* vol. 5, Fall 1977, pp. 95–104.

Rondot, Pierre, "Palestine: peace talks and militancy," *WT,* vol. 30, September 1974, pp. 379–384.

Rouleau, Eric, "The Palestinian quest," *Foreign Affairs,* vol. 53, no. 2, (1975), pp. 261–284.

Sayegh, Fayez A., "The Camp David agreement and the Palestine problem," *JPS,* vol. 8, no. 2, (Winter 1979), pp. 3–40.

"The Soviet attitude to the Palestine problem: from the records of the Syrian Communist Party, 1971–1972," *JPS,* vol. 2, no. 1, (Autumn 1972), pp. 187–212.

Spiegel, Steven L., "Carter and Israel," *Commentary,* vol. 64, no. 1, (July 1977), pp. 35–40.

Stanley, Bruce, "Fragmentation and national liberation movements: the PLO," *Orbis,* (Philadelphia), vol. 22, no. 4, (Winter 1979), pp. 1033–1055.

Trabulsi, Fawwas, "The Palestine problem: Zionism and Imperialism in the Middle East," *New Left Review,* no. 57, September–October 1969, pp. 53–90.

Tuma, Elias, "The Economic Viability of a Palestinian state," *JPS,* vol. 7, no. 3, (Spring 1978), pp. 102–124.

Ya'ari, Ehud, "Al-Fatah's political thinking," *New Outlook,* vol. 11, no. 9, (November–December 1968), pp. 20–33.

Yodfat, Aryeh, "The Soviet Union and the Palestine Guerrillas," *Mizan,* January–February 1969, pp. 8–17.

———, "The USSR, Jordan and Syria," *ibid.,* March–April 1969, pp. 73–93.

———, "Moscow reconsiders Fatah," *NME,* no. 15, December 1969, pp. 15–18.

———, "How strong is the Soviet hold in the Lebanon," *NME,* no. 20, May 1970, pp. 23–27.

———, "The USSR and Arab communist parties," *NME,* no. 32, May 1971, pp. 29–33.

———, "The Soviet presence in Syria," *East Europe,* (New York), vol. 20, no. 7, (July 1971), pp. 9–12.

———, "Why USSR backs the Palestinians," *Soviet Analyst,* (London), vol. 4, no. 8, (April 10, 1975), pp. 2–4.

———, "The People's Republic of China and the Middle East (Part II)," *Asia Quarterly,* (Bruxelles), 1978, no. 1, pp. 67–78.

Periodicals and newspapers

Abbreviations: B – Beirut, C – Cairo, D – Damascus, L – London, M – Moscow, NY – New York, P – Paris, W – Washington DC.

Afro-Asian Affairs, L
Al Ahram, C
Al Akhbar, B
Al Akhbar, C
Al Anwar, B
Arab Palestinian Resistance, (PLA,D)
Arab Report, L
Arab Report and Record, L
Aziya i Afrika Segodniya, M

Al Ba'th, D

Christian Science Monitor, Boston

Daily Report, US Foreign Broadcast Information Service,
Daily Telegraph, L
Department of State Bulletin, W

Economist, L
Events, L

Fateh, B
Financial Times, L
Foreign Affairs, NY
Foreign Policy, NY
Free Palestine, L

Guardian, L

Al Hadaf, (PFLP), B
Al Hawadith, B
Al Hurriyya, (PDFLP), B
Al Hayat, B

International Affairs, M
International Herald Tribune, P and Zurich
International Problems, Tel Aviv
Izvestia, M

Jeune Afrique, P
Journal of Palestine Studies, B

Krasnaya Zvezda, M

The Middle East, L
The Middle East and North Africa, (Yearbook), L
Middle East International, L
Middle East Journal, W
Middle East Record, (Yearbook), Tel Aviv
Middle East Review (formerly: Middle East Information Series), NY
Mizan, L
Monday Morning, B
Le Monde, P
Al Muharrir, B

Al Nahar, B
An Nahar Arab Report, B
New Middle East, L
New Outlook, Tel Aviv
Newsweek, NY
New Times, M
New York Times, NY
Al Nida, B

Observer, L

Peking Review, Peking (Beijing)
Pravda, M

Ruz al Yusuf, C

Sawt al Asifa, (Fath)
Sawt Filastin, (PLA)
Shu'un Filastiniyya, B
Der Spiegel, Hamburg
Summary of World Broadcasts, (British Broadcast Corporation), L

Al Tala'i, (Sa'iqa), D
Al Tala'i wa al Jamahir, (Sa'iqa in Lebanon),
Al Thair al Arabi (ALF),
Al Thawra, D
Al Thawra al Filastiniyya, (Fath), D

Time, NY
Times, L
Tishrin, D
Trud, M

United Nations Monthly Chronicle, NY
US News and World Report, W

Washington Post, W
Weekly Compilation of Presidential Documents, W
World Marxist Review, Prague
The World Today, L

Za Rubezhom, M

Appendix two

List of Documents

1. — The Palestine National Covenant 1968 and 1964.
Source: *Middle East Record*, Vol. IV, 1968.

2. — PLO-Lebanese Secret Agreement, November 3, 1969.
Source: *Al-Nahar,* Beirut, April 20, 1970,

3. — Proceedings of symposium "Democratic Palestinian State".
Source *Al-Anwar,* Beirut, March 8 and 15, 1970;
Al Ahram, Cairo, September 14, 1969.

4. — Proposal by King Husayn for "United Arab Kingdom".
Source: Amman Radio Home Service, March 15, 1972.

5. — UN Security Council Resolution 242.
Source: *UN Monthly Chronicle,* Vol. IV, No. 11.

6. — UN Security Council Resolution 338.
Source: *UN Monthly Chronicle,* Vol. X, No. 10.

7. — Secret Resolutions, Arab Summit, Algiers, November 26—28, 1973.
Source: *Al-Nahar,* Beirut, December 4, 1973.

8. — Draft Programme, Fath, Sa'iqa, PDFLP and PFLP.
Source: *Al-Nahar,* Beirut, March 10, 1974.

9. — Resolutions of 12th Palestine National Council, Cairo, June 1—9, 1974.
Source: Voice of Palestine, Cairo, June 8, 1974.

10. — Sadat-Husayn Statement, July 18, 1974.
Source: Voice of the Arabs, Cairo, July 18, 1974.

11. — Report on Secret Sessions, Arab Summit, Rabat, October 26—29, 1974.
Source: *Akhbar Al Yawm,* Cairo, November 2, 1974.

12. — Resolutions at Arab Summit, Rabat, 1974.
Source: *Al Ahram,* Cairo, October 31, 1974.

13. — UN General Assembly Debate "The Question of Palestine", November, 1974.
Source: *UN Monthly Chronicle,* Vol. XI, No. 11.

14. — UN General Assembly Resolution 3236 (XXIX) on Palestinians' Rights,
November 22, 1974.
Source: *UN Monthly Chronicle,* Vol. XI. No. 11.

15. — UN General Assembly Resolution 3237 (XXIX) on Observer Status for PLO,
November 22, 1974.
Source: *UN Monthly Chronicle,* Vol. XI, No. 11.

16. — Secret Memorandum, signed by Secretary Kissinger and Minister Allon,
September, 1975.

Source: *New York Times,* September 18, 1975.

17. – Statement on Palestinian Issue by Deputy Secretary Saunders, November 12, 1975.
Source: *US Dept. of State Bulletin,* December 1, 1975.

18. – Toward Peace in the Middle East.
Source: *Brookings Institution Report,* Washington, D.C., December, 1975.

19. – Political Declaration, 13th PNC Session, Cairo, March 12–20, 1977.
Source: *MENA,* Cairo, March 20, 1977.

20. – Joint US–USSR Statement, October 1, 1977.
Source: US State Department and Tass and *Pravda*, October 2, 1977.

21. – "Framework for Peace" Camp David Agreement, September 17, 1978.
Source: *US Department of State Publication,* September 1978.

22. – "Moscow Backs Terror Inc."
Source: *Daily Telegraph,* London, July 16, 1979.

Index

222